Epochs of American History

Division and Reunion

1829-1889

BY

WOODROW WILSON, Ph.D., LL.D.

PROFESSOR OF JURISPRUDENCE IN PRINCETON UNIVERSITY
AUTHOR OF "CONGRESSIONAL GOVERNMENT," "THE STATE" ELEMENTS
OF HISTORICAL AND PRACTICAL POLITICS," ETC.

WITH FIVE MAPS

TENTH EDITION

NEW YORK AND LONDON
LONGMANS, GREEN, AND CO.
1898

EDITOR'S PREFACE.

THIS third, and concluding, volume of the EPOCHS OF AMERICAN HISTORY brings down the narrative to the end of President Cleveland's first administration, 1889. Each author has kept his own point of view, and no pains have been taken to harmonize divergences of judgment; but it is believed that all three substantially agree as to the underlying causes of the growth of our beloved country. The bibliographical apparatus of the third volume has been cast into fewer groups; much of the period covered is so recent that trustworthy detailed references are not to be found. The series is an honest effort to put before the American public, in brief compass, an account of the essentials in their own history, — a history rich in striking events and in great characters, but richer as showing the success of a great nation in combining efficient government with a high degree of individual freedom.

ALBERT BUSHNELL HART.

CAMBRIDGE, December 6, 1892.

AUTHOR'S PREFACE.

In this volume, as in the other volumes of the series to which it belongs, only a sketch in broad outline has been attempted. It is not so much a compact narrative as a rapid synopsis — as rapid as possible — of the larger features of public affairs in the crowded space of sixty years that stretches from the election of Andrew Jackson to the end of the first century of the Constitution. The treatment of the first twelve years of that period I have deliberately expanded somewhat beyond the scale of the rest, because those years seem to me a most significant season of beginnings and of critical change. To discuss the events which they contain with some degree of adequacy is to simplify and speed all the rest of the story.

I have endeavored, in dividing the matter into five parts, to block out real periods in the progress of affairs. First there is a troubled period of critical change, during which Jackson and his lieutenants introduce the "spoils system" of appointment to office, destroy the great Bank of the United States, and create a new fiscal policy; during which the tariff question discloses an ominous sectional divergence, and increases the number of unstable compromises between North and South; when a new democratic spirit of unmistakable national purpose and power comes on the stage, at the same moment with the spirit of nullification and local separateness of feeling. Then the slavery question emerges into sinister prominence; there is a struggle for new slave territory; Texas is added to the Union, and the Mexican war is fought to make Texas bigger; that war results in the acquisition of a vast territory besides Texas, and the old question of slavery in the Territories is re-opened, leading to the sharp crisis and questionable compromise of 1850, and finally to the fatal repeal of the Missouri Compromise. Then there is secession and civil war, which for a time disturb every foundation of the government. Reconstruction and a new Union follow, and the government is rehabilitated. These seem to me the natural divisions of the subject.

That the period covered by this volume has opposed many sharp difficulties to any sort of summary treatment need hardly be stated. It was of course a period of misunderstanding and of passion; and I cannot claim to have judged rightly in all cases as between parties. I can claim, however, impartiality of judgment; for impartiality is a matter of the heart, and I know with what disposition I have written.

WOODROW WILSON.

Princeton, N. J., October 24, 1892.

SUGGESTIONS FOR READERS AND TEACHERS.

THE fact that this volume is small and contains a mere outline of events is expected to make it the more useful both to teachers and to the "general reader;" for no subject can be learned from a single book. Only a comparison of authors and a combination of points of view can make any period of history really familiar. The briefer the preliminary sketch the better, if only it be made in just proportion. The use of this book should be to serve as a centre from which to extend reading or inquiry upon particular topics. The teacher should verify its several portions for himself by a critical examination, so far as possible, of the sources of information. His pupils should be made to do the same thing, to some extent, by being sent to standard authors who have written on the same period. The bibliographies prefixed to the several chapters are meant for the pupil rather than for the teacher. They are, for the most part, guides to the best known and most accessible secondary authorities, rather than to the original sources themselves. They ought to be acceptable, therefore, to the general reader also, who is a pupil without a teacher. If he wishes to seek further than these references carry him, he will find the books mentioned a key to all the rest.

The following brief works may serve for reference or comparison, or for class use in the fuller preparation of topics. The set should cost not more than ten dollars.

1. ALEXANDER JOHNSTON: *History of American Politics.* 3d ed. New York. Henry Holt & Co., 1890. — Best brief outline of purely political events.

2-4. JAMES SCHOULER: *History of the United States of America under the Constitution.* Vols. iii.–v. New York: Dodd, Mead & Co., 1889–1891 — A careful narrative, brought down to 1861. It should be used with caution, because of its strong bias of sympathy in the sectional controversy

5, 6. CARL SCHURZ: *Life of Henry Clay (American Statesmen).* 2 vols. Boston & New York · Houghton, Mifflin & Co., 1887. — Covers the period 1777–1852.

7. EDWARD M SHEPARD: *Martin Van Buren (American Statesmen).* Boston & New York: Houghton, Mifflin & Co, 1888. — Critical of political influences

8. EDWARD STANWOOD *A History of Presidential Elections.* 4th ed, revised. Boston & New York: Houghton, Mifflin & Co, 1892. — An account of the political events of each Presidential campaign, with the platforms and a statement of the votes.

9 WILLIAM G. SUMNER : *Andrew Jackson (American Statesmen).* Boston & New York: Houghton, Mifflin & Co., 1882. — Full account of financial questions.

To make up a very good working library of standard reference books, the following works may be added, at an additional cost of probably not more than one hundred and twenty dollars.

10, 11. THOMAS HART BENTON: *Thirty Years' View, or, A History of the Working of the American Government for Thirty Years, from 1820–1850.* 2 vols. New York. D Appleton & Co, 1861, 1862.

12, 13. GEORGE TICKNOR CURTIS: *Life of James Buchanan.* 2 vols New York: Harper & Brothers, 1883 — The best account of the disordered times immediately preceding the Civil War.

14, 15 JEFFERSON DAVIS: *The Rise and Fall of the Confederate Government.* 2 vols. New York· D. Appleton & Co.,
1881.

16. RICHARD T. ELY· *The Labor Movement in America.*
New York : Thomas Y. Crowell & Co, 1886.

17. WILLIAM GOODELL: *Slavery and Antislavery: A History of the Great Struggle in both Hemispheres ; with a View to
the Slavery Question in the United States.* New York. William
Goodell, 1855 — A judicious estimate of the movements of
opinion, based upon extracts from authoritative records.

18. HORACE GREELEY: *A History of the Struggle for
Slavery Extension or Restriction in the United States, from the
Declaration of Independence to the Present Day. Compiled from
the Journals of Congress and other official records.* New York .
Dix, Edwards & Co., 1856.

19, 20. HORACE GREELEY: *The American Conflict A
History of the Great Rebellion in the United States of America,
1860–64; Its Causes, Incidents, and Results.* 2 vols. Hartford .
O. D. Case & Co, 1864–1867 — Abounds in extracts from
speeches and documents

21–23. ALEXANDER JOHNSTON : *Representative American
Orations to illustrate American Political History,* 1775–1881.
3 vols. New York· G. P. Putnam's Sons, 1884.

24–26. JOHN J. LALOR *Cyclopædia of Political Science, Political Economy, and of the Political History of the United States.*
3 vols. Chicago. Rand, McNally & Co., 1883, 1884 — Contains invaluable articles on the history and politics of the
United States, by the late Professor Alexander Johnston.

27. JUDSON S LANDON: *The Constitutional History and
Government of the United States. A Series of Lectures.* Boston
& New York. Houghton, Mifflin & Co., 1889 — An excellent
brief constitutional history.

28–31. JOHN T MORSE, JR., EDITOR: *American Statesmen
Series.* Boston & New York: Houghton, Mifflin & Co., 1882–
1891. In addition to those already mentioned: HERMANN
VON HOLST: *John C. Calhoun,* 1882; HENRY C LODGE

Daniel Webster, 1883, THEODORE ROOSEVELT: *Thomas Hart Benton*, 1887, ANDREW C. McLAUGHLIN: *Lewis Cass*, 1891 — Lives of Lincoln, Seward, Sumner, Charles Francis Adams, and Chase are also announced.

32. EDWARD A. POLLARD: *The Lost Cause; A New Southern History of the War of the Confederates. Drawn from Official Sources* New York: E B Treat & Co, 1866.

33 HENRY J RAYMOND: *Life and Public Services of Abraham Lincoln, together with his State Papers.* New York: Derby & Miller, 1865.

34, 35. JAMES FORD RHODES *History of the United States from the Compromise of* 1850. New York. Harper & Brothers, 1893. — The two volumes published cover the period 1850-1860, with an introductory chapter on Slavery

36, 37. ALEXANDER H STEPHENS: *A Constitutional View of the War between the States Its Causes, Character, Conduct, and Results* 2 vols Philadelphia: National Publishing Co., 1867. — An exceedingly able argumentative statement of the Southern side of the slavery and State sovereignty controversies.

38. WILLIAM G. SUMNER: *History of American Currency.* New York: Henry Holt & Co., 1875.

39. F. W TAUSSIG: *The Tariff History of the United States. A Series of Essays.* New York & London: G. P. Putnam's Sons Revised edition, 1892.

40. GEORGE TUCKER· *The History of the United States from their Colonization to the End of the Twenty-sixth Congress, in* 1841. Vol. iv. Philadelphia: Lippincott, 1857. — A Southern history of admirable temper.

41-46 HERMANN VON HOLST *The Constitutional and Political History of the United States* (1750-1861). Translated from the German by A B Mason, J. J. Lalor, and Paul Shorey Vols. ii.-vii. Chicago Callaghan & Co, 1877-1892 — The narrative begins at about 1828, and ends in 1860.

CONTENTS.

———◆———

CHAPTER III.

THE BANK QUESTION (1829-1837).

CHAPTER IV.

ADMINISTRATION OF VAN BUREN (1837-1841).

III.

THE SLAVERY QUESTION (1842-1856).

CHAPTER V.

THE SLAVERY SYSTEM.

CHAPTER VI.

TEXAS AND THE MEXICAN WAR (1836-1848).

CHAPTER VII.

THE TERRITORIES OPENED TO SLAVERY (1848-1856).

IV.

SECESSION AND CIVIL WAR (1856-1865).

CHAPTER X.

CONSTITUTION AND GOVERNMENT OF THE CONFEDERATE STATES.

V.

REHABILITATION OF THE UNION (1865-1889).

CHAPTER XI.

RECONSTRUCTION (1865-1870).

CHAPTER XII.

RETURN TO NORMAL CONDITIONS (1870-1876).

CHAPTER XIII.

THE NEW UNION (1876-1889).

LIST OF MAPS.

EPOCHS OF AMERICAN HISTORY.

DIVISION AND REUNION.
1829-1889.

I.

INTRODUCTORY.

1. References.

Bibliographies. — Hart's Formation of the Union, §§ 69, 81, 93, 106, 118, 130; Lalor's Cyclopædia of Political Science (Johnston's articles on the several political parties); Foster's References to the History of Presidential Administrations, 22-26; C. K. Adams's Manual of Historical Literature, 566 *et seq.*, Gilman's Monroe, Appendix, 255 ; Winsor's Narrative and Critical History of America, vii. 255-266, 294-310, viii. 469 *et seq.*, 491 *et seq.*

Historical Maps. — Thwaites's Colonies, Map 1; Hart's Formation of the Union, Maps 1, 3, 5 (Epoch Maps, Nos. 1, 6, 7, 10); Scudder's History of the United States, Frontispiece (topographical); MacCoun's Historical Geography of the United States, series "National Growth" and "Development of the Commonwealth;" Scribner's Statistical Atlas, Plates 1 (topographical), 13, 14; Johnston's School History of the United States, p. 218.

Special Histories. — Johnston's History of American Politics, chaps. i.-x ; Stanwood's History of Presidential Elections, chaps. i -xi.; Henry Adams's John Randolph, 268-306 ; J. T. Morse's John Quincy Adams, 226-250, A. C. McLaughlin's Lewis Cass, 86-129, Carl Schurz's Henry Clay, 258-310; Theodore Roosevelt's Thomas H. Benton, 1-87; Tucker's History of the United States, iv. 409-515.

General Accounts. — Pitkin's History of the United States; McMaster's History of the People of the United States; Von Holst's Constitutional and Political History of the United States, ii. 1-31; Schouler's History of the United States, iv. 1-31; Henry Adams's History of the United States, ix. 175-242 ; W. G. Sumner's Jackson, 1-135 (chaps. i.-vi.), Henry A. Wise, Seven Decades of the Union, chap. v.

1

Contemporary Accounts. — Michel Chevalier's Society, Manners, and Politics in the United States, Albert Gallatin's Writings, ii ; Josiah Quincy's Figures of the Past, Daniel Webster's Correspondence; Thomas H. Benton's Thirty Years' View, i. 70-118, John Quincy Adams's Memoirs, vi. 5-104, Alexander Johnston's Representative American Orations, Alexis de Tocqueville's Democracy in America, Bowen's Translation, i. 1-72; Ben Perley Poore, Perley's Reminiscences, i. 88-199; Sargent's Public Men and Events, i. 116-171; Mrs. Frances Trollope's Domestic Manners of the Americans ; Martin Van Buren's Inquiry into the Origin and Course of Political Parties, chapters v., vi ; W. W. Story's Life and Letters of Joseph Story, i.

CHAPTER I.

THE STAGE OF DEVELOPMENT (1829).

2. A New Epoch.

MANY circumstances combine to mark the year 1829 as a turning point in the history of the United States. In that year profound political changes occurred, *Changed conditions.* produced by the forces of a great and singular national development, — forces long operative, but hitherto only in part disclosed. The revolution in politics which signalizes the presidency of Andrew Jackson as a new epoch in the history of the country was the culmination of a process of material growth and institutional expansion. The population of the country had increased from about four millions to almost thirteen millions within the forty years which had elapsed since the formation of the federal government in 1789. The new nation was now in the first flush of assured success. It had definitively succeeded in planting new homes and creating new States *Political instincts* throughout the wide stretches of the continent which lay between the eastern mountains and the Mississippi. It had once more proved the capacity of the English race to combine the rude strength and bold

initiative that can subdue a wilderness with those self-
controlling habits of ordered government that can build free
and permanent states. Its blood was warm with a new
ardor, its power heartened into a new confidence. Party
strength and discipline in the mercantile and maritime
States of the eastern coast could no longer always avail to
decide the courses of politics. A new nation had been
born and nurtured into self-reliant strength in the West,
and it was now to set out upon a characteristic career.

The increase of population in the United States has
from the first been extraordinarily rapid. In only a single

*Population
and immi-
gration.*

decennial period, — that in which the great
civil war occurred, — has the increase fallen
below the rate of thirty per cent. Generally
it has considerably exceeded that ratio. Before 1830
very little of this increase was due to immigration : probably not more than four hundred thousand immigrants
are to be reckoned in the increase of nearly nine millions
which took place between 1790 and 1830; but within that
period the pace was set for the great migration into the
interior of the continent.

At first that migration was infinitely difficult and painful. It had to make its way over the mountains, and

*The west-
ward move-
ment.*

through the almost impenetrable wilderness
of forest that lay upon and beyond them, in
lumbering vehicles which must needs have
wide ways cut for them, and which, whether on smooth or
on rough roads, vexed the slow oxen or jaded horses
that drew them. Or else it must try the rivers in raft-like
boats which could barely be pushed against the currents
by dint of muscular use of long poles.

3. A Material Ideal.

It was an awkward, cumbersome business to subdue a
continent in such wise, — hard to plan, and very likely

impossible to execute   Under such circumstances, Nature was much bigger and stronger than man.   She would
Struggle   suffer no sudden highways to be thrown across
with Nature.   her spaces; she abated not an inch of her
mountains, compromised not a foot of her forests.   Still,
she did not daunt the designs of the new nation born on
the sea-edge of her wilds.   Here is the secret, — a secret
so open, it would seem, as to baffle the penetration of
none, — which many witnesses of the material growth and
territorial expansion of the United States have strangely
failed to divine.   The history of the country and the
ambitions of its people have been deemed both sordid
Inspiration   and mean, inspired by nothing better than a
of the task.   desire for the gross comforts of material abundance; and it has been pronounced grotesque that mere
bigness and wealth should be put forward as the most
prominent grounds for the boast of greatness.   The
obvious fact is that for the creation of the nation the
conquest of her proper territory from Nature was first
necessary; and this task, which is hardly yet completed,
has been idealized in the popular mind.   A bold race has
derived inspiration from the size, the difficulty, the danger
of the task.

Expansion has meant nationalization; nationalization
has meant strength and elevation of view.

" Be strong-backed, brown-handed, upright as your pines;
  By the scale of a hemisphere shape your designs,"

is the spirited command of enthusiasm for the great
physical undertaking upon which political success was
conditioned.

4. Speed and Character of Growth.

Whatever fortune might have attended that undertaking by other instrumentalities, it is very clear that it was

steam, and steam alone, that gave it speed and full assurance of ultimate success   Fulton had successfully applied
Steam   steam to navigation in 1807, and immediately
navigation   the immense practical value of his invention
in the building up of a nation became evident.   By 1811
steamboats had appeared in considerable numbers on the
great river highways of the West ; and with their assistance the river valleys began rapidly to fill up with settlers.
Kentucky, Tennessee, and Ohio, indeed, the first fruits
of western settlement, had been created without the aid
of steam, and were an earnest of what the nation had
meant to accomplish, whether Nature were compliant or
not.   But it was not until 1810 that States began rapidly
New States. to spring up.   Within the period of little more
than nine years, from April, 1812, to August,
1821, seven States were admitted to the Union; and by
the latter date there were already eleven new States
associated with the original thirteen in the conduct of the
federal government.

For fifteen years after the admission of Missouri no
other State was created.   During those years the popula-
Distribution tion was being compacted rather than extended.
of the people. Not only were those districts entered and filled
which settlement had hitherto left untouched in its hasty
progress, but the density of population within the regions
already occupied showed a marked rate of increase.   The
aggregate population of the nine States which had been
created toward the west was already almost half as great
as the aggregate population of the States which had
formed the Union in 1789.

5. A Rural Nation.

This growth of population, it is important to note, had
not been creative of cities so much as of simple and for
the most part sparsely settled agricultural communities,

living each its own arduous, narrow life in comparative isolation. Railways were just beginning to be built in 1830; travellers moved slowly and with difficulty from place to place; news was sluggish, extended communication almost impossible. It was a time when local prejudices could be nursed in security; when old opinion was safe against disturbance; when discussion must be ill informed and dogmatic. The whole people, moreover, were self-absorbed, their entire energies consumed in the dull, prosaic tasks imposed upon them by their incomplete civilization. Everything was both doing and to be done There was no store of things accomplished, and there must needs be haste in progress. Not many manufactures had been developed; comparatively little agricultural produce was sent abroad. Exports there were, indeed, but more imports. Neither of these, moreover, bore any direct proportion to the increase of population. When foreign wars or the failure of crops in Europe created prices in transatlantic markets which greatly tempted to exportation, exportation of course took place, was even for a year or two greatly stimulated, — as, for example, in 1807. But presently it would fall to its old level again The total value of the exports of 1829 was no greater than the total value of those of 1798. Manufactures, too, had been developed only upon a small scale by the War of 1812 and the restrictive commercial policy which had attended and followed it. Jackson came to the presidency at the beginning of a new industrial era, when railways were about to quicken every movement of commercial enterprise and political intercourse, and when manufactures were about to be developed on the great scale, but before these changes had been accomplished or generally foreseen. Hitherto the country had dreamed little of the economic and social revolution that was to

(margin notes:) Rural communities

Manufactures and commerce

come. It was full of strength, but it was not various in
its equipment. It was a big, ungainly, rural nation; alert
but uncultured; honest and manly, but a bit vulgar and
quite without poise; self-conscious, but not self-contained,
— a race of homespun provincials.

6 Limitations upon Culture.

There was, of course, not a little culture and refinement in
some parts of the country. Among the wealthy planters
of the South there was to be seen, along with
simple modes of rural life, a courtliness of
bearing, a knowledge of the world and of books, and an
easy adaptability to different kinds of society which exhibited only enough of the provincial to give them fresh-
ness and piquancy. New Englanders of all sorts and
conditions had been affected by a system of popular education, although they had by no means all partaken of it;
and those of the better sort had received a college training that had put them in the way of the higher means of
culture. Books as well as life, old knowledge as well as
new experience, schools as well as struggles with Nature,
had gone to make up the American of the time. There
were cultured families everywhere, and in some communities even a cultivated class. But everything was conditioned by the newness of the country Judged
by the standards of the older society of Europe,
the life of Americans in their homes, and their behavior
in public, seemed primitive and rude. Their manners were
too free and noisy, their information touching things that
did not immediately concern themselves too limited, their
inquisitiveness too little guarded by delicacy, their eti-
quette too accidental. Their whole life, though interesting by reason of its ceaseless activity and movement, and
inspiriting by reason of its personal courage and initiative, was ungainly, unsuited to the drawing-room. There

Education.

American society.

was too much strain, and too little grace.   Men took their
work too seriously, and did not take social amenities seriously enough.   Their energy was fine, but had too little
dignity and repose.

In the literature of culture and imagination, Americans
had as yet done almost nothing.   Their literary work, like
Literature.   their work of settlement and institutional development, had hitherto been subject to the
stress of theology and politics.   Their best minds had
bent themselves to the thoughts that might make for progress, to the task of constructing systems of conduct and
devising safe plans of reform.   A literature of wisdom
had grown up; but there had been no burst of song, no
ardor of creative imagination.   Oratory, deserving to
rank with that already classical, flourished as almost the
only form of imaginative art

In brief, the nation had not yet come into possession
either of leisure or of refinement   Its strength was rough
and ready; its thought chastened only in those spheres
Intellectual   in which it had had experience.   It had been
conditions   making history and constructing systems of
politics, and in such fields its thinking was informed and
practised.   But there was too much haste and noise for
the more delicate faculties of the mind; men could not
pause long enough for profound contemplation; and there
was very little in the strenuous life about them to quicken
the quieter and more subtle powers of poetic interpretation.   The country was as yet, moreover, neither homogeneous nor united.   Its elements were being stirred hotly
together.   A keen and perilous ferment was necessary ere
the pure, fine wine of ultimate national principle should
be produced.   With full, complex, pulsing life, penetrated
by the sharp and intricate interplay of various forces, and
yet consciously single and organic, was to come also the
literature of insight and creation.

7. Political Conditions in 1829.

The election of Andrew Jackson marked a point of significant change in American politics, — a change in New political *personnel* and in spirit, in substance and in characteristics. method.   Colonial America, seeking to construct a union, had become national America, seeking to realize and develop her united strength, and to express her new life in a new course of politics.   The States which had originally drawn together to form the Union now found themselves caught in a great national drift, the direction of their development determined by forces as pervasive and irresistible as they were singular and ominous.   Almost immediately upon entering the period of Jackson's administrations, the student finds himself, as if by a sudden turn, in the great highway of legislative and executive policy which leads directly to the period of the civil war, and, beyond that, to the United States of our own day.   The tariff becomes a question of sectional irritation; the great Bank of the United States is destroyed, and our subsequent fiscal policy made necessary; the Indians are refused protection within the States, and given over to the tender mercies of border agencies; the slavery question enters its period of petition and public agitation, fulfilling the warning of the Missouri debates.   More significant still, a new spirit and method appear in the contests of parties.   The "spoils system" of appointment to office is introduced into national administration, and personal allegiance is made the discipline of national party organization.   All signs indicate the beginning of a new period.

During the forty years of federal organization which had preceded 1829, the government had remained under the influence of the generation of statesmen which had conceived and framed the Constitution   It had been

conducted with all the conservatism of an old government. Washington, John Adams, Jefferson, Madison, and

Original
spirit of
politics.

Monroe, the first five Presidents, were all of
them men whose principles had been imbibed
while the colonies were still subject to England. Their first training in affairs had been derived
from experience acquired in communities whose politics
had long run in lines parallel with the politics of their
mother-country, whose institutions got their spirit and
pattern from old-world originals. They were, in a sense,
old-world politicians. Their views were clarified and
their purposes elevated, no doubt, by their association
with the purer and more elementary conditions of life in
new communities; but they displayed a steady conservative habit in the conduct of affairs which distinguishes
them from all subsequent generations of public men in
the United States. John Quincy Adams, the sixth President, though of a new generation, was not of a new strain.
His training had worked the principles of his father's
school into every fibre of his stiff structure. His ideas
of public duty were the old tonic, with the addition of a
little acid.

Despite the apparent " revolution " involved in separation from England, there had really been an almost un-

New political
conditions.

broken continuity in our politics from the first
until 1824. Immigration from Europe did
not begin seriously to affect the original strain of blood
amongst us till the first generation of national statesmen was passing away. Not till then, either, did expansion westward, and the erection of new States remote
from the coast, begin to tell upon our politics by the
infusion of a decided flavor of newness. The colonial
States were of course themselves a bit raw and callow as
compared with the seasoned growths of European history ; but even they had acquired some of the mellowness

and sedateness of age The new States, on the other
hand, which came rapidly into being after the Revolution,
Expansion   were at a much greater remove from old tradi-
and change.   tion and settled habit, and were in direct contact
with difficulties such as breed rough strength and a bold
spirit of innovation. They brought into our national life
a sort of frontier self-assertion which quickly told upon
our politics, shaking the government out of its old
sobriety, and adding a spice of daring personal initiative,
a power also of blind personal allegiance, to public life.
The inauguration of Jackson brought a new class of men
into leadership, and marks the beginning, for good or for
ill, of a distinctively American order of politics, begotten
of the crude forces of a new nationality A change of
political weather, long preparing, had finally set in. The
new generation which asserted itself in Jackson was not
in the least regardful of conservative tradition. It had
no taint of antiquity about it. It was distinctively new
and buoyantly expectant.

Moreover, the public stage had been cleared for it.
The old school of politicians had been greatly thinned
Political   by death, and was soon to disappear alto-
leaders   gether. Only Madison, Marshall, Monroe,
and Gallatin remained, and only Marshall remained in
authority. Monroe had but two more years to live.
Madison, who had retired from active life in 1817, was
drawing towards the end even of his final function of
mild and conciliatory oracle. Gallatin was to live till
1849, but nobody was to call upon him again for public
service. The generation to which these men belonged
did not, indeed, altogether fail of successors The tradi-
tions of statesmanship which they had cherished were to
lose neither dignity nor vigor in the speech and conduct
of men like Webster and the better New England Federalists; but they were to be constrained to adapt them

selves to radically novel circumstances. Underneath the conservative initiative and policy of the earlier years of the government there had all along been working the potent leaven of democracy, slowly but radically changing conditions both social and political, foreshadowing a revolution in political method, presaging the overthrow of the "money-power" of the Federalist mercantile classes, and antagonism towards all too conspicuous vested interests.

8. Development of Parties (1789-1824).

The federal government was not by intention a democratic government. In plan and structure it had been

Original character of the government

meant to check the sweep and power of popular majorities The Senate, it was believed, would be a stronghold of conservatism, if not of aristocracy and wealth. The President, it was expected, would be the choice of representative men acting in the electoral college, and not of the people. The federal Judiciary was looked to, with its virtually permanent membership, to hold the entire structure of national politics in nice balance against all disturbing influences, whether of popular impulse or of official overbearance. Only in the House of Representatives were the people to be accorded an immediate audience and a direct means of making their will effective in affairs The government had, in fact, been originated and organized upon the initiative and primarily in the interest of the mercantile and wealthy classes. Originally conceived in an effort to accommodate commercial disputes between the States, it had been urged to adoption by a minority, under the concerted and aggressive leadership of able men representing a ruling class. The Federalists not only had on their side the power of convincing argument, but also the pressure of a strong and intelligent class.

possessed of unity and informed by a conscious solidarity
of material interest.

Hamilton, not only the chief administrative architect
of the government, but also the author of the graver and
Federal   more lasting parts of its policy in the critical
hierarchy.   formative period of its infancy, had consciously
and avowedly sought to commend it by its measures first
of all and principally to the moneyed classes, — to the
men of the cities, to whom it must look for financial support.   That such a policy was eminently wise there can of
course be no question   But it was not eminently democratic.   There can be a moneyed aristocracy, but there
cannot be a moneyed democracy.   There were ruling
classes in that day, and it was imperatively necessary
that their interest should be at once and thoroughly en
listed.   But there was a majority also, and it was from
that majority that the nation was to derive its real energy
and character.   During the administrations of Washington and John Adams the old federal hierarchy remained
virtually intact; the conservative, cultivated, propertied
classes of New England and the South practically held
the government as their own.   But with Jefferson there
came the first assertion of the force which was to transform American politics, — the force of democracy.

So early did these forces form themselves for ascendency that, had foreign influences been shut out, and the
normal conditions of domestic politics preserved, the
First demo-   Federalists would probably have been forced
cratic move-   from power after the second administration
ment.   of Washington, and John Adams would have
been excluded from the presidency.   But the identifica-
tion of the Democrats with the cause of the revolutionary
party in France delayed their accession to power.   At
first sympathy with the French revolutionists had been
the predominant sentiment in America.   Even Washing

ton's popularity was in a marked degree diminished by
his committing the country to neutrality when France
went to war with England.   When, in addition to this, he
signed Jay's treaty, which secured commercial privileges,
indeed, in our trade with the English, but which gave up
unquestionable international rights, indignation turned to
wrath; and the man who had been universally revered
as the savior of his country was freely and most cruelly
denounced as little better than a traitor.   But the tide

Reaction. turned.   The commercial advantages secured
by Jay's treaty proved more considerable
than had been thought, and placated not a few among
the opposition.   The insane impudence of Genet and the
excesses of his Republican supporters had alienated the
moderate and the thoughtful.   John Adams was elected
President, and his party once more gained a majority in
Congress.   France, too, straightway did all she could to
strengthen the reaction.   By insulting and hostile measures she brought about an actual conflict of arms with
the United States, and Federalist ascendency was apparently once more assured.

But the war spirit thus so suddenly and unexpectedly
created in their behalf only lured the Federalists to their

Fall of the own destruction.   Blinded by the ardor and
Federalists self-confidence of the moment, they forced
through Congress the arbitrary Alien and Sedition Laws.
These laws excited the liveliest hostility and fear throughout the country.   Virginia and Kentucky, at the suggestion of no less persons than Jefferson and Madison,
uttered their famous Resolutions.   The Federalists had
added to their original sin of representing the moneyed
and aristocratic classes, and to their later fault of hostility to France and friendship for England, the final offence of using the powers of the federal government to
suppress freedom of speech and trial by jury.   It was a

huge and fatal blunder, and it was never retrieved. With the close of John Adams's administration the power of the Federalists came to an end.

Jefferson was the fittest possible representative of the reaction against them. Not only did he accept quite Thomas Jefferson. completely the abstract French democratic philosophy which had proved so hot an influence in the blood of his fellow Republicans while they sought to support the revolution in France; he also shared quite heartily the jealousy felt by the agricultural South and West towards cities, with their rich merchants and manufacturers, towards the concentration of capital, towards all "special interests." Both in dogma and in instinctive sympathies he was a typical Democrat.

The future, it turned out, was with the Republican party. The expansion of the country proved to be an Democracy predominant. expansion also of democratic feeling and method. Slowly, steadily, the growth of new communities went on, — communities chiefly agricultural, sturdily self-reliant, strenuously aggressive, absorbed in their own material development, not a little jealous of the trading power in the East. The old Federalist party, the party of banks, of commercial treaties, of conservative tradition, was not destined to live in a country every day developing a larger "West," tending some day to be chiefly "West.") For, as was to have been expected, the political example of the new States was altogether and Extension of suffrage. unreservedly on the side of unrestricted popular privilege. In all of the original thirteen States there were at first important limitations upon the suffrage. In this point their constitutions were not copied by the new States; these from the first made their suffrage universal. And their example reacted powerfully upon the East. Constitutional revision soon began in the old States, and constitutional revision in every case meant, among other things, an extension of the suffrage. Parties in the East speedily felt the change. No longer protected by a property qualification, aristocracies like that of New England, where the clergy and the lawyers held respectable people together in ordered party array, went rapidly to pieces, and popular majorities began everywhere to make their weight tell in the conduct of affairs.

Monroe's terms of office served as a sort of intermediate season for parties, — a period of disintegration and germination. Apparently it was a time of political unity, an "era of good feeling," when all men were of one party Monroe's and of one mind. But this was only upon the presidency. surface. The Federalist party was a wreck, and had left the title "Federalist" a name of ill-repute which few any longer chose to bear; but the Federalist spirit and the Federalist conception of politics were not dead. These were still vital in the minds of all who wished to see the material and political development of the country quickened by a liberal construction and progressive employment of the powers of the general government. Such germs were quick, therefore, to spring up into that National Republican party which was to become known in later days as "Whig," and which was to carry on the old Federalist tradition of strong powers extensively employed. While Monroe remained President such divisions as existed showed themselves for the most part merely as individual differences of opinion and personal rivalries. Divergent proposals of policy there were, votes and counter-votes; Congress by no means presented the picture of a happy family. In the very middle of the period, indeed, came the sharp contest over the admission of Missouri as a slave State, with its startling threat of sectional alienation. But party lines did not grow distinct; party organization was slow to take form.

9. Election of 1824, 1825.

By the presidential campaign of 1824 party politics were given a more definite form and direction. That

Nominations. campaign has, with more force than elegance, been described as "the scrub race for the presidency." The old parties were no longer in existence; the old party machinery would no longer work. It had been customary to give party candidates their nomination by congressional caucus; but the caucus which now got together to nominate William H. Crawford of Georgia consisted of a mere handful of his personal friends. New England made it known that her candidate was John Quincy Adams; Clay was put forward by political friends in the Legislatures of Kentucky, Louisiana, Missouri, Illinois, and Ohio; the legislators of Tennessee and many State conventions in other parts of the country put Andrew Jackson in nomination. A bitter personal contest ensued between men all nominally of the same party. So far as it turned upon principles at all, it was generally understood that Clay and Adams were in favor of a broad construction of the Constitution, and a liberal expenditure of the federal revenue for internal improvements; while Crawford and Jackson were strict constructionists, and therefore inclined to deny the constitutionality of such outlays. The results of the election were

Results of not a little novel and startling. It had been a
the election. great innovation that a man like Andrew Jackson should be nominated at all. No other candidate had ever been put forward who had not served a long apprenticeship, and won honorable reputation as a statesman in the public service. There had even been established a sort of succession to the presidency. Jefferson had been Washington's Secretary of State; Madison, Jefferson's; Monroe, Madison's. In this line of succession John

Quincy Adams was the only legitimate candidate, for he was Secretary of State under Monroe. Jackson had never been anything of national importance except a successful soldier. It was unprecedented that one so conspicuously outside the ranks of administrative and legislative service should seek the highest civil office in the gift of the people. It was absolutely startling that he should receive more electoral votes than any of the other candidates. And yet so it happened. Jackson received 99 votes, while only 84 were cast for Adams, 41 for Crawford, 37 for Clay. It was perhaps significant. too, that these votes came more directly from the people than ever before. Until 1820, presidential electors had been chosen in almost all the States by the state legislatures; but in 1824 they were so chosen in only six States out of the twenty-four. In the rest they were elected directly by the people, and it was possible to estimate that almost fifty thousand more votes had been cast for the Jackson electors than for those who had voted for Adams. No one of the candidates having received an absolute majority of the electoral vote, the election went into the House of Representatives, where, with the aid of Clay's friends, Adams was chosen. It was then that the significance of the popular majority received its full emphasis. The friends of Jackson protested that the popular will had been disregarded, and their candidate shamefully, even corruptly, they believed, cheated of his rights. The dogma of popular sovereignty received a new and extraordinary application, fraught with important consequences. Jackson, it was argued, being the choice of the people, was "entitled" to the presidency. From a constitutional point of view the doctrine was nothing less than revolutionary. It marked the rise of a democratic theory very far advanced beyond that of Jefferson's party, and destined again and again to assert itself as against strict constitutional principle.

Choice by the House.

10. The Accession of Jackson (1825-1829).

Adams being seated in the presidential chair, the crystallization of parties went rapidly forward. Groups tended more and more to coalesce as parties. The personal traits of Adams doubtless contributed to hasten the process. His character, cold, unbending, uncompanionable, harsh, acted like an acid upon the party mixture of the Re-formation of parties. day, precipitating all the elements hitherto held in solution. He would placate no antagonisms, he would arrange no compromises, he sought no friends. His administration, moreover, startled and alienated conservative persons by its latitudinarianism upon constitutional questions. It was frankly liberal in its views ; it showed the governing, as opposed to the popular, habit. It frightened those who, like the Southerners, had peculiar privileges to protect, and it provoked the jealousy of those whom it had so narrowly defeated, the personal admirers and followers of Jackson.

The supporters of Jackson did not for a moment accept the event of the election of 1825 as decisive. The "sovereignty of the people," — that is, of the vote cast for Jackson, — should yet be vindicated. The new administration Campaign of 1828. was hardly seven months old before the Legislature of Tennessee renewed its nomination of Jackson for the presidency. The "campaign of 1828" may be said to have begun in 1825. For three whole years a contest, characterized by unprecedented virulence, and pushed in some quarters by novel and ominous methods, stirred the country into keen partisan excitement. The President found his office stripped in part of its weight and prestige. For the first time since 1801 the presidential messages failed to suggest and shape the business of Congress : Adams fared as leader of a faction, not as head of the government. Old party discipline and allegiance had disappeared; there was now nothing but the sharp and indecisive struggle of rival groups and coteries. And by one of these a new discipline and principle of allegiance was introduced into national politics. In New York and Pennsylvania there had already sprung into existence that machinery of local committees, nominating caucuses, primaries, and conventions with which later times have made us so familiar; and then, as now, this was a machinery whose use and reason for existence were revealed in the distribution of offices as rewards for party service. The chief masters of its uses were "Jackson men," and the success of their party in 1828 resulted in the nationalization of their methods.

Jackson carried New York, Pennsylvania, and the West and South against New Jersey and New England, and could claim a popular majority of almost one hundred and forty thousand. In 1828 the electors were voted for directly in every State, except Delaware and South Carolina. Jackson could claim with sufficient plausibility that the popular will had at last been vindicated. That the people are sovereign had been the central dogma of democratic thought ever since the day of Jefferson and the triumph under him of the "Democratic-Republican" party; but it had not received at the hands of that party its full logical expansion and application. The party of Jefferson, created by opposition to the vigorous centralizing measures of the Federalists, held as its cardinal, distinctive tenet the principle that the Constitution should be strictly, even literally, construed; that its checks and balances should be made and kept effective; that the federal authorities should learn and observe moderation, abstention from meddlesome activity. But the logic of popular sovereignty operated, under other circumstances, in a quite opposite direction, as presently

appeared. When, in 1824 Jackson, after having received
a plurality of the electoral votes, backed by what was
thought to be a virtual popular majority, had nevertheless
been defeated in the House of Representatives, the cry
of his followers had been that there was a conspiracy to
defeat the will of the people. Beyond all question the
election of Adams had been perfectly constitutional. It
could not be doubted that the Constitution had intended
the House to exercise a real choice as between the three
candidates who had received the highest number of votes
when the electors had failed to give to any one a majority. The position of the Jackson men was plainly incompatible with any valid interpretation of the Constitution,
most of all with a strict and literal construction of it. The
plain intent of their doctrine was that the votes of popular
majorities should command the action of every department of the government. It meant national popular
verdicts; it meant nationalization.

The democracy of Jefferson had been very different.
It had entertained very ardently the conviction that government must emanate from the people and be conducted
in their interest; but the Jeffersonians had deemed it the
essence of democracy to confine government to the little
home areas of local administration, and to have as little
governing anywhere as possible. ' It was not a theory
of omnipotence to which they held, but a theory of
method and sanction. They could not have imagined
the Jacksonian dogma, that anything that the people
willed was right; that there could not be too much omnipotence, if only it were the omnipotence of the mass, the
might of majorities. They were analysts, not absolutists.

II.

A PERIOD OF CRITICAL CHANGE
(1829–1837).

11. References.

Bibliographies. — Sumner's Andrew Jackson, *passim;* **Foster's** References to the History of Presidential Administrations, 22–26; Lalor's Cyclopædia of Political Science (Johnston's articles, "Democratic Party," "Nullification," "Bank Controversies," "Whig Party," etc) ; Adams's Manual of Historical Literature, 566 *et seq* . Winsor's Narrative and Critical History, vii. 255–266, 294–310, viii. 469 *et seq* ; W. F. Allen's History Topics, 109–111 , Notes to Von Holst's United States and Schouler's United States.

Historical Maps. — A. B Hart's Formation of the Union, Map 3; this volume, Map 1 (Epoch Maps, 7, 8), MacCoun's Historical Geography of the United States, series "National Growth," 1821–1845; series "Development of the Commonwealth," 1830, 1840 ; Scribner's Statistical Atlas, plates 1 (topographical), 15, and series ix. ; H. E. Scudder's History of the United States, frontispiece (topographical).

General Accounts. — H von Holst's Constitutional and Political History of the United States, ii.; James Schouler's History of the United States, iii., iv., chaps xiii., xiv.; George Tucker's History of the United States, iv , chaps. xxvi.–xxix.; Alexander Johnston's History of American Politics, chaps. xi.–xiv.; Edward Stanwood's History of Presidential Elections, chaps. xii.–xiv.; John T. Morse's John Quincy Adams, 226–291 ; Theodore Roosevelt's Thomas Hart Benton, 69–183 ; A. C. McLaughlin's Lewis Cass, 130–169 ; Andrew W. Young's The American Statesman, chaps xxviii.–liv.; Josiah Quincy's Memoir of the Life of John Quincy Adams, chaps. viii , ix.; Henry A. Wise's Seven Decades of the Union, chaps vi., vii.

Special Histories. — Carl Schurz's Henry Clay, i. 311–383, ii. 1–127, W. G. Sumner's Andrew Jackson, 119–386; Ormsby's History of the Whig Party; Patton's Democratic Party; Hammond's History of Political Parties, Holmes's Parties and their Principles; Byrdsall's History of the Loco-foco, or Equal Rights, Party; F. W

Taussig's Tariff History of the United States; W. G. Sumner's History of American Currency; James Parton's Life of Andrew Jackson, H. Von Holst's Calhoun, 62-183, E. V. Shepard's Martin Van Buren; Mackenzie's Life and Times of Van Buren; G. T. Curtis's Life of Webster; H. C. Lodge's Daniel Webster; R. T. Ely's Labor Movement in America.

Contemporary Accounts. — John Quincy Adams's Memoirs, vii.-ix. (chaps. xv.-xviii.); Thomas H. Benton's Thirty Years' View, i.; Amos Kendall's Autobiography and Life of Jackson; Martin Van Buren's Origin of Political Parties in the United States; Nathan Sargent's Public Men and Events, i., chaps. iii., iv; Chevalier's Society, Manners, and Politics in the United States; Harriet Martineau's Society in America, Josiah Quincy's Figures of the Past; Daniel Webster's Correspondence; Private Correspondence of Henry Clay; J A Hamilton's Reminiscences; Ben Perley Poore's Perley's Reminiscences, i. 88-198; Alexander Johnston's Representative American Orations, ii.; Garrisons' William Lloyd Garrison, i.

CHAPTER II.

PARTY SPIRIT AND POLICY UNDER JACKSON (1829-1833).

12. The New President (1829).

THE character of Jackson created everywhere its own environment, bred everywhere conditions suitable to it-

Jackson's character.
self and its own singular, self-willed existence. It was as simple and invariable in its operations as a law of nature. He was wholly a product of frontier life. Born in one of the least developed districts of North Carolina, of humble Scotch-Irish parents but just come from County Antrim he had in early manhood gone to the still more primitive settlements of that Western District of North Carolina which was presently to become the State of Tennessee. As a boy he had almost no instruction even in the elements of an edu

cation; had been obliged to eke out a shabby livelihood by saddle-making and work in the fields; had preferred horse-racing, cock-fighting, rough jests, and all rude and heedless sport to steady labor; and then had gone into the West, with a little knowledge of the law such as all young men who meant to get on in the world were then used to pick up, to assist in the administration of justice in the boisterous communities beyond the mountains. He speedily commended himself to his new neighbors for leading parts in their common life. He became a member of the convention which framed the first constitution of Tennessee, and was that State's first representative in the Federal House. He was afterwards for a short time in the Senate. He was even made a member of the Supreme Court of his State More appropriately, he was chosen major-general of militia. Offices fell to him, not because of his ambition, but rather because the imperative qualities of his character thrust him forward as a natural leader of men. He was in every way a type of the headstrong, aggressive, insubordinate, and yet honest and healthy, democracy to which he belonged. He found his proper *rôle*, at last, in the war with the Creek Indians and in the war with England, which followed. He hated the Indian and the Englishman, and he loved to fight. At forty-seven he had repulsed the British at New Orleans, and won a military reputation which was to gain for him no less a prize than the Presidency.

Jackson's public experience.

13. New Political Forces (1829).

Such were the origin and nurture of the character which was to dominate the politics of the country from 1829 to 1837, — one of the most important and critical periods in the history of the government. It is necessary to know the man in order to understand the politics of the time: a man of the type of Daniel Boone, John Sevier, and Sam Houston; cast in the mould of the men of daring, sagacity, and resource, who were winning the western wilderness for civilization, but who were themselves impatient of the very forces of order and authority in whose interest they were hewing roads and making "clearings." Such a man naturally stands forward in the development of a new and democratic nation. He impersonated the agencies which were to nationalize the government. Those agencies may be summarily indicated in two words, "the West." They were agencies of ardor and muscle, without sensibility or caution. Timid people might well look at them askance. They undoubtedly racked the nicely adjusted framework of the government almost to the point of breaking. No wonder that conservative people were alienated who had never before seen things done so strenuously or passionately. But they were forces of health, hasty because young, possessing the sound but unsensitive conscience which belongs to those who are always confident in action.

The West.

14. Causes of Jackson's Success (1829–1837).

Our democracy has not by becoming big lost the characteristic democratic temperament. That is a temperament of hopefulness, but it is also a temperament of suspicion. The South, in 1828, saw the tariff policy of the party of the East forcing her agricultural interests more and more into a position of disadvantage, and feared other aggressions still more serious. The West was tired of the "artificial system of cabinet succession to the presidency," which seemed to be keeping the greatest of the national offices in the hands of a coterie of eastern statesmen. The whole country had grown jealous of the control of presi-

The sections.

dential nominations which Congress had for long exercised through its party caucuses. It seemed to many as if national politics were getting into ruts, and as if those who had long been prominent in affairs were coming to Political im- regard the management of the offices as a patience. private cult, necessitating the choice only of the initiated by the people. " If a link in the chain of successive secretary dynasties be not broken now," said the Pennsylvania convention which nominated Jackson in 1824, " then may we be fettered by it forever." It was even suspected that the group of public men for whom the great offices were always reserved were harboring corruption as well as the pride and exclusiveness of power. Perhaps some man sent out from the " bosom of the people," without taint of the politician's trade, might discover many things amiss, and set all things right. It was not a campaign of reason, it was a campaign of feeling, summed up in an " Hurrah for Jackson." It was easier for the mass of the people to cheer for this man, whose character seemed evident, and dignified by a fresh and open sincerity, than for any one of the accomplished gentlemen, his opponents, who had been so long before the country. It was hoped, by electing Jackson, to effect a gentle revolution.

15. Appointments to Office (1829, 1830).

And indeed many phenomena of radical change were at once visible at the seat of government when he had taken Altered   the oath of office. The whole country perconditions. ceived them, and seemed to feel the thrill and consciousness of altered conditions. It had felt the hand of western men before this, but differently. Clay had brought with him into politics an imagination for great schemes, an ardor for progress on the great scale, a

quick sympathy with the plainer sort of strong, sagacious
men, and a personal force of initiative which marked him
from the first as a man bred among those who were wresting the continent from Nature for their own uses.   Benton, too, was on every point of political doctrine clearly a
man of the West.   But Clay acquired a politic habit of
compromise, and Benton studied classical models of style
and conduct.   Neither of them had the direct and terrible
energy or the intense narrowness of Jackson   Jackson's
election was the people's revolution; and he brought the
people to Washington with him.   Those who were known
to speak for him had said that, whatever his policy in
other respects, it might confidently be expected that he
would " reward his friends and punish his enemies.")For
Office-
seeking
the first time in the history of the country,
Washington swarmed with office-seekers.   It
was believed that the people had at last inherited the government, and they had come to enter into possession.   Not
only those who sought appointment to the better sort of
offices came, but the politically covetous of every degree.
Jackson saw to it that they got all that there was to give.
For the old office-holders there set in a veritable reign of
terror.) Official faithfulness and skilled capacity did not
shield them; long tenure was construed against them.
The President and his lieutenants must have the offices
for the friends who had served them in the campaign.
The Tenure of Office Act, passed in 1820, facilitated the
new policy.   That Act had created a four-year term for
a large number of offices which had before that time been
held by an indefinite tenure of good behavior. ˙ Monroe
and Adams had not taken advantage of it; they had simply reappointed such officers as had not proved unfaithful.
But it smoothed the way for the new methods of appointment introduced by Jackson.   It made removals in many
cases unnecessary : offices fell vacant of themselves.

16. Jackson's Advisers (1829, 1830).

The result was, of course, an almost entirely new civil service, made up of men without experience, and interested only in the political side of their new profession. The new discipline, too, was in the hands of new captains. In choosing his cabinet officers, Jackson did not altogether depart from custom. The men he selected were, it

The cabinet. is true, with but one exception, inconspicuous and without the usual title to high office; but they had at any rate all been members of Congress, and engaged in national affairs. Martin Van Buren, who had but a few months before been elected governor of New York, was made Secretary of State, and though a politician of the new order of managers, rather than of the old order of statesmen, possessed talents not unworthy of the place. John H. Eaton of Tennessee was made Secretary of War because he was a personal friend of Jackson's. The Secretaries of the Treasury and of the Navy and the Attorney-General owed their preferment to the fact that they were friends of Calhoun, the Vice-President, who was the leader of the Southern contingent of the Jackson forces. The Postmaster-General had recently been a candidate for the governorship of Kentucky, in the Jackson interest, and had been defeated by the candidate of the party of Clay.

It was of little significance, however, as it turned out, who held these offices. Jackson was intimate with Eaton, and came more and more to confide in Van Buren;

"Kitchen Cabinet." but he sought advice for the most part outside the cabinet. Jackson was never afraid of responsibility, and never had any respect for custom. He therefore took whom he pleased into his confidence, ridding himself without a touch of compunction of the cabinet meetings which most of his predecessors had felt it their duty to hold. Instead of confiding in his "constitutional advisers," he drew about him a body of men which the press of the day dubbed his "Kitchen Cabinet." By far the most able members of this group were William B. Lewis. Jackson's relative and neighbor, and now for twelve years or more his confidential friend and political coach and manager, and Amos Kendall, a political soldier of fortune. Lewis was a born manager of men, a master of the difficult dramatic art of creating "situations" useful to his friends. Kendall had the intellectual gifts and the literary style which fitted him for writing the higher kind of state-papers; the pity of it was that he had also the taste and talent for supplying the baser sort of writing necessary for the effective editing of partisan newspapers. These private advisers, whatever may have been their individual virtues, were gotten together to effect that combination between national policy and party management which has ever since been the bane and reproach of American politics.

No wonder political leaders of the old stamp were alarmed. It must have seemed as if the foundations of

Disharmony in the government

political morals had broken away; as if the whole character of the government were threatened with sinister change. The President's frontier mind made a personal matter of all opposition to him. Congress and the President had hitherto acted together as co-operative parts of an harmoniously integrated system of government; there had seldom been more than the inevitable and desirable friction between those who supported and those who opposed the measures of the administration. Until John Quincy Adams became President, Congress had even allowed its business to be shaped in most matters by the suggestions of the Executive. But since parties had divided upon lines of personal rivalry in the campaign of 1824, affairs had worn a much altered complexion; and the election of Jackson to the presidency seemed to make the change permanent. It began to be felt, by those who opposed him, that party struggles for the future affected, not so much measures, as the very structure of the government.

17. The "Spoils System" (1829, 1830).

It was in such an atmosphere and under such circumstances that the business of the country was resumed by **Patronage.** the Twenty-first Congress on December 7, 1829. The nine months which had elapsed since Jackson's inauguration had disclosed many evidences of what the new administration was to be, and the Houses came together in an anxious frame of mind, conscious that there were delicate questions to be handled. The radical reconstruction of the civil service in the interest of those who had actively supported Jackson for the presidency had startled and repelled not a few even of the Jackson men; for many of these had chosen to believe that their chief was to represent a conservative constitutional policy; had refused to see that he was not a politician at all, but only an imperative person whose conduct it would always be difficult either to foresee or control. It was estimated that when Congress met, more **Removals.** than a thousand removals from office had already taken place, as against seventy-three at most for all previous administrations put together; and John Quincy Adams uttered a very common judgment when he wrote in his Journal: "Very few reputable appointments have been made, and those confined to persons who were indispensably necessary to the office." "The appointments are exclusively of violent partisans," he declares, "and every editor of a scurrilous and slanderous newspaper is provided for." "The administration," exclaimed Webster, when the whole scope

and significance of the new system of appointment had
been disclosed, " the administration has seized into its
own hands a patronage most pernicious and corrupting,
an authority over men's means of living most tyrannical
and odious. and a power to punish free men for political
opinions altogether intolerable."

A good deal of solicitude had once and again found
expression concerning executive patronage, especially of

Crisis in the
public ser-
vice.

late years, as the number of Federal offices ran
higher and higher into the thousands; but
the fears that had been felt had seemed idle
and exaggerated in the presence of the steady conservatism and integrity of the Presidents hitherto in the exercise of their removing power. Now, at length, however, the abuses that had been dreaded had come. " We
give no reasons for our removals," said Van Buren; but
the reasons were generally plain enough. Friends were
to be rewarded, enemies punished; and inasmuch as the
number of needy friends greatly exceeded the number of
avowed enemies to be found in office, even those who
could not be shown to deserve punishment were removed,
to provide places for those who were deemed to deserve
reward. The Senate rejected some of the worst names
submitted to it; it cast anxiously about for some means
of defeating the unprecedented schemes of the President; but all to no avail. Its resistance only exasperated Jackson; there were even alarming indications that
the President gained in popularity almost in direct pro
portion to the vigor and stubbornness with which he
stood out against the Senate in the assertion of what he
deemed the prerogatives of his office.

The President's first message to Congress showed a
consciousness that some explanation was due to the
country; but the explanation offered was very vague. It
asserted the corrupting influence of long terms of office,

and denied that any one ever acquired a right to an office by holding it; but it did not attempt to show that long tenure had actually corrupted those who had been removed, or that those who had been substituted had the necessary title of capacity. Probably Jackson was not personally responsible for the choice of unworthy men. He asserted just before his death, indeed, that he had himself made only one removal of a subordinate official " by an act of direct personal authority." There can be no question that he thought that many of those in office at his advent were dishonest; and no one who understands his character can doubt that he wished trustworthy men to be put in their places. But it was impossible to appoint so many without mistakes, — impossible to make appointments at all upon the ground of personal or party allegiance without an almost unbroken series of mistakes.

(Marginal note: The President's reasons.)

18. Responsibility for the System (1829, 1830).

It is possible now to assign the responsibility for the introduction of these pernicious practices into national politics quite definitely. Unquestionably it must rest upon those who advised Jackson, rather than upon Jackson himself. Jackson loved his friends and hated his enemies, after the hearty, straightforward manner of the frontier. He was, moreover, a soldier, and a soldier whose knowledge of war and discipline had been acquired in the rough border warfare in which the cohesion of comradeship and personal devotion is more effective than the drill and orderly obedience of regular troops. Temperament and experience alike explain his declaration, " I am no politician ; but if I were one, I would be a New York politician." New York politics had produced that system of party organization whose chief instrument was the nominating convention,

(Marginal note: Jackson's advisers.)

made up of delegates selected, in caucus, by local political managers, and organized to carry out the plans of a
coterie of leaders at the State capital (Formation of the
Union, § 131). This coterie was known in New York as
The Albany the "Albany Regency," and its guiding spirit
Regency was Martin Van Buren, whom Jackson had
called from the governor's chair to be Secretary of State
and his trusted personal friend and adviser. The system which Mr Van Buren represented had come to completion with the extension of the suffrage. A great mass
of voters, unable of themselves to act in concert or with
intelligent and independent judgment, might by careful
management and a watchful sagacity be organized in the
interest of those who wished to control the offices and
policy of the State. Neither the idea nor the practice
was confined to New York. Pennsylvania also had
attained to almost as great perfection in such matters.

The means by which the leading coteries of politicians
in these States controlled the action of caucuses and con-
Means of ventions were not always or necessarily cor-
management. rupt. It is probable, indeed, that in the youth
of these party organizations actually corrupt practices
were uncommon. The offices of the State government
were used, it is true, as prizes to be given to those who
had rendered faithful party service, in due submission to
those in command ; and there were pecuniary rewards to
be had, too, in the shape of lucrative contracts for public
works or the State's printing. But very honorable men
were to be found acting as masters of the new management. "When they are contending for victory," said
Mr. Marcy in the Senate, speaking of the group of New
York politicians to which he himself belonged, "they
avow the intention of enjoying the fruits of it. If they
are defeated, they expect to retire from office. If they
are successful, they claim, as a matter of right, the

advantages of success. They see nothing wrong in the
rule that to the victors belong the spoils of the enemy."
There was nothing consciously sinister in this avowal. It
was, on the contrary, the language of an upright, if not a
very wise, man; and it contained a creed which Jackson
accepted at once, by natural instinct, without perceiving
either the demoralizing or the corrupt meaning of it. He
loved men who would stand together in hearty loyalty,
shoulder to shoulder, and submit to discipline. He
believed that it was right to see to it that every public
servant, of whatever grade of the service, adhered to the
right men and held to the right political opinions. He
put himself in the hands, therefore, of the new order of
politicians, some of whom had views and purposes which
he was too honest and upright to perceive. It was thus
unwittingly that he debauched national politics.

19. The Democratic Programme (1829).

The question of appointment to office was not the only
question which was given a new aspect by the policy of
Jackson's   the new administration. The President's first
policy.   message to Congress was full of important
matter aggressively put forward. It was in almost every
point clear, straightforward, explicit; and it subsequently
turned out to have been meant as a serious programme,
marking lines of policy which the President was to pursue
resolutely — stubbornly when necessary — to the end.
It gave warning that the President doubted the constitutionality of the charter of the Bank of the United States,
which everybody supposed had been finally established
by the decision of the Supreme Court in the case of
McCulloch vs. *Maryland* (Formation of the Union, § 125);
and thus foreshadowed his purpose to lay inexperienced
hands on the finances of the country. It bespoke his

purpose to rid the States of their Indian population. It declared also, very impressively, his respect for the independent powers of the States under the Constitution, and his opinion that the surplus revenue about to accrue to the national treasury ought to be turned into their several exchequers, rather than spent by Congress upon internal improvements under a doubtful interpretation of the Constitution. It assumed a firm and dignified attitude towards foreign affairs, which promised gratifying results. Only Popular on the tariff did it speak with uncertain support. sound. It was a characteristic document. Its hostility to the Bank reflected a popular sentiment and a political instinct with which the friends of the Bank had not sufficiently reckoned hitherto. Its desire that the surplus funds of the federal government should be distributed among the States had a touch of the same meaning. Its utterance concerning the policy of the government towards the Indians gave voice to Jackson's own feeling about the relative rights of white men and red in the border States, and betokened that he would be no less effective an opponent of the Indian as President than he had been as commander in the Creek and Seminole wars. Its language touching foreign affairs spoke the military confidence and the bold patriotism of the old soldier.

20. The Indian Question (1802-1838).

All frontiersmen loved autonomy in local government, and were by instinct "states-rights" men; and of none was this truer than of the men of Kentucky and Frontiersmen. Tennessee. When the federal government had hesitated about purchasing Louisiana, and thus gaining control of the Mississippi, they had threatened to break away from their allegiance and take independent action. They had been impatient of the slackness and

delays of the authorities in Washington when their lives
and property were in jeopardy because of the Indians, and
the wars with the southwestern tribes had been largely
of their own undertaking.   The Southerners who had
supported Jackson for the presidency were not mistaken,
therefore, when they reckoned the Tennessee general a
friend of the powers of the States, though it was dangerous, as it turned out, to presume too far upon his sympathies in this regard while he was himself at the head of
the federal government.   To resist the federal authority
was then to resist Jackson himself, and the instinct of
masterful authority in him was stronger than the instinct
of "states-rights."

In Georgia the Indian question had just passed one
sharp crisis (Formation of the Union, § 137) when Jackson
Georgia   came to the presidency, and was entering
Indians.   upon a second and final crisis.   The State had
again and again demanded that the federal authorities
should take action in the matter, in fulfilment of their
promise of 1802, that the Indian titles should be ex-
tinguished as soon as possible; but the Indians had
steadily refused to treat.   The State authorities had
grown impatient, had violated the treaty rights of the
Indians; had even threatened to defy federal authority
and drive the red men out at all hazards.   Finally, federal commissioners had obtained the Georgian lands of
the Creeks, in 1826, probably by bribing the chiefs of the
tribe, and Congress had provided a new place of settlement for them beyond the Mississippi.

But the Cherokees remained, and it was a much more
serious inconvenience to Georgia to have the Cherokees
Cherokees.   remain than it would have been to fail to get
rid of the Creeks.   There were more than
thirteen thousand Cherokees in the State.   They occupied an extensive and very fertile region in the northwest

portion of her territory; they had acquired a degree of civilization and of ordered self-government which rendered it impossible to deal with them as with savages; every circumstance threatened to fix them as a permanent independent community within the State. The Georgians were very naturally determined that nothing of the sort should take place. So soon as it was known that Jackson had been elected President, an Act was passed by the Georgia Legislature extending the laws of the State over the Cherokee territory, and dividing that territory into counties. In 1829 Alabama followed suit. Jackson approved. "I informed the Indians inhabiting parts of Georgia and Alabama," he told Congress in his first message, "that their attempt to establish an independent government would not be countenanced by the Executive of the United States, and advised them to migrate beyond the Mississippi or to submit to the laws of those States." When the governor of Georgia requested him to withdraw the federal troops which had been sent down to protect the Indians, he complied. In 1830 Congress passed an Act to encourage and assist the Indians to remove beyond the Mississippi Three several times between the opening of the year 1830 and the close of the year 1832 were the claims of the Indians taken by appeal from the Georgia courts to the Supreme Court of the United States, and as often did that court decide in favor of the Indians as claimants under treaties with the United States; but the Executive declined to enforce its judgments. The last appeal that was taken having been decided in 1832, when a new presidential election was at hand, Jackson declared that he would leave the decision as to the legality of his conduct in this matter to the people, thus making bold avowal of his extraordinary constitutional theory, that a vote of the people must override the action of all con-

Jackson's attitude.

stituted authorities when it could be construed to approve what they had condemned   In 1834 an Indian Territory was roughly defined by Act of Congress beyond the Mississippi.   By 1838 the Indians were almost wholly driven from the Gulf States.

Jackson had, it should be remembered, in his message of December, 1829, taken his stand upon the Constitution A point   in regard to this question.   Those who would of law   judge for themselves between Georgia and the Cherokees must resolve this point of law : if the power of the federal executive to negotiate treaties be added to the power of Congress to regulate commerce with the Indian tribes, do they together furnish a sanction for the erection of a permanent independent state within the territory of one of the members of the Union, and so override that other provision of the Constitution which declares that " no new State shall be formed or erected within the jurisdiction of any other State " without the express consent of the Legislature of that State and of Congress?   Judgment was passed upon the law of the case by the Supreme Court, and Jackson should unquestionably have yielded obedience to that judgment; but the point of law is a nice one.

21. Internal Improvements (1829-1837).

In the matter of internal improvements (Formation of the Union, § 136) Jackson gave early and frequent proof Jackson's   that he was in favor of a strict construction of position.   the Constitution and a scrupulous regard for the separate powers of the States.   He declared his purpose to stand upon the constitutional principles that had governed Madison and Monroe in this question, — upon the ground, namely, that no expenditure by the federal government was legitimate which was not made for an object clearly national in character ; and that, inasmuch

as it must always be very difficult to determine whether
the public works which the United States was constantly
being urged to undertake were really of national importance, it was best to be exceedingly chary of agreeing to
such outlays. He had urged in his first message the
very great importance of the functions of the States in
the national system of government, and had solemnly
warned Congress "against all encroachments upon the
legitimate sphere of state sovereignty." He had in this
way given emphasis to his proposal that instead of applying the surplus revenue of the federal government by
the vote of Congress to the construction of public works,
it should be distributed among the States, to be employed at their discretion. And this continued to be his
attitude throughout the years of his presidency. (The
appropriations made by Congress for internal improvements during those years were large, but they
were not made by distinct Acts of appropriation for that specific purpose. They were made as items
in the general Appropriation Bills, which the President
must have vetoed as a whole in order to reach the obnoxious items. It was only thus that the President's
opposition to such expenditures could be thwarted.

"Riders."

22. Sectional Divergence.

John Quincy Adams had been while President an outspoken and even urgent advocate of national expenditures for internal improvements, a firm sup-
porter of the treaty rights of the Indians in
the Gulf States, and an avowed friend of the system of
protective tariffs; and his position upon these questions
had completely alienated the South from him. In 1824
he had received some support in the South for the presidency; but in 1828 he had received practically none at all

Division un-
der Adams

outside of Maryland. All of the southern votes which
had been cast for Crawford or Clay in the election of
Jackson's   1824 were transferred in 1828 to Jackson; and
attitude.   in the matter of his treatment of the Indians
and his attitude towards internal improvements the South
had had no reason to repent of its choice. Jackson
fulfilled its hopes by drawing about him a party firmly,
consistently, even courageously devoted to the principle
of strict construction in the interpretation of the constitutional powers of the federal government, and the South
had good reason to be satisfied with the local autonomy
thus secured to it.

But there were influences afoot which were to force
sectional divergences, nevertheless. The tariff law of
Southern   1828 (Formation of the Union, § 138) had
commercial committed the country to the fullest extent to
interests   the policy of commercial restrictions in favor
of domestic manufactures; and such a policy could not
but subject the South to a serious, if not fatal, economic
loss. For her system of slavery shut her out from the
development of manufactures. Her only hope of wealth
lay in the maintenance of a free commerce, which should
take her agricultural products, and, most important, her
cotton, to any market of the world, foreign or domestic, that might offer. The era of railway construction
was just dawning, and that era was to witness vast and
sudden changes in the economic condition of the country which would operate to expand and transform the
industrial North and West speedily and upon an enormous scale, but which were to affect the South scarcely
at all. The northern and southern groups of States, already profoundly different in life and social structure,
were to be rendered still more radically unlike. A sharp
and almost immediate divergence between them, both in
interest and in opinion, was inevitable.

23. The Public Land Question (1829, 1830).

Jackson came to the presidency at the very moment when, for the first time since the Missouri debates, symptoms of this divergence were becoming acute.
Political
significance. During the first session of the first Congress of his term a debate upon the public land question brought out in the most striking manner possible the antagonism already existing between the two sections. The public land question had two very distinct sides. On the one hand, it was a question of administration, of the management of the national property; on the other hand, it was a question of politics, of the creation of new States and the limitation or extension of the area of settlement. From the point of view of institutions, it was also a question of the extension or limitation of slavery. It was in its latter aspect that it had provoked debate upon the occasion of the admission of Missouri to the Union; and it was in this aspect also that it called forth the "great debate" of 1830. That debate took place upon a resolution introduced by Mr. Foot of Connecticut, who proposed that an official inquiry
Foot's Resolution. should be instituted for the purpose of determining the expediency of the policy of rapid sales of the public lands which had been pursued hitherto, and of ascertaining whether these sales might not, at least for a period, be with advantage limited to lands already surveyed and on the market. The resolution meant that the eastern States, which were trying to foster a new industrial system of manufactures, were hostile to the policy of creating new agricultural communities in the West, at any rate rapidly and upon an unlimited scale. If the federal government continued to survey and police the western lands, and thus prepare them for settlement, inviting all classes to purchase, the while, by means of

prices meant merely to cover the actual expenses of the government in making this preparation for settlement, not only those who had capital, but also the better part of the laboring classes would be constantly drawn away from the East, and her industrial system greatly embarrassed, if not rendered impossible. (What was the use of protective tariffs which shut out foreign competition, if wages were to be perpetually kept at a maximum by this drain of population towards the West? Here was a serious issue between East and West, — a serious issue also, as it turned out, between the eastern States and the South; for in this matter the South stood with the West.

It is not easy without a somewhat close scrutiny of the situation to perceive why this should have been the case. Apparently the interests of the South would not be greatly advanced by the rapid settlement and develop-

Sympathy of South and West.

ment of the West; for it was already evident that the political interests of the South were inextricably bound up with the maintenance and even the extension of the system of slavery, and the Missouri Compromise had shut slavery out from the greater part of the Western territory. At the time of the debate on Foot's resolution, however, other considerations were predominant. The protective tariff law of 1828 had been taken by the South to mean that the eastern States intended, at whatever hazards of fortune to other portions of the Union, to control the revenue policy of the federal government in their own interest. When Foot introduced his resolution Benton had sprung forward to declare with hot indignation that such propositions were but further proof of the spirit, — a spirit now of neglect and again of jealousy, — which the New England States had always manifested towards the West. The South, therefore, smarting under a restrictive tariff which it

regarded as a New England measure, and the West
chafing under the selfish jealousy which, it seemed to her,
New England was always showing towards Western interests, it was natural that they should draw together in
policy, as they had done in personal preferences when
they had united to support Jackson.

24. The Debate on Foot's Resolution (1830).

But it is what was said in this memorable debate,
even more than what was done for the amalgamation of
parties by the feelings which it aroused, that made it
one of the most significant in the annals of Congress.
It brought out, for the first time on the floor of Congress, a distinct statement of the constitutional principles
upon which North and South were to diverge. Senator
Hayne of South Carolina. speaking for his
State, and, it was feared, for the South as a
whole, plainly declared that, in case of aggressions which
seemed deliberate, palpable, and dangerous violations of
the rights reserved to the States under the Constitution,
any State would be justified, when her solemn protests
failed of effect, in resisting the efforts of the federal government to put the measures complained of into execution
within her jurisdiction. He appealed, for authority, to
the Virginia and Kentucky Resolutions of 1798 and 1799
(Formation of the Union, § 90), which had seemed to
give voice to a common sentiment when holding in their
day similar doctrine. He claimed that the Constitution
of the Union was a compact between the States; that to
make the federal government the sole judge, through its
judiciary, of the extent of its own powers was to leave
the States utterly without guarantee of the rights reserved
to them, and might result in destroying the federal character of the government altogether; and that if the

States could not defend themselves in cases where the unconstitutionality of acts of the Federal Government seemed to them deliberate and palpable, the government might be consolidated to a point of intolerable tyranny. To these arguments Mr. Webster replied in a speech full of power and of high purpose, and illuminated by a chastened eloquence which renders it worthy of being preserved among classical specimens of oratory. (He maintained that the great fundamental instrument of the Union was not a compact, but in the fullest and strictest sense of the word a constitution, meant, not to effect an arrangement, but to found a government; and that this government had been purposely equipped at all points with self-sustaining powers. It was not a creature of the States, but the organ of the nation, acting directly upon individuals, and not to be checked in the exercise of its powers save by such processes and upon such principles of law as should be sanctioned by its own Supreme Court, which the Constitution had itself designated as the sole interpreter of its meaning.

Mr. Webster.

It would be difficult to exaggerate the significance of this discussion. It was the formal opening of the great controversy between the North and South concerning the nature of the Constitution which bound them together. This controversy was destined to be stimulated by the subsequent course of events to greater and greater heat, more and more intense bitterness, until it should culminate in war. At its heart lay a question, the merits of which are now seldom explored with impartiality. Statesmanlike wisdom unquestionably spoke in the contention of Webster, that the Constitution had created, not a dissoluble, illusory partnership between the States, but a single federal state, complete in itself, enacting legislation which was the supreme law of the land, and dissoluble only by revolution. No other doctrine could

Political importance

have stood the strain of the political and economic experiment we were making. If we were not to possess the continent as a nation, and as a nation build up the great fabric of free institutions upon which we had made so fair a beginning, we were to fail at all points. Upon any other plan we should have neither wealth nor peace sufficient for the completion of our great task, but only discord and wasted resources to show for the struggle. It may, nevertheless, be doubted whether this was the doctrine upon which the Union had been founded. It seems impossible to deny that the argument of Hayne contained much more nearly the sentiment of 1787-89. The Virginia and Kentucky Resolutions (Formation of the Union, § 90), whether they spoke any purpose of actual resistance or not, had certainly called the federal Constitution a compact, and had declared, in language which Senator Hayne adopted, " that in case of a deliberate, palpable, and dangerous exercise of other powers, not granted by the said compact, the States, who are members thereof, have the right, and are in duty bound, to interpose, for arresting the progress of the evil, and for maintaining within their respective limits the authorities, rights, and liberties appertaining to them " There are no indications that these Resolutions were considered treasonable at the time they were passed; they do not even seem to have shocked the public sense of constitutional duty. Indeed, the doctrine that the States had individually become sovereign bodies when they emerged from their condition of subjection to Great Britain as colonies, and that they had not lost their individual sovereignty by entering the Union, was a doctrine accepted almost without question, even by the courts, for quite thirty years after the formation of the government. Those who worked the theory out to its logical consequences described the sovereignty

Historical merits of the question.

of the federal government as merely an emanation from
the sovereignty of the States. Even those public men who
Early sen- loved the Union most, yielded theoretical as-
timents. sent to the opinion that a State might legally
withdraw from the government at her own option, and
had only practical and patriotic objections to urge. Every
State or group of States which had a grievance against
the national government bethought itself of its right to
secede. The so-called Whiskey Rebellion in Pennsylvania had been symptomatic of disunion in that quarter ;
Virginia and Kentucky had plainly hinted at it in their
protests against the Alien and Sedition Laws ; and New
England had more than once threatened it when she
deemed the federal policy destructive of her own interests. She had doubted whether she would remain in
the Union after the purchase of Louisiana, — a territory
in which, she foresaw, States were to grow up which might
care nothing for the interests of the East ; and she had
talked of secession when the embargo of 1807 and the
Threats of War of 1812 had brought her commerce to a
secession. standstill (Formation of the Union, § 115).
" It is my deliberate opinion," Josiah Quincy of Massachusetts had said in the House of Representatives, when
it was considering the admission of the first State from
the great Louisiana purchase, " it is my deliberate opinion that if this bill passes, the bonds of the Union are
virtually dissolved ; that the States which compose it are
free from their moral obligations ; and that, as it will be
the right of all, so it will be the duty of some, to prepare
definitely for a separation, — amicably if they can, violently
if they must ; " and the House had seen nothing in the
speech to warrant a formal censure. Even so late as the
period of the Missouri Compromise, " the Union was still,
in some respects, regarded as an experiment," and specu-
lations about the advisability of dissolving it did not

appear to the popular mind either "politically treasonable or morally heinous."

The ground which Webster took, in short, was new ground; that which Hayne occupied, old ground. But Strength of Webster's position was one toward which the Webster. greater part of the nation was steadily advancing, while Hayne's position was one which the South would presently stand quite alone in occupying. Conditions had changed in the North, and were to change in the immediate future with great and unprecedented speed; but the conditions of the South, whether political or economic, had remained the same, and opinion had remained stationary with them. The North was now beginning to insist upon a national government; the South was continuing to insist upon the original understanding Nullification of the Constitution: that was all. The right upon which Hayne insisted, indeed, was not the right of his State to secede from the Union, but the singular right to declare a law of the United States null and void by Act of her own Legislature, and remain in the Union while denying the validity of its statutes. There were many public men, even in South Carolina, who held such claims to be ridiculous. They believed in the right to secede: that seemed a perfectly logical inference from the accepted doctrine of state sovereignty, but they did not believe in the right to disregard the laws of the Union without seceding: that seemed both bad logic and bad statesmanship. It was, in truth, a poor, half-way inference, prompted, no doubt, by love of the Union, and genuine reluctance to withdraw from it. Those who held it, wished to secure their States against aggression, but did not wish to destroy the federal arrangement Webster found little difficulty in overwhelming the argument for "nullification;" it was the argument for state sovereignty, the major premise of the argument for nullification, which he was unable to dislodge from its historical position. It was to be overwhelmed only by the power that makes and modifies constitutions, — by the force of national sentiment.

25. Tariff Legislation (1816-1828).

South Carolina, nevertheless, meant to put this novel doctrine of nullification to the test of practical experi-
Tariff policy.   ment. Her grievance had no immediate con-
nection with the question of the public lands; it arose out of the tariff policy of the federal government. The question of western settlement was part of the economic situation as a whole; but the central question of that situation was the tariff; and the latest tariff legislation had, in the opinion of Carolinians, been the worst. Certainly the South had abundant reason to be dissatisfied with the operation of protective tariffs; and cer-
Act of 1828   tainly the protective tariff of 1828 was a monstrosity of its kind (Formation of the Union, § 138). It was not equitable even when judged by the standard of its own purposes; it was not so much as self-consistent. It was a complex of compromises, and bore upon its face evidences of the notorious fact that it was the product of a selfish contest between several sections of the country for an economic advantage. The awkward part of the situation for the southern members was that they had themselves been in part responsible for this very law, and in a way that it was very embarrassing to defend. They had used their influence to fill the bill with as many provisions as possible that would be obnoxious to New England, and had then used their votes to prevent amendments, in order that the New England members might be forced to vote with them at the last against the adoption of the measure. They had

played a dangerous game for a political advantage, with a view to the presidential election just at hand, and they had lost the game; for a sufficient number of the New England members voted for the bill to carry it.

All this, however, though it embarrassed the southern argument against the measure, did not change the char-

Elements of acter of the tariff law of 1828, or alter its signi-
the struggle. ficance as an object lesson in such legislation.
It had evidently been the result of a scramble among rival interests for a selfish advantage. Until 1816 the duties imposed upon imports had been primarily intended to yield a revenue to the government; they were only

Act of 1816. incidentally protective. The tariff of 1816
had been more directly meant to afford protection to industries which had sprung up during the period of the embargo and the War of 1812-14, when all foreign commerce was practically cut off, and domestic manufactures made necessary (Formation of the Union, § 122). The moderate duties then imposed, however, had not prevented a flood of importation after the war, or a rapid rise in the prices of agricultural products in consequence of repeated failures in the European crops They had not mended the vicious currency system of the country. They had not furnished any remedy for specu-lation or any specific against the results of a return of good crops in Europe. In 1819, therefore, there came a financial crash. Public opinion insisted upon a series of protective measures; and the Tariff Act of 1828 was the culmination of the series.

26. Effect of the Tariff upon the South (1816-1829).

The particular provisions of these various tariff mea-sures were of comparatively little consequence, so far as the South was concerned. The Act of 1816 had had

4

little importance for her; but when subsequent tariffs increased duty after duty and more and more restrained
Southern interests.   importation, it became very evident that she was to suffer almost in direct proportion as other sections of the country gained advantage from such legislation. And assuredly she was making contributions to the wealth and commerce of the country which entitled her to consideration in the matter. The total value of the exports from the United States in 1829 was $55,700,193, and to this total the southern States contributed no less
Southern exports   than $34,072,655 in cotton, tobacco, and rice. The contribution of the South appears still more striking if it be compared with the total value of agricultural exports, which was a little under $44,000,000. Three-fourths of the agricultural exports of the country, in short, came from the South; and very nearly three-fifths of all the exports. The value of the exports of manufactured articles reached only about $6,000,000. High duties on hemp and flax, on wool, on lead and iron, meant that those who contributed most to the external commerce of the country were to have their markets restricted for the benefit of those who contributed very little.)The value of the exports of manufactured iron in 1829 was only $70,767; of the exports of lead, only $8,417.

Moreover, if there was reason for complaint, South Carolina was entitled to be spokesman for the South.
Exports from South Carolina   The exports from South Carolina in 1829 reached the sum of $8,175,586, — figures exceeded only by the figures for New York and Louisiana, and, by a few thousands, by those for Massachusetts. The total value of the exports of cotton in that year was $26,575,311; that of cotton manufactured goods exported, only $1,258,000. It was urged, of course, that by stimulating domestic industries the resources of the

country were being augmented and a great home market created for the products of the South; but this home market for cotton and rice and tobacco seemed a remote and doubtful good to the southern planters when balanced against the great and present value of their foreign market.

27. Constitutional Question of the Tariff (1829).

It was this gross inequality in the operation of the tariff, this burden thrown upon a particular section from which the other sections were exempt, that gave emphasis to the claim of the southern leaders that such legislation was unconstitutional, even "deliberately and palpably" unconstitutional. The Constitution of the United States explicitly bestows upon the federal Congress both the power to levy taxes of all kinds and the power to regulate commerce with foreign nations. The only limitation imposed is that all taxation shall be uniform throughout the United States, and that its object shall be either to pay the debts or to provide for the common defence or general welfare of the country. Plainly it would seem to be within the right of Congress to regulate commerce by means of duties or imposts in any way that seemed to it calculated to promote the general welfare of the nation. At any rate, such an exercise of power on its part could certainly not be deemed within reason a deliberate and palpable violation of the Constitution. And yet to stop here is not to state the whole case which the South had to urge. Incidental, or even direct, protection of domestic industry by means of tariffs, it might be urged, was one thing; but the adoption of a system which notoriously bore with its whole weight upon a single section of the country was quite a different thing. Such taxation was not uniform in its incidence, neither did it promote the

The Southern view.

A system of protection.

general welfare.   It might even be urged that any selection of specific interests for protection made the constitutionality of the policy doubtful by deliberately **making** the burdens of taxation unequal   At any rate. it was **not** easy to answer such objections; a serious doubt could be cast upon protective tariffs by representing them **as** acts of special legislation such as the Constitution could not have contemplated in connection with the power of laying taxes.   Such legislation unquestionably constituted, so far as the South was concerned, a very substantial grievance indeed; and, like other parties with a grievance, the southern party fell back upon the doctrine of state sovereignty.

28. Calhoun and Jackson (1818-1831).

The real leader of the South in its action against the tariff policy of Congress was not Senator Hayne, but the Hayne's Vice-President, Calhoun.   Hayne's speech function. upon Foot's resolution, though its brilliancy and force were all his own, was recognized as a manifesto of the group of southern statesmen who stood about Calhoun   Possibly it was tentative, meant to try the temper of Congress and of the country with regard to the policy which the southern men were meditating. Their next step was to test the feeling of Jackson.   At a great Democratic banquet given on the 13th April, 1830, the birthday of Thomas Jefferson, toasts were proposed which smacked very strongly of state sovereignty. Southern spokesmen responded to them warmly; and then the President, who was of course the principal guest of the occasion, was called upon to volunteer a Jackson's sentiment   He did so with characteristic directness and emphasis.   His toast was, " Our Federal Union : it must be preserved."   The South Caro-

lina leaders had misjudged their man.   General Jackson
was in favor of a strict construction of the Constitution
and a studied respect for the rights of the States; but he
had the quick executive instinct of the soldier.   He both
knew and relished his duty with regard to the laws of the
United States.   " Yes," he said to a member of Congress
from South Carolina who had called upon him, and who
asked him upon leaving whether he had any commands
for his friends in South Carolina, " Yes, I have; please
give my compliments to my friends in your State, and
say to them that if a single drop of blood shall be shed
there in opposition to the laws of the United States, I
will hang the first man I can lay my hand on engaged in
such treasonable conduct, upon the first tree I can reach."
The issue was made up so far as the President was concerned : the nullification party knew what to expect from
the Executive.

Practical test of the issue was hastened by a personal
breach between Jackson and Calhoun.   Calhoun had
Calhoun's re- supported Jackson for the presidency, had
lations with been elected Vice-President as his friend,
Jackson. and was regarded as his natural successor
in the presidency.   But his political fortunes, as it turned
out, depended upon the personal favor of Jackson, whose
individual popularity had created the new Democratic
party; and the intriguing rivals of Calhoun presently set
facts before the President which caused an immediate
breach with Calhoun.   Calhoun had been Secretary of
War in Monroe's cabinet in 1818, when Jackson, in prosecution of the war against the Seminole Indians, had, after
his own thorough and arbitrary manner of conducting
Question of a warfare, wantonly disregarded the neutral
court-martial. rights of Spain upon the Florida peninsula, and
had, besides, hanged two British subjects whom he found
among the Indians and suspected of inciting the tribes to

hostilities against the United States. He had acted in direct disobedience to orders from the War Department, and he had embroiled the government with two neutral powers. When the matter was discussed in the cabinet, Calhoun, as Secretary of War, had naturally proposed that Jackson should be censured for his extraordinary insubordination. But the majority of his colleagues would not brave the universal popularity of the man, or impeach his motives by such an action; and Calhoun was directed to write the insubordinate commander an official letter of thanks and congratulation. In Jackson's mind, with its frontier standards in such matters, no man could be his friend and yet censure his conduct. The attitude of the cabinet towards his course in the Seminole War was a point of special sensitiveness with him, for he knew and resented the fact that his censure had been debated. In 1831 a betrayal of confidence on the part of another member of the cabinet of Monroe in-

Calhoun out of favor. formed Jackson of what he had not suspected, that Mr. Calhoun had favored, had even pro-posed, the censure. It was in vain that Calhoun pro-tested that he had, nevertheless, been Jackson's personal friend throughout, even while seeking to vindicate his own official authority as head of the War Department. Such a friend Jackson regarded as a traitor. The breach was immediate and final, and Calhoun and his friends were read out of the Jackson party.

29. Reconstruction of the Cabinet (1831).

The quarrel came opportunely for the reconstruction of his cabinet, which Jackson now desired on other grounds, also personal in their nature. He

Mrs. Eaton had not found his cabinet either harmonious or docile. It was not made up of those who were really his confidential advisers ﹛ The wives of several of the secretaries had refused social recognition to Mrs. Eaton, the wife of the Secretary of War, because before her marriage with General Eaton she had not enjoyed an enviable reputation ; and the President had warmly taken her part   It was not long since he had lost his own wife, whom he had loved after a tender and knightly fashion. Scandalous things had been said about her, too, most unjustly, and he was in a mood to espouse the cause of any woman whose name was aspersed. The officers of whom he wished in any case to rid himself were either unable or unwilling to command the conduct of their wives towards Mrs. Eaton. It was therefore the more pleasant to dismiss them, Calhoun men and all, and make up his

A new cabinet. cabinet afresh. Van Buren and Eaton withdrew, to facilitate the process, and during the spring and summer of 1831 the cabinet places were filled with men who were the real forces of the Jackson party: Edward Livingston of New York (Department of State), Louis McLane of Delaware (Treasury), Lewis Cass of Michigan (War), Levi Woodbury of New Hampshire (Navy), and Roger B. Taney of Maryland (Attorney-General). Only Barry of the Post Office was retained. The administration was now organically whole.

30. South Carolina's Protests against the Tariff (1828-1832).

But Calhoun and his friends were at the same time freed from entangling alliances, and left at liberty to pur-

Calhoun's motives. sue their own course without party responsibility. It seemed to men of that day who were watching with suspicion and alarm the movements of the South Carolina party that Calhoun and his friends were hatching a deliberate conspiracy against the Union ; but now that the whole of the careers of the men concerned, and the entire history of the measures taken, are

open to scrutiny, it is impossible to justify so harsh a
judgment.   Men's lives offer strange paradoxes and con-
tradictions, and it is evident now that the most urgent
sentiment of Calhoun's heart was love for the Union, in
1831 when he was advocating nullification, no less than
in his earlier days in Congress, when he was throwing his
whole soul into every project that was liberal and national.
But in his mind the Union meant state sovereignty no
less than it meant national expansion and united power.
His devotion was reserved for the original ideal, as he
conceived it; for a Union of free States, not a national
government set over subject States.   He thought to preserve the Union by checking a course of events which
threatened, as it seemed to him, to pervert it from its
original and better plan.   If he loses his early liberality
of view as his years advance, if he grows stern and turns
bitter in his moods, if he draws away from questions of
national politics to devote himself wholly to the promo-
tion of sectional objects, it is the more pathetic. ⌈His
career may be pronounced tragical, but it cannot justly
be pronounced false.   He meant to the last to save the
Union, and he died as if with a broken heart when it
became evident, even to himself, that he could not save
it by the means he had chosen and had deemed right.
Webster had certainly been able to prove the doctrine
of nullification — the paradoxical doctrine of peaceful
and legal disobedience to the law — an absurd and mis-
chievous tenet.   It was indeed a desperate and perverse
remedy; but it was not dishonestly used by those who
proposed it.

In the summer of 1828 Calhoun prepared a careful and
elaborate statement of the theory of nullification for the
The " Ex-   use of the Legislature of South Carolina, which
position "   presently adopted and promulgated it as an
official manifesto.   It became known as the " South Caro-

lina Exposition " It explains the whole attitude of Calhoun and his friends in the most explicit terms, and in
terms of evident sincerity. It declares, what was only
too true, that there is a permanent dissimilarity of interest
between the South and the rest of the Union, because
the southern States are "staple States," exclusively devoted to agriculture, and destined always to remain so
because of their " soil, climate, habits, and peculiar labor,"
while the other States of the Union may diversify their
industry and their resources as they please. The southern
States, in other words, were in the position of a minority,
whose advantage could never wholly coincide with the
advantage of the majority in respect of the commercial
policy of the country. Under such circumstances, the
" Exposition " argued, Congress should be the more careful, the more punctilious, to keep strictly within the plain
letter of its constitutional powers. And if it should seem
to one of the States of the minority that those powers
were evidently exceeded in any case, it must be within
her privilege to veto the legislation in question, and so
_{Suspension} suspend its operation so far as she herself
_{of the tariff} was concerned until an amendment to the
federal Constitution, specifically granting the power disputed, should have been prepared and accepted by three-
fourths of the States. It was nevertheless pronounced
by the "Exposition " to be inexpedient to adopt such
measures of suspension at once; time ought to be allowed for "further consideration and reflection, in the
hope that a returning sense of justice on the part of the
majority, when they came to reflect on the wrongs which
this and the other staple States have suffered and are
suffering, may repeal the obnoxious and unconstitutional
Acts, and thereby prevent the necessity of interposing
the veto of the State; " especially since it was hoped
that the "great political revolution " which was to dis-

place the Adams administration on the following 4th of March, and "bring in an eminent citizen, distinguished for his services to the country and his justice and patriotism," might be "followed up, under his influence, with a complete restoration of the pure principles of our government." When Jackson's words at the Jefferson banquet made it plain that the nullification movement could count upon no sympathy from him, Calhoun prepared and published in one of the newspapers of his State Calhoun's "An Address to the People of South Caro- "Address." lina," dated from Fort Hill, his South Carolina home, July 26, 1831, in which he re-argued the matter of the "Exposition." He dwelt again upon the great dissimilarity and even contrariety of interests which existed between the different parts of the country; he again interpreted the Constitution as being meant to establish an equilibrium of powers between the state and federal governments, — a delicate poise of interests very difficult to maintain; and he spoke with greater boldness than before of the remedy of nullification. Deep feelings were excited in South Carolina and throughout the South; there were many ominous signs of grave discontent; there were even unmistakable signs that nullification was actually to be tried, unless Congress should take steps to remove the tariff grievance.

Almost the entire attention of Congress, therefore, was given to the tariff question during the session of 1831–1832. Tariff Act It was not difficult to make sentiment in favor of 1832. of changing the tariff law of 1828: it was very generally admitted to be a "tariff of abominations," by reason of its method without principle, its miscellaneous protecting, without regard to any consistent principle of protection. There had been protests against it in the North as well as in the South. Accordingly, in July, 832, a new tariff measure, passed by very large major

ities, became law. It did away with almost all the
" abominations " of the law of 1828. Taken as a whole,
it may be said to have sought to effect, substantially, a
return to the tariff of 1824 It maintained the principle of protection, but abandoned previous vagaries in
applying it. It was to go into effect March 3, 1833.

31. Nullification (1832).

It was to the principle of protection, however, rather
than to any particular applications of it that the South
Continued   objected. The revision of 1832 showed that
opposition   the majority in Congress were willing to see
the policy of protection temperately and reasonably employed, but did not give any promise that they would
ever consent to abandon it. It rather fixed the policy
upon a firmer basis by ridding it of its extravagances
Calhoun immediately took steps to prevent its going into
operation. He wrote an elaborate letter to James Hamil-
Calhoun's   ton, the governor of South Carolina, dated
position.   Fort Hill, August 28, 1832, again setting forth
his views on the right of the State to defend her reserved
powers against the encroachments of the general government. Once more he stated, with consummate clear-
ness and force, the historical argument for state sovereignty. He maintained that the central government was
the agent of the States ; that the people of each State
were obliged to obey the laws of the Union because their
State in joining the Union had established their obligation to do so; but that, as each State had established
this obligation for its citizens, it could also declare its extent so far as they were concerned, and that such a declaration would be as binding upon them as the original
Act of adherence to the Union. He argued that a declaration on the part of the State defining the extent of its

obligation under the Constitution which it had accepted, might be made by a convention of the people; that such a declaration would be similar to the Act by which the State had entered the Union, of like solemnity, and as much a part of her fundamental law; and he could find nothing in the Constitution which could warrant the federal government in coercing a State for any purpose Nullification or in any manner whatever. Nullification, he not secession insisted, was not, as some contended, the same thing as secession. "Secession is a withdrawal from the Union, . . . a dissolution of the partnership;" "nullification, on the contrary, presupposes the relation of principal and agent, . . . and is simply a declaration, made in due form, that an act of the agent transcending his power is null and void." He thought the one power as logical a deduction from the premises of state sovereignty as the other. The only majority which could, he conceived, under our federal system, avail to overcome the opposition of a State to the exercise of the contested power was the majority which could amend the Constitution : that majority, and not the majority of Congress, could override nullification, by the process of amendment, inasmuch as the Union was a confederation of interests, not a mere combination of individuals. Our system was meant to fortify the constitution-making power against the law-making.

In the minds of the public men of South Carolina this letter was conclusive, not only as to what ought to be held, but also as to what ought to be done. The State Legislature came together in October and formally called a convention for the following month. The convention was immediately chosen, and convened in Columbia on Ordinance of November 19. On November 24 it passed an nullification ordinance of nullification, which declared the Tariff Acts of 1828 and 1832 null and void and without force within the jurisdiction of South Carolina; prohibited the payment of duties under those laws within the State after the first day of the following February; forbade, under penalties, appeals upon the questions involved to the courts of the United States; and declared that any attempt on the part of the federal government to enforce the nullified laws in South Carolina would sever the State's connection with the Union and force her to organize a separate government.   Meantime (November 6) Jackson had sent instructions to the collector of the port of Charleston to collect the duties at all hazards, if necessary by the use of force, — as much force as might be needed.   When the convention promulgated its ordinance, he issued a proclamation (December 11), couched in terms characteristically direct and vehement.   It argued the manifest practical difficulties of the doctrine of nullification, and very firmly denounced it as "incompatible with the existence of the Union, contradicted expressly by the letter of the Constitution, unauthorized by its spirit, inconsistent with every principle on which it was founded, and destructive of the great object for which it was formed."   He exhorted the people of South Carolina to yield, but he offered no compromise.   "The laws of the United States," declared the President, "must be executed   I have no discretionary power on the subject, — my duty is emphatically pronounced in the Constitution.   Those who told you that you might peacefully prevent their execution deceived you . . . Their object is disunion, and disunion by armed force is treason."   The state authorities, nevertheless, did not flinch even in the face of this ominous proclamation.   A new legislature, in which the nullifiers had secured an overwhelming majority, met in Columbia the same month, and called Mr. Hayne from the Senate to assume the governorship of

Jackson's proclamation.

South Carolina defiant.

the State; and one of the first acts of the new governor
was to issue a proclamation of his own, denouncing the
utterance of the President, and calling upon the people
of the State to stand firm in their opposition to its pernicious doctrines. During these transactions Calhoun
resigned the office of Vice-President to accept Hayne's
vacated seat upon the floor of the Senate He must be
in the arena itself, where part of the battle was to be
fought.

32. The Presidential Election of 1832.

In the mean time there had been a new presidential
election; the President had "taken the sense of the country," and regarded the result as a triumph
both for himself and for his avowed principles
of government. This election is notable for
several reasons. It marks the beginning of the system
of national nominating conventions; it gave Jackson a
second term of office, in which he was to display his
peculiar qualities more conspicuously than ever; it compacted and gave distinct character to the new Democratic
party; and it practically settled directly the fate of the
Bank of the United States, and indirectly the question of
nullification. Jackson was easily re-elected, for he had
established a great popularity, and the opposition was
divided.

A new party came into the field, and marked its advent by originating the national nominating convention.
This was the Anti-Masonic party. In 1826
one William Morgan, who had ventured to
make public the secrets of the Masonic order,
was abducted, and, it was alleged, murdered. The event
created great excitement, and led, singularly enough, to
the formation of a political party whose first tenet was
the duty of excluding Freemasons from public office.

Importance of the election

A national nominating convention.

This party spread so rapidly that within four years it assumed something like the proportions of a national organization. By September, 1831, it was able to muster a national nominating convention, in which more than half the States were represented. This convention put in nomination William Wirt of Virginia, formerly Attorney-General. The National Republicans, following suit, met in a similar convention in December of the same year, and by unanimous vote nominated Henry Clay of Kentucky, already once before Jackson's rival for the presidency.) A "national assembly of young men" also met in Washington in May, 1832, at the suggestion of members of the Clay party, to indorse the National Republican nominations, and to add another point to subsequent practice by adopting a set of formal resolutions defining its position on the issues of the campaign, "the first platform ever adopted by a national convention." These resolutions denounced Jackson for most of the acts of his administration; declared that the Supreme Court of the United States (rather than the President, or the leading public men in South Carolina) was the proper tribunal "for deciding in the last resort all questions arising under the Constitution and laws of the United States;" and favored the policy of protection. The Democrats, in their turn, also held a convention in May, 1832, without hesitation renominated Jackson for the presidency, and, with considerably less spontaneity, Martin Van Buren for the vice-presidency. Mr. Van Buren was Jackson's choice for the office, and it was Jackson's preference that forced him upon the party, many of whose members would have been glad to have some one else. Calhoun had fallen out from the line of succession since his breach with the President; his position at the time with reference to nullification practically severed his connection with parties altogether.

The first "platform."

Van Buren

The result of the election was decisive. The electoral votes of all the southern States even, except those of South Carolina and five out of the eight votes of Maryland, were cast for Jackson, whose total was 219. Only 49 votes were cast for Clay; South Carolina threw away her eleven votes on John Floyd of Virginia; and Vermont alone was carried by the Anti-Masons.

Upon Jackson, with his somewhat Napoleonic instincts, the election acted like the tonic of a favorable *plébiscite*. Significance He was incapable of entertaining any purpose of the result. to overthrow the Constitution, or even to act in contravention of its provisions; but he did claim the right to read and interpret that instrument for himself, without the assistance either of the courts or of the leaders of politics; and he took his second election to mean that the people gave him *carte blanche* to act as their representative, on that theory. The chief issue of the election had been the question of the re-charter of the Bank of the United States, — a question which we shall presently discuss. The tariff question had entered only in a subordinate degree, for Jackson was not fully committed with regard to it, and the nullification troubles had not come to a head until too late to affect the vote materially. It was Jackson's immense popularity, the divisions among his opponents, his successes, and their lack of unity that determined the result. But Jackson made no close analysis of the result. He was heartened by the Effect upon consciousness that he had been such a President Jackson. dent as the people liked and were ready to support It was probably this feeling that contributed to give its clear ring of determination to the proclamation which he issued against the nullifiers in December. In January he asked Congress for special powers to enforce the revenue laws. He wished to be authorized to alter revenue districts as he thought best, to change the locality of custom houses when necessary, and to use the land and naval forces of the government to prevent unlawful interference with the powers of collectors. There was evident need that such powers should be conferred upon the Executive, for the legislature of South Carolina, after electing Hayne governor, had passed Acts practically resuming some of the powers expressly withheld from the States by the federal Constitution, and had taken steps to put the State in a condition of military preparation against the time of federal action in February. A bill to enforce the tariff laws was therefore introduced into

"Force Bill."

Congress in response to the President's request, and became known as the "Force Bill."

33. Compromise and Reconciliation (1832, 1833).

While the employment of force was proposed, however, conciliation also was attempted, — at the suggestion of

Verplanck's tariff bill.

the administration itself. The Secretary of the Treasury had recommended in his annual report that the duties be lowered to the revenue standard, and on December 27 Mr. Verplanck, chairman of the Committee of Ways and Means, had reported to the House a bill meant to effect a return to the tariff of 1816. The protectionists of the House, however, subjected the measure to a raking fire of debate and amendment which very soon disfigured it beyond recognition, and which delayed final action upon it until within two weeks of the end of the session. The Senate did not wait for the action of the House. On February 12, Mr. Clay intro-

Clay's compromise.

duced a compromise measure in the Senate, intended at once to save the principle of protection and to stave off civil difficulties. Taking the tariff of 1832 as a basis, it provided that all duties which,

5

under the provisions of that tariff, exceeded twenty per cent should be reduced by one tenth of that excess on the 1st of January, 1834, and of each alternate year till 1840, and that then, on the 1st of January, 1842, one half of the remaining excess should be taken off, and on the 1st of July, 1842, the other half, so that after the first day of July, 1842, there should be a uniform duty of twenty per cent on all articles.   South Carolina had early given notice that such an horizontal rate was the least concession that would satisfy her   To Mr. Clay's measure, after a little hesitation, all parties assented.   On February 26 the House dropped its own bill and took up the Senate measure, which it speedily passed   Passing the Senate also, the bill became law on March 2, 1833, the day before the tariff law of 1832 was to have gone into effect. The " Force Bill " became law one day earlier, on the first of March.

What had been happening in South Carolina in the mean time ?   The nullification ordinance was to have gone into effect on the first of February.   It had unquestionably been intended, however, to force, not war, but concession; and it would have been in the highest degree

Suspension of the ordinance.

unwise and maladroit to attempt to put it forcibly into operation while Congress was actually debating concession.   Virginia, moreover, when she saw preparations a-making for actual conflict between South Carolina and the federal authorities, had undertaken the part of mediator.   Her legislature passed resolutions which reiterated the principles of the celebrated Resolutions of 1798, — while expressing the opinion that those principles sanctioned neither the action of South Carolina nor the proclamation of the President, — and which begged South Carolina at least to suspend her ordinance until after the close of the session of Congress.   But the convention which had passed the ordinance had dispersed, and no power existed which, under the theory of nullification, was authorized to repeal it. Under such circumstances, since nothing regular could be done, something very irregular was resolved upon, which no conceivable theory of constitutional law could justify, but which prudence and practical wisdom nevertheless demanded. Governor Hayne replied to the overtures of Virginia that the ordinance would be suspended by common consent, and a private meeting of leading public men was held in Charleston late in January, which declared the ordinance suspended until Congress should adjourn. The federal officers collected the duties after the first day of February as before. On March 11, the nullification convention reassembled at the call of the governor, and, reciting the concessions of Congress, Repeal of the repealed the ordinance nullifying the tariff ordinance. laws. At the same time, however, it passed another ordinance nullifying the Force Bill, which there was then no longer any reason for putting into operation.

The outcome of the matter could not be wholly satisfactory to either party. South Carolina had obtained the concessions which she had demanded; but the Force Bill was still unrepealed, and stood as a flat denial of the whole principle for which the nullifiers had contended. The federal authorities had collected the revenue at the ports of South Carolina, and enforced the law which she The result. had attempted to nullify; but then they had immediately withdrawn that law and acceded to the State's demands. Nullification had succeeded in its immediate practical object by getting rid of the laws at which it had been aimed; but it had failed in the much greater matter of establishing itself as an acknowledged principle. What is most striking in the whole affair for the student of institutions is, that it gave to the practical politics of an English people a theoretical cast such as the politics of no English community had ever worn before. Practical considerations, hitherto conclusive in all matters of English development, were now for the first time compelled to contest their right with refined theories of government; had a cunning net of logical inference from a written document thrown about them by a master of logic, and were bidden to extricate themselves without breaking the net.

CHAPTER III.

THE BANK QUESTION (1829-1837).

34. The Bank of the United States (1789-1816).

THE re-election of Jackson in 1832 sealed the fate of the Bank of the United States, and ultimately resulted Currency in a complete revolution in the fiscal policy of question the government. The Constitution may be said to have been in large part created by a fiscal question. Tariff wars between the States and the dangers of an unsound currency had been prominent among the causes which led to the formation of a strengthened federal government in 1789. One of the chief objects of those who advocated and framed the new government was to create an authority which could supply the country with a safe currency (Formation of the Union, § 53). The Congress of the Confederation and the governments of the States had demoralized commerce and industry by unlimited issues of irredeemable paper money, and the Constitution of 1787 was meant to secure the country against like folly in the future It vested in Congress Federal alone the power to coin money and regulate the convention. value of coin; it explicitly forbade the States to emit bills of credit; and it nowhere granted the power to emit such bills to Congress. A proposition to confer that power upon Congress had been defeated in the constitutional convention by a heavy majority. There remained, however, a device for issuing paper money. It was promptly held by the courts that this power, which the States could not directly exercise, they could exercise indirectly through the instrumentality of banks. While state legislatures could not vote government issues, they could incorporate banks and authorize them, State banks. as joint-stock companies, to issue paper in any amount they chose, without restriction or safeguard, and that even when the State itself arranged to become the chief or only stockholder. The only way in which the federal government could check such operations, apparently, was by going into the field of competition itself and dominating unsound state banks by means of a sound national bank whose issues would be extensive and accepted with confidence.

The first Bank of the United States had been established, at the suggestion of Hamilton, for several purposes : not only in order to furnish the country with at least one sound and stable currency, Bank of the United States but also in order to serve as the fiscal agent of the government in handling its revenues and floating its loans, and in order to interest men with money in the new federal government (Formation of the Union, § 78). That it did act as a check upon the less reliable state banks is made sufficiently manifest by the opposition offered to the renewal of its twenty-year charter, which expired in 1811. After experiencing for five years, however, the combined financial effects of war and state banking, the country was glad to see a second Bank of the United States chartered in 1816 (Formation of the Union, § 120).

35. Constitutionality of the Bank (1789–1819).

The constitutionality of a bank chartered by Congress had early been called in question. Where, it was asked, did Congress, exercising only specified powers, get the authority to grant charters ? And, even if it could grant charters, whence did it derive the right to charter a bank and give to it the handling of the national revenues? The Constitution gave to Congress the power to lay and collect taxes, duties, imposts, and excises, to pay the debts and provide for the common defence and general welfare of the United States; the power to borrow money on the credit of the United States; and the power to coin money and regulate the value of both foreign and domestic coin. But how, from any one of these powers, or from all of them put together, could it argue its right to create a great semi-governmental bank? The last clause of the article of the Constitution conferring powers upon Congress did indeed say that Congress might make " all laws which should be necessary and proper for carrying into execution the foregoing powers; " but could this bank be said to be both necessary and proper for carrying into execution the limited fiscal functions of the federal government? Washington had thought these questions worthy of consideration before signing the bill which created the first national bank in 1791, and had obtained careful written opinions from Hamilton and Jefferson. Hamilton had argued strongly in favor of the constitutionality of the bank, Jefferson as strongly against it; but Washington had accepted the reasoning of Hamilton (Formation of the Union, § 78), and in 1819 the Supreme Court of the United States, in the leading case of *McCulloch* vs. *Maryland*, sustained the Act creating the second Bank of the United States upon substantially the same grounds that Hamilton had urged (Formation of the Union, § 125). It held that, while it was true that the government of the United States was a government of specified powers only, it must nevertheless be deemed to be sovereign within the sphere assigned to it by the Constitution; that the powers granted must be taken to include every privilege incidental to their exercise, the choice of

Early views.

Decision of the Supreme Court.

the means by which the ends of the government were to be reached lying in every case within the discretion of Congress, and not being subject to be restrained by the courts. The Bank had been chartered as a fiscal agent of the government: whether the creation of such an agency was necessary and proper to the exercise of its fiscal functions it was for Congress, not for the courts, to judge. A "sound construction of the Constitution must allow to the national legislature that discretion with respect to the means by which the powers it confers are to be carried into execution, which will enable that body to perform the high duties assigned to it, in the manner most beneficial to the people."

36. Jackson's Hostility to the Bank (1829, 1830).

Such a decision was of course conclusive of all legal controversy. But it had not by any means satisfied all Opposition minds. Many still dreaded the effects of the to the Bank exercise of such powers by Congress, even when they did not doubt their constitutionality They dreaded the power of this great corporation which the federal government had set up to dominate the money transactions of the country. Jackson was of the number of those who felt uneasy about the influence of the Bank. Moreover, he never considered any question settled merely because the Supreme Court had passed upon it. He did not, therefore, hesitate to speak of the Bank in disparaging terms of covert hostility in the very first message he sent to Congress. The charter of the Bank was not to expire until 1836, and the term of office for which Jackson had been elected when he wrote the message of December, 1829, was to end in 1833. It was singular that he should call the attention of Congress to a matter with the final settlement of which he might have

nothing to do. But delicacy did not weigh with Jackson
any more than the judgments of the Supreme Court.
He attacked the Bank at once, and the terms in which he
did so deserve transcription as a suitable text
First attack.   for the controversies that were to follow.
" The charter of the Bank of the United States expires
in 1836, and its stockholders will most probably apply
for a renewal of their privileges. In order to avoid the
evils resulting from precipitancy in a measure involving
such important principles and such deep pecuniary interests, I feel that I cannot, in justice to the parties interested, too soon present it to the deliberate consideration
of the legislature and the people. Both the constitutionality and the expediency of the law creating this Bank are
well questioned by a large portion of our fellow-citizens ;
and it must be admitted by all that it has failed in the
great end of establishing a uniform and sound currency.
Under these circumstances, if such an instrument is
deemed essential to the fiscal operations of the government, I submit to the wisdom of the legislature whether
a national one, founded upon the credit of the government and its revenues, might not be devised, which would
avoid all constitutional difficulties, and at the same time
secure all the advantages to the government and the
country that were expected to result from the present
Bank." These sentences forecast a great deal that was
to follow. There was more feeling and determination
back of them, they were spoken with much more definiteness of purpose, than appeared upon their smooth
surface. Congress at first attached no importance to
these utterances of the President ; but again and again,
in subsequent messages, Jackson returned to the subject,
his language becoming constantly more and more explicit
in its hostility, until at length decisive measures of self-
defence were forced upon the friends of the Bank.

Jackson's feelings towards the Bank were compounded of many elements, and it is impossible to assign to these Objections their relative importance in shaping his pur-
examined. poses. His declaration that the Bank had failed to establish a sound currency was notoriously without reasonable foundation. Every observant man was convinced that the Bank had gone far towards accomplishing that very object. But he hit upon a very widespread sentiment, and so was upon firmer ground, when, at a later stage of the controversy, he stigmatized the Bank as an "un-American monopoly."

37. History of Banking in the United States (1783-1829).

The history of banking corporations in the United States has shown the power of economic errors to perpetuate themselves when they happen to fall in with certain democratic notions entertained by the masses of the people. The debtor class in all parts of the country, and all classes in the newer settlements, had a marked partiality Paper for paper money. Abundant money, even if
money. unsound, seemed to furnish the capital which the newer communities so much needed for their development. The control which the possession of real capital gave those who possessed it over the fortunes of those who needed it was hated as the "money power." That shrewd capital should be able to make its own hard terms with the plain and earnest men who were seeking to get at the riches of the new continent, but lacked the means neccessary to supplement their muscle, seemed a grinding monopoly, essentially undemocratic, because enjoyed by very few persons. It was a delightful, even if a delusive, discovery, therefore, that by authorizing certain individuals to issue their promises to pay, you could create the means of buying cattle and ploughs and

seed without awaiting the slow accumulation of super-
abundant, loanable wealth; and it seemed a great hardship that the usefulness of this discovery should be
hampered by the setting up of a great corporation by
the federal government possessing such resources and
power as to be able to discredit and embarrass local banks
in carrying out their beneficent function of distributing
fictitious and prospective wealth.

Moreover, there was a grave element of party politics
in the whole question. The chartering of banks, during
all the earlier history of the country, was effected exclusively by direct act of legislature. It was not open
Political   to every one to obtain a charter, — that was a
charters.   privilege which would be bestowed only by
favor; and many state legislatures were in the habit of
conferring banking powers only upon the party friends
of the majority. The persons thus favored, having
received their charters as a political trust, employed the
privileges enjoyed under them in a partisan spirit,
granted accommodations much more readily and on
much easier terms to fellow partisans than to adherents
of the opposite party, — willing to prove themselves
worthy of the confidence their friends in the legislature
had reposed in them. Such practices had been common
enough to generate an atmosphere of suspicion. Partisan banking was expected; a sort of presumption was
created that corrupt influences tainted the whole system
of charters and privileges of issue. There seems unquestionably to have been a widespread feeling of jealousy and suspicion, accordingly, in the minds of the
people with regard to the Bank of the United States;
at any rate, a widespread readiness to suspect and be
jealous, both because the national Bank was known to
check the operations of the state banks, and because it
was taken almost for granted that it would use the great

power which it possessed for political purposes, — to control elections, when necessary, in its own interest, and to buy the favor of influential public men.

38. The Branch Bank at Portsmouth (1829).

These were impressions which Jackson seems to have shared in some degree from the first, though probably

Hill and Mason. they did not take clear shape in his mind until his hostility to the Bank was otherwise aroused. His purposeful convictions about the Bank were formed during the first summer of his presidency, the summer of 1829. It was then that what seemed to him a clear case of improper political motive in the management of the Bank was brought to his notice. Isaac Hill and Levi Woodbury were Jackson leaders in New Hampshire. They had won the State over to the Jackson interest. Woodbury entered the Senate, and Hill left his newspaper and his state bank at Concord to enter the "Kitchen Cabinet." It was matter of deep chagrin to them that Jeremiah Mason, Webster's friend and their own most formidable opponent, an earnest and eloquent man of the ancient Federalist faith, should have been made president of the branch of the Bank of the United States at Portsmouth, with financial power in their State, and that he should distress some of their friends by insisting upon strict business methods, to the discouragement of all special pecuniary favors to anybody. In the summer of 1829 Woodbury wrote to

Complaints against Mason Ingham, Secretary of the Treasury, making complaints of Mason, as not only harsh in his administration of the Bank, but guilty of partiality also in making loans and insisting upon collections. He could not specifically charge, but he wished to insinuate, political motives and partialities. At about the same time Amos Kendall repeated to the Secretary

certain rumors which had reached his ears of an improper use of money by officers of the Bank in Kentucky to influence the election of 1825 in that State.

The Secretary wrote to Mr. Nicholas Biddle, the president of the Bank of the United States, and called his
Ingham's   attention to the charges which had been made
criticisms.   against Mason, assuming a tone which im-
plied that the Bank was in some way responsible to the
administration in all its affairs. His letter seemed to
take it for granted that Mr. Mason had been appointed
because of his political views, — because, in short, the
Bank was hostile to the Jackson interest in New Hampshire. It intimated that the theory upon which the Bank
was understood to have been founded, and upon which
it was now thought to be managed, was that the "arm of
wealth" ought to be strengthened, in order to "counter-
poise the influence of extended suffrage in the disposition
of public affairs," and that the only way in which to remove the suspicion that this was the theory and policy
of the institution was to make choice of its officers
from both national parties, without discrimination. Mr.
Biddle's   Biddle replied with natural indignation, refut-
defence   ing the charges against Mason, asserting the
perfectly non-partisan character of the administration of
the Bank, and declaring, courteously but warmly, that,
being non-partisan, it recognized no political responsibility either to the Secretary of the Treasury or to any
one else. But his indignation, however natural, was im-
politic; it savored too much of defiance and contempt
to suit the temper of a Jackson administration. The
Secretary startled Mr. Biddle by reminding him that it
was within the privilege of the Secretary of the Treasury
to remove the deposits of public money from the Bank;
and the contents of the President's first message indicated the impression that had been made upon him

39. Constitution of the Bank (1816-1832).

Charges of all sorts began to be heaped up against the Bank; and although they were, almost without exception, again and again wholly disproved, they told at last against its reputation among the people at large by mere force of reiteration. During the first two years of the history of the Bank there had been gross mismanagement, which had disgusted even those who had voted for its charter; but by 1829 these early errors had been long ago corrected, and the Bank had established such a reputation for safe business methods that its only enemies were those who were jealous of its business privileges, or those who wished in vain to bring it to their assistance in politics. Its constitution made its connection with the federal government quite close. The federal Treasury had subscribed seven millions to its capital stock of thirty-five millions; its other stockholders were privileged to make up three-fourths of their subscriptions in United States stock; five of its twenty-five directors were appointed by the President; and it was the depository of the public funds. In return for these privileges the Bank had paid a million and a half dollars, and agreed to negotiate the loans of the government free of charge. No other bank, its charter promised, was to be established by Congress during the twenty years that charter was to run. The Secretary of the Treasury was authorized to withdraw the public moneys from the Bank in case he deemed it necessary to do so at any time, stating his reasons for his action to Congress at its next session. It was privileged to issue circulating notes, and these notes were made receivable for all dues to the United States; but it was obliged by law to redeem its notes in specie on demand The obligations of this

(marginal notes: Management of the Bank. — Connection with the government.)

charter it had kept; but in the eyes of the Jackson managers it was too closely connected with the government to be kept out of politics. It had too much at stake: if it was not active for the administration, it must, they argued, be active against it.

40. The Fight for Re-charter (1832).

Just before the political campaign of 1832 the administration seemed for a moment to relent in its pursuit of A lull in the Bank: McLane, who had taken Ingham's the attack. place at the Treasury Department after the breach between Jackson and Calhoun, made a report to Congress in December, 1831, in which he strongly favored the Bank, and it began to look as if the administration were going, for a season at least, to let the bank question drop. But Clay was not wise enough to let this happen He thought that he saw in the bank controversy a capital means of putting Jackson in the wrong in the eyes of the country, and defeating him in the election. The Whigs, at Clay's suggestion, made their advocacy of the Bank prominent in the address which they issued to the people in Charter bill making their nominations in December, 1831, passes Con- and, upon Clay's urgent advice, the friends gress. of the Bank applied to Congress for a renewal of its charter during the session of Congress immediately preceding the campaign. A bill renewing the charter passed the Senate in June, 1832, by a vote of 28 to 20, and the House in July by a vote of 109 to 76 Jackson vetoed it in " a message of great ability, which was mainly The veto devoted to proving the Bank, as then constituted, to be an unnecessary, useless, expensive, un-American monopoly, always hostile to the interests of the people, and possibly dangerous to the government as well." The majorities for the bill in Con-

gress were not large enough to pass it over the veto, and
the two parties "went to the country" to obtain its verdict in the elections of November, 1832.

41. Removal of the Deposits (1832-1833).

The result showed the folly of which Clay had been
guilty in supposing that respect for a great and useful
Jackson   moneyed corporation would be as universal or
re-elected   as powerful a motive among the voters as
appreciation of General Jackson, the man of the people.
It was madness to stake the existence of a great bank on
the popular vote. When the result was known, Jackson
of course interpreted it to mean that he had a commission from the people to destroy the Bank; and he almost immediately proceeded to destroy it. In his message
of December, 1832, to the Congress which had attempted
to re-charter the Bank, he intimated grave doubts as to
its solvency, which nobody had yet dreamed of doubting,
and suggested that its affairs ought to be investigated
by Congress, especially for the purpose of ascertaining
whether the deposits of the United States ought to be
allowed to remain in it, in view of its disordered and perhaps precarious condition. The House decided, by a
very large majority, that the deposits were safe. But the
President was convinced that the Bank had gone into
politics in the campaign of 1832, if never before, and
that the public funds were not safe in the hands of the
managers of "an electioneering machine." He determined to take the responsibility of withdrawing them.
In May, 1833, he appointed Livingston, the Secretary of
State, minister to France, transferred McLane, a friend
of the Bank, to the State Department, and appointed
William J Duane of Pennsylvania, an opponent of the
Bank, Secretary of the Treasury. It was necessary that

he should get a Secretary of the Treasury who would serve him in the business, for the law had conferred the

Removal of the Secretaries.

authority to remove the deposits, not upon the President, but upon the Secretary of the Treasury, and had made him directly responsible for the exercise of it to Congress. / The new Secretary, however, did not prove a pliant instrument; when requested to order the removal he declined, and made an earnest protest against the policy. He did not believe that the President ought to act in a matter of so great importance without first obtaining the assent of Congress to the action he proposed to take; and he saw that the sudden removal of the government deposits might cause a serious disturbance in the money market and jeopard important business interests. From no one, indeed, whose opinion was worth taking did Jackson receive the least encouragement to take the step he was contemplat-

"Paper read to the cabinet"

ing. But his mind was made up, and that was the end of the matter. In September he informed the cabinet that the removal of the deposits had been irrevocably determined upon, that it was his own decision, should be his own act, and he would take the responsibility. Duane declined to make way for the carrying out of the design by resigning; Jackson therefore dismissed him, and put in his place the Attorney-General, Roger B. Taney of Maryland, who was known to assent to the President's plan. Almost immediately an order issued from the Treasury directing that the nearly ten millions of public money then in the Bank of the United States should be gradually drawn upon, as usual, to meet the expenses of the government, but that no more should be deposited. Certain state banks were selected instead as depositories of the revenues. The Bank of the United States was at once compelled to curtail its loans, to enable it to bear

6

the drain, and there was distress, almost a panic, in the money market)

When Congress met in December, 1833, the President frankly explained why this extraordinary step had been **Jackson's** taken. He declared that he had received from **reasons.** the government directors of the Bank "an official report, establishing beyond question that this great and powerful institution had been actively engaged in attempting to influence the elections of the public officers by means of its money; and that, in violation of the express provisions of its charter, it had by a formal resolution placed its funds at the disposition of its president, to be employed in sustaining the political power of the Bank." It seemed to him that "the question was distinctly presented whether the people of the United States are to govern through representatives chosen by their unbiassed suffrages, or whether the power and money of a great corporation are to be secretly exerted to influence their judgment and control their decisions." In everything that the Bank did, even in its curtailment of its loans to meet the withdrawal of the funds of the government, he saw nothing but trickery and a struggle for illegitimate power. It seems clear, too, that these were his real convictions. (Probably there was now at last some truth in the charges he made against the Bank. Although it was not the monster he pictured it, it had unquestionably gone into politics; it had spent money in the elections, liberally, though probably not corruptly. Clay had destroyed it by forcing it to stake its life upon a political campaign, and so justify its enemies in their opinion of it.) The Bank had submitted to a vote, and the vote had gone against it: that was the Jacksonian logic. It was the same doctrine of popular sovereignty with which the Jackson party had started out upon its career.

42. Censure and Protest (1833, 1834).

The House of Representatives to which Jackson explained his motives in directing the removal of the deposits was the House which had been elected in 1832, and in it his party possessed a decided majority. It approved his action, of course. Not so with the Senate. There his opponents controlled the majority, and were led by the best talent of the country; and there Mr. Clay introduced resolutions censuring the President for dismissing a Secretary of the Treasury for refusing to act contrary to his sense of duty; and attacking the new Secretary for removing the deposits for reasons " unsatisfactory and insufficient."

Clay's resolutions.

Jackson would by no means submit to a public rebuke. He sent to the Senate a protest against its resolutions which constitutes one of the most remarkable documents in the public records of the country. Taken in connection with the message of July, 1832, vetoing the bill which granted a renewal of the charter of the Bank, it furnishes a complete exposition of the Jacksonian theory of the government. The veto message had declared that the President was not bound in his judgment of what was or was not constitutional either by precedent or by the decisions of the Supreme Court. " Mere precedent," it said, " is a dangerous source of authority, and should not be regarded as deciding questions of constitutional power except where the acquiescence of the people and the States can be considered as well settled." Congress, it showed, had itself wavered in its view of the matter, and the state legislatures were probably " as four to one " against the Bank. " The opinion of the judges has no more authority over Congress than the opinion of Congress has over the judges; and, on that point, the President is

Jackson's reply.

Jacksonian doctrine.

independent of both." The decisions of the Supreme Court must be permitted "to have only such influence as the force of their reasoning may deserve." (The protest added that it was not within the constitutional privilege of one of the Houses of Congress to condemn the President in any manner except by the process of impeachment; that the President, not the Secretaries, constituted the executive of the United States; and that the President — at any rate the President now in office — was the direct representative of the people, their organ, spokesman, and embodiment.) Such was Jackson's construction of the Constitution.

Two years later the friends of General Jackson commanded a majority in the Senate, and on January 16, 1837, the resolutions of censure were expunged from the journal of that body.

The Bank of the United States quietly arranged its affairs against the expiration of its national charter, Expiration obtained a charter as a state bank from the of charter legislature of Pennsylvania, and passed for the time out of general view.

43. Diplomatic Successes (1829-1831).

Perhaps the most satisfactory part of Jackson's record as President is to be found in his settlement of two interesting and important questions affecting the foreign relations of the country. Guided by Van Buren in matters which required delicacy, he exhibited the same initiative and energy in diplomacy that characterized him in dealing with questions of domestic policy.

Trade with the West India Islands had seemed ever since colonial times the natural and rightful outlet of our commerce; but when the States ceased to be colonies they parted with the privileges as well as with the disadvantages

of belonging to the British Empire, and began to be
excluded from their former free intercourse with neigh-
West India boring British possessions (Formation of the
trade   Union, §§ 47, 56, 63.) Until 1825 England kept steadily to her policy of favoring her own
ships in trade with all her colonial ports, and laying
all manner of restrictions upon ships of other nations,
and there seemed no hope of ever breaking down her exclusive navigation system. The only thing that could be
done, according to the notions of the time in such matters,
was done. countervailing restrictions were laid upon English ships in their trade with American ports. (In 1825,
however, under the influence of Huskisson, England offered to open her ports and the ports of her colonies to the
vessels of any nation that would open her own ports to
English vessels, upon the same terms that should be extended to the latter. The offer was to be left open for one
year. Congress did not take advantage of it; and when
Gallatin, for the Adams administration, proposed, after the
close of the period, to negotiate the question of the trade
relationships between the two countries, England declined. Jackson saw the value of the West India trade
to the United States, and he saw the only means of securing it.) He moved towards his object with his usual
directness. (He sent McLane to England to say that the
Adams administration had been rejected by the American people; that the new administration was of a new
mind; that the United States would repeal all her own
restrictions upon the carrying trade of England if England would remove hers upon the carrying trade of the
United States to the West India ports./ Congress, the
while (May 29, 1830), passed an Act to the same effect.
Lord Aberdeen said that that was all that England had
ever demanded, and the affair was settled.

The other question arose out of the claims of the

United States upon France for depredations upon American commerce during the Napoleonic wars, known as the French spoliation claims. These Jackson undertook to press, and circumstances favored the success of the negotiations which he set on foot. 1830 witnessed a revolution in France, the elevation of Louis Philippe to the throne, and the establishment of a constitutional government. The claims of the United States this government recognized as just, and it was agreed that they should be paid. The United States had claims also against other European powers for injuries done citizens of the Union during the same period, and these too were liquidated through the efforts of the Jackson administration.

French spoliation claims.

These successes gained for Jackson great credit with the country, for they not only obtained money and commercial advantage, but also maintained the dignity of the government, which foreign powers had hitherto never shown themselves very prompt to respect. Whenever directness and energy could succeed, Jackson was sure of success; and he certainly deserves credit in these transactions for a clear perception of what ought to be done and a straightforward confidence in doing it, even when it took the un-Jacksonian form of asking favors.

Jackson's reputation.

44. Distribution of the Surplus (1833–1836).

Whatever may be said of Jackson's charges against the Bank of the United States or of his method of effecting its ruin, it was probably a wise instinct that led him to destroy it. The country was on the eve of a great industrial development, when business was to enter upon a period of unparalleled expansion, and when a new force of speculative adventure was to hurry men beyond all rational reckonings, and make

Danger from the Bank

enterprise often as unwise as it was eager. In such a period, with such an atmosphere, when prudence could scarcely anywhere keep its head, it would have been indeed perilous to leave so great, so dominating a financial power in the hands of a giant private corporation like the Bank of the United States.

On the other hand, however, it could do nothing but harm to destroy such an institution suddenly, with an ignorant and almost brutal disregard of the damage that would thereby be done to the delicate fabric of commercial credit. ¶If it was the right thing to do, Jackson did it in the worst possible way. The effect of it was to produce at once and of a sudden, and to leave without check or guidance of any kind, the very madness of speculation and of bubble banking that the great presiding bank might in some measure have moderated and restrained.

Danger from destroying the Bank.

No sooner had the policy of withholding the federal deposits from the Bank of the United States been determined upon than every circumstance, whether good or bad in itself, seemed to conspire with every other to precipitate a financial crisis. Even the paying off of the national debt indirectly contributed to that result. By the close of the year 1835 all the obligations of the Federal Government had been paid, and it was entirely free from debt. At once the question arose, What is to be done with the surplus revenue? The receipts of the government could not very well be reduced, because they came chiefly from the customs duties, and the customs duties were levied under the compromise Tariff Act of 1833, which was a pledge of peace between parties and could not in good faith be touched. The proposal which found most favor under the circumstances was, that the surplus should be distributed among the States. (Accordingly, in June, 1836, an Act was

Surplus

passed which provided that on and after January 1st,
1837, all surplus funds remaining in the Treasury in
Deposit Act.   excess of $5,000,000 should be distributed in
quarterly payments to the States. There
were known to be scruples in some quarters about
making direct gifts in aid to the States, and in these
scruples the President was known to share. (The distribution was declared by the Act, therefore, to be of
the nature of loans to the States, though without interest,
to be recalled at the pleasure of Congress.) Jackson
signed the bill, and three quarterly payments were
made under it, the total sum distributed amounting to
$28,000,000.   After that, as it turned out, there was no
surplus to distribute.   Reckless speculation brought fatal
disaster, and the government suffered with the country.

45. The " Pet Banks " (1833-1836).

When the deposits of the federal government were
withdrawn from the Bank of the United States, the
Places of   Treasury Department selected certain state
deposit.   banks to take the place of the "monster"
corporation as custodians of the funds.   These the
political slang of the time promptly dubbed the "pet
banks." They were chosen, evidently, not according to
any criterion of soundness, but on the principle which
had hitherto been followed in the States in the granting
of bank charters, the principle, namely, of party fidelity.
The deposits were placed with Democratic banks in the
South and West, — where there was either little capital
and a good deal of speculation, or no capital at all and
a vast deal of speculation, — rather than with "Whig
banks" in the North and East.   There followed, of
course, eager, even bitter, competition on the part of Democratic bankers everywhere for admission to the select

company of custodians.   All sorts of influences were
brought to bear, and all sorts of influences were successful in swelling the number of favored depositories.

Stimulated not a little by such chances of lucrative
favors from the government, and given almost a clear
field by the destruction of the Bank of the
United States at a time when enterprise was
in all parts of the country assuming a new
boldness and adventuring a new magnitude of plan, a
passion for the establishment of banks of issue manifested itself everywhere. Charters were granted wholesale by the States, without deliberation or prudence, and
without effort to effect any system or exercise any control. Hundreds of banks, with no capital at all, issued
their notes as boldly and as freely as the few banks that
had real resources and tried to keep a specie reserve.
Even while the Bank of the United States continued to
exercise a certain presidency and control in such matters,
the aggregate circulation of the state banks had been
several times greater than its own; and now that the
influence and power of the great bank were withdrawn,
the volume of bank paper swelled to a portentous bulk.

*Multiplica-
tion of banks
of issue.*

46. Inflation (1833-1836).

Speculation of every sort, and particularly of every
unsound sort, received an immense impetus.   Money
was abundant and, inasmuch as it did not
represent capital, was easy to obtain.   The
Treasury chose its depositories, not where
money was needed for legitimate purposes or could be
used to the best advantage, but where there were faithful
Democratic bankers; and those who received it felt bound
to find borrowers who would use it. The paper notes
of the local banks were not good to travel with, they

*Effect of
government
deposits*

rapidly depreciated as they left the neighborhood of the
bank of issue. Only a very few banks were either known
or trusted throughout any large part of the country;
but the issues of every bank could be disposed of, and
fatally facilitated the starting of enterprises of all kinds.
The distribution of the surplus among the States embarrassed the banks of deposit, because they had to meet
Effect of   the quarterly payments; but although it ar-
distribution   bitrarily shifted the locality of speculation, it
did not decrease its bulk or seriously diminish its spirit
The States themselves found schemes to put the money
into, and that answered the same purpose; enterprise
was made the more confident, if anything, and the more
universal: the bubble of inflation grew all the bigger
and all the thinner. Railroads, too, were now beginning
to suggest the rapid extension of the area of enterprise;
everywhere the cry was, "Develop the country."

Jackson made trial of the efficacy of a small pill
against the earthquake. It had not been his intention
Jackson on   to clear the field of sound money and make
the currency.   way for the reign of paper credit. He took
occasion to avow his opinion that gold and silver were
the "true constitutional currency" of the country, and
a distinct effort was made by the administration to force
the output of the national mints into circulation. The
Gold coinage.   coinage of 1833 amounted to less than four
                millions; that of 1834 considerably exceeded
seven millions, the increase being almost altogether in
the gold coinage; and arrangements were made with the
deposit banks that they should issue no notes of less
than twenty dollars, at the same time that one-third of
their circulation should represent specie. A great many
of the States, too, were induced to forbid the issue of
notes of the smaller denominations by the state banks.
But no small expedients could stay the rising tide of

bank circulation, could provide capital to uphold that circulation, or assuage the fever of speculation that had fallen upon the country.

47. The " Specie Circular " (1836).

The situation, too, as was to have been expected, speedily became perilous for the government. Its revenues were being received in the paper of the banks, which exhibited all varieties and stages of depreciation. Sale of public lands. Speculation began to have an extraordinary effect upon the sales of the public lands. In 1834 less than five millions accrued from their sale; but in 1835 more than fourteen millions, and in 1836 nearly twenty-five millions; and these sales of course brought a flood of depreciated paper into the Treasury. Jackson was alarmed, and determined that, so far at any rate as the federal government was concerned, the "true constitutional currency" should be restored   July 11, 1836, The circular. accordingly, there issued from the Treasury the celebrated "Specie Circular," which directed that thereafter nothing but specie should be taken by the land agents in payment for public lands. The receipt by the Treasury of any notes but those of specie-paying banks was already prohibited by statute. The President doubtless had good reason to believe that there were no longer any specie-paying banks: he would assure the Treasury of sound money by confining the receipts to gold and silver. This measure, like the removal of the deposits, was his own, taken against the advice of the cabinet and on his own responsibility.

Before the full effects of this violent and arbitrary interference with exchanges could make themselves felt, Jackson's second term of office came to an end, and Van Buren succeeded to the presidency. Van Buren was Jackson's own choice

Van Buren succeeds Jackson.

for the succession; but he came in with a much reduced
following, and received from his predecessor a heritage
of bad policy which was to overwhelm him.   His majority
in the electoral college was forty-six, as against Jackson's
majority of one hundred and fifty-nine four years before;
his popular majority, 25,000, as against a majority of
157,000 for Jackson.   He did not lead, or constitute, a
party as Jackson did, and he deliberately emphasized
his subordination by implicit public pledges that he
would in all respects follow carefully in Jackson's foot-
steps.   He thus made himself responsible for all the
effects of the specie circular upon the business of the
country, and shouldered, besides, the burden of every
other mistake that Jackson had made.

CHAPTER IV.

ADMINISTRATION OF VAN BUREN (1837-1841).

48. Financial Crisis (1837).

THE financial storm had already fairly begun to break upon the country when Van Buren assumed the chief Commercial post of the federal government. Business crisis. was already upon the threshold of the crisis of 1837. The volume of paper currency which had gone West for the purchase of lands was thrown back upon the East for redemption, or to add still further to the plethora of circulation already existing there. Credit had received a stunning blow, under which it first staggered, and then fell. There was a sudden rise in prices. There had been a very rapid increase in the amount of imports since 1832, and considerable sums of specie had been sent abroad to meet balances. Flour rose from five dollars (1834) to eleven dollars per barrel (1837); corn from fifty-three cents to one dollar and fifteen cents per bushel. In February and March, 1837, there were bread riots in New York. The banks were everywhere driven to a suspension of specie payments, the deposit banks going down with the rest, in May. On May 15 the President called an extra session of Congress, for the first Monday in September, to consider measures of relief.

So far as he himself was concerned, the President evidently did not believe that relief should be sought in Policy of an abandonment of the policy of the specie Van Buren. circular. He himself issued a circular of similar import with regard to the transactions of the

Post Office Department; and when Congress met he had
no suggestion of retreat to make. Silas Wright of New
York was the authoritative spokesman of the administration. He had hinted at the advisability of a currency
wholly metallic in 1834, in the debates which followed
the removal of the deposits; and now that Van Buren was
at the head of the government, a party emerged from behind Jackson as the advocate of a stubborn adherence
to the policy of "hard money." Of this party Silas
Wright was one of the conspicuous leaders. Congress
had tried to effect a repeal of Jackson's specie circular in
its session of 1836–1837. Calhoun had declined to vote
on the bill, on the ground that he believed the state of the
currency to be "almost incurably bad, so that it was very
doubtful whether the highest skill and wisdom could re-
store it to soundness. An explosion he considered inevitable, and so much the greater the longer it should be
delayed." And this seems to have been the feeling of
the administration. Better insist on the specie circular,
and bring on the revolution, than try to postpone it by
makeshifts.

This was the negative side of the policy of this new
political combination. It had also positive proposals to
Sub Treas- make. It suggested a complete divorce of the
ury scheme. government from the banks, and proposed that
this divorce should be effected by leaving the revenues
of the government in the hands of the collecting officers, to be disbursed, transferred, and accounted for by
them under bonds of sufficient amount to secure their
fidelity. This was not a plan to regulate the currency
or to relieve the financial distress. It was purely administrative in character, meant to save the government from loss, and to secure it against embarrassment
by separating its affairs entirely from the hazards of
banking. The Senate accepted these proposals, even

adding a clause directing that all dues to the government should be paid in gold and silver; but the House tabled the measure. The four years of Van Buren's administration were spent in a persistent effort to get this bill through Congress. There were strong forces working for it, though they would seem not to have been forces of party principle so much as influences of individual opinion. Men like Benton, for whom the policy of the government in respect of the public lands had a vitality of interest such as it did not possess for the public men of the East, felt very keenly the need for some such heroic remedy for speculation as Jackson's circular supplied; men like Calhoun saw no use in trying to amend the bank system, and thought the maladies of the currency incurable except by acute suffering and a thorough natural purging of all morbid humors. Jackson, probably at Benton's suggestion, had committed his party to a definite course; Van Buren meant to follow him consistently in what he had done; and the party leaders had nothing else to suggest.

49. Banking Reform (1837–1841).

The only group of politicians, apparently, which then knew its own mind with reference to financial policy was "Loco-foco" principles. made up of those Democrats, originally a local faction in New York and dubbed " Locofocos," who thought that they detected the chief danger in the corruption incident upon the granting of bank charters in the States, and in the folly of the unlimited powers of note-issue conferred by those charters. They plainly avowed their "unqualified hostility to bank notes and paper money as a circulating medium" and to all special grants of incorporation by state legislatures They mustered strong enough to exercise a very considerable influence upon the state elections in New

York; the President, Silas Wright, and Senator Benton, although not openly of their party, practically entertained their principles; and when they presently disappeared within the general body of the Democratic party, it was rather because they had drawn it to themselves than because it had absorbed or defeated them.

The "Loco-foco" principles, indeed, were symptomatic of a common movement of opinion. Some efforts towards New York the reform of the banking system had already safety fund. been made in New York, and it is noteworthy that Van Buren had played a very wise and intelligent part in what had been attempted there. It was in accordance with suggestions contained in his message to the legislature of New York as governor, in 1829, that the "safety-fund" law had been passed, which required all the banks which had been chartered by the State to pay into the state treasury a certain percentage of their capital stock to serve as a fund out of which the liabilities of any of them that might fail should be made good. The deposit required proved too small, and a different system was presently found preferable; but the safety-fund was the beginning of reform.

In 1838 New York established a "free-banking" system, which set the fashion of reform elsewhere, and New York which, as subsequently amended, served as a free banking model for the excellent federal banking law of 1863. Under this system the practice of granting special charters was abandoned; it was to be free to any persons to form a banking company who should conform to the requirements of the Act, the leading and most important requirement being that each company should deposit securities with the State to the full amount of its circulating notes. Other States. sooner or later, entered upon the same line of policy. The follies and disasters of unregulated banking were at last telling upon the minds of legislators; and New York, the most party-ridden of States, led in the reform.

50. The Independent Treasury (1840).

Again and again did the administration party press the "Independent Treasury" scheme upon Congress: Financial three times was it adopted by the Senate and distress. rejected by the House. On the fourth trial it passed both houses, and became law July 4, 1840 Meantime nothing positive had been done for the relief of the financial distress of the country, and nothing permanent for the relief of the Treasury. The failure of the deposit banks, coming at the same time with the distribution of the surplus among the States, had brought actual pecuniary distress upon the government. Twice was it necessary, accordingly, to authorize the issue of Treasury notes. In the interval between the suspension of the banks of deposit and the determination by Congress of the policy of the Treasury in the matter of the custody of the revenues, a sort of extra-legal independent treasury arrangement had been inevitable; there was no safe place of deposit provided, and the moneys collected had to be retained by the Treasury agents.

The Independent Treasury Act, as finally passed, "directed rooms, vaults, and safes to be provided for the Treasury, in which the public money The Act. should be kept; provided for four receivers-general, at New York, Boston, Charleston, and St. Louis, and made the United States Mint and the branch mint at New Orleans places of deposit; directed the treasurers of the United States and of the mints, the receivers-general, and all other officers charged with the custody of public money, to give proper bonds for its care and for its transfer when ordered by the Secretary

7

of the Treasury or Postmaster-General; and enacted that after June 30, 1843, all payments to or by the United States should be in gold and silver exclusively." The system was to be presently repealed, for Van Buren and his party were to suffer immediate and overwhelming defeat; but it was to be restored, and was to become the permanent system of federal financial administration.

From the very first, all popular influences in politics went against Van Buren. The whole " bank war " had Unpopularity served to deepen the impression that Congress of Van Buren and the Federal Government as a whole was in some very direct way responsible for the financial condition of the country. Jackson's bank veto and his removal of the deposits had killed the Bank of the United States, against the protests of Congress; his transference of the public moneys to the state banks had led to the multiplication of local banking companies and the still more unhealthy stimulation of speculation; and then, after ostentatiously trusting the local banks, he had at a single wanton blow destroyed them, and with them all credit, by his specie circular. And now his successor would mend nothing, would propose nothing, except that the government take care of itself by keeping its own moneys, and have nothing whatever to do with any banks at all. Those of his party, the while, who said anything distinctly, said that gold and silver must be the currency of the country, at a time when there was no gold or silver to be had. As for the people, they still believed in legislative panaceas for pecuniary distress, and were beyond measure exasperated with the administration.

51. The Democrats discredited (1840).

There were other causes of irritation, other influences of alienation, too, between the government and the people.

The policy of arbitrary removals and partisan appointments which Jackson had adopted had early borne its nat-

Jobbery and
the "Spoils
System."

ural fruit; but its demoralizing results were
not fully disclosed until the administration of
the ill-fated Van Buren. Then many serious
cases of mismanagement, jobbery, peculation, and fraud
were discovered, and the particulars made public. Van
Buren seems to have sought no concealments, to have
made no effort to shield any offender; but he got no
credit for his uprightness, — he only received blame for
the establishment of a system which had made such demoralization of the civil service inevitable. It was commonly believed that he had been chiefly instrumental in
importing the "spoils system" of New York politics into
the national administration; for he had been one of the
most influential members of that "Albany Regency"
which had so long and so successfully controlled the public patronage in New York, and he was known to have
been the leading spirit of Jackson's administration. The

Van Buren's
responsibility

suspicion was unjust. Van Buren had used the
patronage in New York, but he had not fostered the misuse of it. He had acquiesced in Jackson's
methods, as did all who served Jackson; but he had not
introduced these methods, and he had done something to
discountenance their employment in his own Department
so long as he remained a member of the cabinet, —
as much, doubtless, as his too diplomatic nature permitted. But the suspicion, although unjust, was natural.
was universal, was ineradicable. It damaged him as
much in the general esteem as if it had rested upon
demonstration.

Every question that arose seemed to bring with it

Other causes
of irritation.

some loss of prestige for the administration.
A small but earnest and intense anti-slavery
party had been growing and agitating since 1831. Under

the influence of the feeling it had aroused, Congress was deluged with anti-slavery petitions, chiefly aimed at slavery and the slave trade in the District of Columbia, and the Democratic party had discredited itself by refusing to hear any petitions on the subject. In the closing months of 1835 Texas had declared her independence of Mexico,

Texas. and the next year Jackson accorded her diplomatic recognition. Now she was manœuvring for admission into the Union, with all the southern interest behind her. Northern men thought with alarm of her vast territory, out of which five slave States might be made; anti-slavery feeling was intense against any dealings or parleyings with her at all. Van Buren declined overtures of annexation, and declared the neutrality of the United States as between Texas and Mexico; but he did it, as he did all things, mildly and with prudent reserve, and was thought by his opponents to do it against his secret desire in the matter.

He handled with prudence and good judgment the troubles which had arisen upon the northeast frontier

Canada. because of a boundary dispute with England, complicated by an insurrection in Canada and by lawless attempts on the part of citizens of the United States to assist the insurgents; but he exasperated the men concerned by his justice towards the rights of England. It was under his administration that the last war

Seminoles. with the Seminole Indians of Florida was brought to a close; but it was a costly and cruel business, and, like other things, brought only criticism to the President and his advisers. These things might have been viewed more justly had the country not been passing through the fires of a prolonged financial

Popular feeling. crisis, and had it not seemed to find in the administration, not only an unwillingness to do anything to relieve the distress which Jackson had caused,

but obduracy and insensibility in its stubborn pursuit of
its single policy of an independent Treasury and hard
money for the general government, with or without a
banking system and a practicable currency for the people. Van Buren unquestionably showed throughout a fine
courage and a certain elevation of view ; but he was not
imperative or impressive, as Jackson was. The country
had made up its mind that he was a small, selfish, incapable politician, and it judged him accordingly.

Throughout the four years of the administration the
influence of the Whigs grew apace. Again and again
they carried States which had been of the Jackson following. In 1838 they elected William H. Seward, their candidate for governor, in Van Buren's own State of New
York, by a majority of ten thousand. For
Presidential
campaign of the campaign of 1840 they again nominated
1840. General William Henry Harrison for President, as they had done four years before, and John Tyler
of Virginia for Vice-President. The Democrats nominated Van Buren and Johnson. General Harrison had
served the country honorably both in civil and in military
capacities, was well known, and had, moreover, a certain homely modesty and candor which commended him
to the mass of plain men. His party proclaimed no principles except opposition to Van Buren and the Democrats. But this was enough. After a campaign of
unparalleled excitement and enthusiasm, Harrison was
elected by two hundred and thirty-four electoral votes,
to sixty for his opponent, carrying nineteen States, as
against seven for Van Buren ; although his popular
majority was less than one hundred and fifty thousand
in a total vote of nearly two millions and a half. The
Whigs, too, were to have a majority of forty-seven in the
House, and of seven in the Senate.

52. A New Era of Material Development (1830-1840).

The bold directness and almost lawless energy of Jackson's character were the more appreciated by his contemporaries because they seemed to epitomize the active spirit of personal initiative which quickened the whole country in his day. The decade 1830–1840 witnessed the beginnings of an industrial revolution in the United States. Railways began to be built.

Railways

The railway map of the United States in 1830 shows four short roads, with an aggregate length of twenty-three miles; on the map of 1840 there are lines representing an aggregate railway mileage of two thousand eight hundred and eighteen. These were small beginnings, but deeply significant of what was to come. The railway mileage of the country was to double thereafter every five years until the period of the Civil War. Steamboats multiplied with great rapidity upon the western rivers and on the Lakes, in response to the impulse which was being given to movements of population. The navigation of the ocean by vessels propelled by steam had become an established success by 1838, the utilization of anthracite coal in the production of steam (1836) and the invention of the screw-propeller (1836–38) contributing not a little to the result.

Steam navigation.

On every side mechanical invention was busy. Anthracite coal was successfully employed in the manufacture of iron in 1836. Nasmyth's steam-hammer was invented in 1838. The McCormick reaper, invented in 1834, at once simplified the cultivation of large farms with a small force of laborers, and assured the development of the great grain lands of the Northwest. Even friction matches, invented in 1829, ought to be mentioned, as removing one of the minor inconveniences of a civilization demanding all the light it could get.

Invention

This rapid multiplication and diversification of labor-saving machinery effected a radical change in economic and social conditions. While railways were to extend population, manufacturing industries were to compact it

Changes in manners and industry. The homely, rural nation which in 1828 chose Andrew Jackson to be its President, was now about to produce a vast and complex urban civilization. Its old habits were to be thoroughly broken up. Its railways were to produce a ceaseless movement of population, section interchanging people with section, the whole country thrown open to be visited easily and quickly by all who chose to travel, local prejudices dislodged by familiar knowledge of men and affairs elsewhere; opinions, manners, purposes made common and alike throughout great stretches of the land by reason of constant intercourse and united effort. The laboring classes, who had hitherto worked chiefly upon their own initiative and responsibility, were now to be drawn together into great factories, to be directed by others, the captains of industry, so that dangerous contrasts both of fortune and of opportunity should presently be created between capitalist and employee. Individual enterprise and simple partnerships were to give place on all hands

Corporations. to corporations The first signs of a day of capitalistic combinations and of monopoly on the great scale began to become visible, and it is noteworthy that Jackson, with his instinctive dread of the bank monopoly, was one of the first to perceive them. The nation, hitherto singularly uniform in its conditions of life, exhibiting almost everywhere equal opportunities of success, few large fortunes, and an easy livelihood for all who were industrious, was now about to witness sudden enormous accumulations of wealth, to perceive sharp contrasts between poverty and abundance, an ominous breaking up of economic levels. The aggregate material power of the country was to be greatly increased; but individual opportunity was to become unequal, society was to exchange its simple for a complex structure, fruitful of new problems of life, full of new capacities for disorder and disease.

It is during this decade, accordingly, that labor organizations first assume importance in the United States, in Labor organ- opposition to "capital, banks, and monopo-
izations. lies." During the financial distresses of the period, when every hardship of fortune was accentuated, strikes, mobs, and riots became frequent, and spoke of a general social ferment.

53. Economic Changes and the South (1829–1841).

The rapid material development of the period had, moreover, this profound political significance, that it has-
Irregular de- tened the final sharp divergence between the
velopment of North and the South. When it is considered
the nation. that the power of steam upon iron rails and in the water, and the multiplied forces of industry created by invention in aid of the mechanic arts, meant the accelerated growth of the West, a still more rapid development and diversification of the undertakings of manufacture, a still huger volume and a still quicker pace for commerce, and that in almost none of these things did the South as a section have any direct share whatever, it will be seen how inevitable it was that political dissension should follow such an economic separation. The South of course
The South made large contributions out of her wealth
and the West and her population to the development of the West; but this movement of southern people did not extend the South into the West. The southerner mixed in the new country with men from the other sections, and their habits and preferences insensibly affected his own

He was forced either to adopt ways of life suitable to the task of subduing a new soil and establishing new communities under novel conditions, or to give over competing for a hold upon the West. He was in most sections of the new territory, moreover, hindered by federal law from employing slave labor. In spite of all preferences or prepossessions, he ceased to be a southerner, and became a "westerner;" and the South remained a peculiar section, with no real prospect of any territorial addition, except on the side of Texas.

54. Structure of Southern Society (1829-1841).

The existence of slavery in the South fixed classes there in a hard crystallization, and rendered it impossible Social effect that the industrial revolution, elsewhere work-of slavery ing changes so profound, should materially affect the structure of her own society. Wherever slaves perform all the labor of a community, and all free men refrain, as of course, from the meaner sorts of work, a stubborn pride of class privilege will exist, and a watchful jealousy of interference from any quarter, either with that privilege itself or with any part of the life which environs and supports it. Wherever there is a vast multitude of slaves, said Burke, with his habitual profound insight into political forces, "those who are free are by far the most proud and jealous of their freedom. Freedom is to them not only an enjoyment, but a kind of rank and privilege. Not seeing there that freedom, as in countries where it is a common blessing, and as broad and general as the air, may be united with much abject toil, with great misery, with all the exterior of servitude, liberty looks, amongst them, like something that is more liberal and noble. I do not mean to commend the superior morality of this sentiment, which has at least as much pride as virtue in it:

but . . . the fact is so. . . . In such a people the haughti
ness of domination combines with the spirit of freedom,
fortifies it, and renders it invincible." Southern society

Resistance had from the first resolutely, almost passion-
to change ately, resisted change. It steadily retained
the same organization, the same opinions, and the same
political principles throughout all the period of seventy-
two years that stretched from the establishment of the
federal government to the opening of the war for its
preservation.

The structure of southern society unquestionably
created an aristocracy, but not such an aristocracy as

Southern the world had seen before. It was, so to say,
aristocracy a democratic aristocracy. It did not create
a system which jeoparded liberty among those who were
free, or which excluded democratic principles from the
conduct of affairs. It was an aristocracy, not of blood,
but of influence, and of influence exercised among
equals. It was based upon wealth, but not upon the use
of wealth. Wealth gave a man broad acres, numerous
slaves, an easy, expansive life of neighborly hospitality,
position, and influence in his county, and, if he chose to
extend it, in his State; but power consisted of opportunity, and not of the pressure of the wealthy upon the
poor, the coercive and corrupting efficacy of money. It
was, in fact, not a money wealth: it was not founded
upon a money economy. It was a wealth of resource
and of leisured living.

The life of a southern planter was in no sense a life of
magnificence or luxury. It was a life of simple and

Simple life. plain abundance· a life companioned with
books not infrequently, oftentimes ornamented
with household plate and handsome family portraits; but
there was none of the detail of luxury. A generous
plenty of the larger necessaries and comforts and a leis-

ure simply employed, these were its dominant features. There was little attention to the small comforts which we call conveniences. There were abounding hospitality and generous intercourse; but the intercourse was free, unstudied in its manners, straightforward, hearty, unconstrained, and full of a truly democratic instinct and sentiment of equality. Many of the most distinguished southern families were without ancient lineage; had gained position and influence by their own honorable successes in the New World; and the small farmer, as well as the great planter, enjoyed full and unquestioned membership in the free citizenship of the State.

As Burke said, all who were free enjoyed rank, and title to be respected. There was a body of privileged persons, but it could scarcely be called a class, for it embraced all free men of any substance or thrift. Of course not all of southern society was rural. There was the population of the towns, the lawyers and doctors and tradesmen and master mechanics, among whom the professional men and the men of culture led and in a sense controlled, but where the mechanic and the tradesman also had full political privilege. The sentiments that characterized the rural population, however, also penetrated and dominated the towns. There was throughout
Solidarity. southern society something like a reproduction of that solidarity of feeling and of interest which existed in the ancient classical republics, set above whose slaves there was a proud but various democracy of citizenship and privilege Such was the society which, by the compulsion of its own nature, had always resisted change, and was to resist it until change and even its own destruction were forced upon it by war.

Although the population of the country increased in the decade 1830-1840 from thirteen to seventeen millions, and although immigration trebled between 1830 and 1837,

the population of the older southern States increased
scarcely at all. In 1830 Virginia had 1,211,405 inhabitants; in 1840, 1,239,797. In 1830 South Car-
Population.   olina had 581,000; in 1840, 594,000. North
Carolina had 737,000 in 1830, 753,000 in 1840. Georgia
had done better: had increased her population by more
than one hundred and seventy-four thousand, and had
gone up from tenth to ninth place in the ranking of the
States by population. Mississippi and Alabama had
grown like the frontier States they were. The increase
of population in the northern States had in almost every
case been very much greater; while an enormous growth
had taken place in the West. Ohio almost doubled her
population, and Indiana quite doubled hers. Two new
States also were admitted, — Arkansas in June, 1836,
and Michigan in January, 1837.

55. An Intellectual Awakening (1829-1841).

The same period witnessed a very notable development
in the intellectual life and literary activity of the country.
The world's   It was a time when the world at large was
movement.   quivering under the impact of new forces,
both moral and intellectual. The year 1830 marks not
only a period of sharp political revolution in Europe,
but also a season of awakened social conscience everywhere. Nowhere were the new forces more profoundly
felt than in England, where political progress has always
managed to be beforehand with revolution. In 1828 the
Corporation and Test Acts were repealed; in 1829
Catholic emancipation was effected; in 1832 the first
reform bill was passed; in 1833 slavery was abolished
throughout the British Empire; in 1834 the system of
poor relief was reformed; in 1835 the long needed re-
constitution of the government of municipal corpora-

tions was accomplished; and in 1836 the Act for the commutation of tithes was adopted. Everywhere philanthropic movements showed the spirit of the age; and in these movements the United States were particularly

Social reforms in America

forward: for their liberal constitutions had already secured the political changes with which foreign nations were busy. Americans were among the first to undertake a serious and thoroughgoing reform of the system of prison discipline. It was the fame of the new penitentiary system of the United States that brought De Tocqueville and Beaumont to this country in 1831, on that tour which gave us the inimitable "Democracy in America." In the same year William Lloyd Garrison established his celebrated paper, "The Liberator," and the anti-slavery movement assumed a new shape, to which additional importance was given in 1833 by the formation of the Anti-Slavery Society. Everywhere a new thoughtfulness and humanity entered into legislation, purging institutions of old wrongs, enlarging the views of statesmen and the liberties of the people. The general spiritual ferment manifested itself in such religious movements as that which came to be known as Transcendentalism; in such social schemes as those of Robert Owen and the distinguished group of enthusiasts who established Brook Farm; in a child-like readiness on the part of all generous or imaginative minds to accept any new fad of doctrine that promised plausibly the regeneration of society.

It was to be expected that an age in which both the minds and the hearts of men were being subjected to new

New writers.

excitements and stirred to new energies should see new life enter also into literature. A whole generation of new writers of originality and power, accordingly, came suddenly into prominence in this decade. Hawthorne began to publish in 1828, Poe in 1829, Whittier in 1831, Longfellow in 1833, Bancroft in 1834, Emerson and Holmes in 1836. Prescott was already giving promise of what he was to do in his essays in the "North American Review." It was just without this decade, in 1841, that Lowell's first volume of youthful poems was given to the public. Law writings, too, were being published which were to become classical. Kent's "Commentaries on American Law" appeared between 1826 and 1830; Mr. Justice Story began to publish in 1833, and by 1838 had practically completed his great contributions to legal literature; Wheaton's "Elements of International Law" was published in 1836. Professor Lieber put forth his first works upon the theory of law and politics in 1838. Henry C Carey's "Rate of Wages" appeared in 1835, and his "Principles of Political Economy" between 1837 and 1840. These were the years also of Audubon's contributions to natural history, and of Asa Gray's first essays in botany. In 1838 James Smithson provided the endowment of the Smithsonian Institution

All this meant something besides a general quickening of thought. America was beginning to have a little more
Cultivation. leisure. As the material resources of the eastern States multiplied, and wealth and fortune became more diffused and common, classes slowly came into existence who were not wholly absorbed by the struggle for a livelihood There began to be time for the cultivation of taste. A higher standard of comfort and elegance soon prevailed, of which books were a natural accompaniment. Miss Martineau did not find European culture in the United States when she visited them in 1834, but she found almost universal intelligence and an insatiable intellectual curiosity. Native writers embodied the new ideals of the nation, and spoke a new and whimsical wit. The country brought forth its own historians and story-tellers, as well as its own mystics,

like Emerson, and its own singers to a cause, like Whittier. "You are a new era, my man, in your huge country,"
wrote Carlyle to Emerson.

Newspapers, too, began to take on a new form. The
life of the nation had grown too hasty, too various and
complex, too impatient to know the news and
to canvass all new opinions, to put up any
longer with the old and cumbersome sheets of the style
inherited from colonial times Papers like the "Sun"
and the "Herald" were established in New York, which
showed an energy and shrewdness in the collection of
news, and an aggressiveness in assuming the leadership
in opinion, that marked a revolution in journalism. They
created the omnipresent reporter and the omniscient editor who now help and hinder, stimulate and exasperate,
us so much. It was a new era, and all progress had
struck into a new pace.

Newspapers.

56. The Extension of the Suffrage.

In the colonies the suffrage had very commonly been
based upon a freehold tenure of property; and where no
property qualification existed, it was customary to limit the suffrage to those who were
tax-payers. In most of the older States such regulations
had survived the Revolution. But nowhere did they very
long remain. The new States forming in the
West bid for population by offering unlimited
political privileges to all comers; cities grew up in which
wealth was not landed, but commercial; French doctrines
of the "rights of man" crept in through the phrases of
the Declaration of Independence; demagogues, too, became ready to offer anything for votes in the "fierce
competition of parties careful for the next election, if
neglectful of the next generation;" and so everywhere,

Colonial

*Influences of
extension*

except in the South, a broad manhood suffrage presently came to prevail. By the close of Jackson's second term no northern State retained any property restriction except Connecticut, Rhode Island, and New Jersey, and no western State except Ohio.

57. The Re-formation of Parties (1829-1841).

Parties had taken form again while Jackson reigned. It was not easy to see the Democratic party as a whole Jackson's   while Jackson was President. His person-
influence   ality was too dominant, and the influences of the time were too personal, too complex, too obscure, to make it possible to say with confidence just how much of the policy of the administration was Jackson's own, just how much suggested to him by those who enjoyed his friendship.   When Van Buren becomes President, how-ever, the party emerges from behind Jackson; Van Buren's figure hides no other man's; and we see, by reading backwards, that a party of definite principles had for some time been forming.

We perceive that some of the measures of Jackson's time were his own, but that the objects aimed at were not his The Demo-   alone, but those of a group of party leaders
crats.   who stood behind him: Van Buren, Taney, Benton, Woodbury, Cass, and others; the group for which Silas Wright spoke in Congress when he intro-duced the Independent Treasury plan.   These men would have destroyed the United States Bank, but they would never have originated the plan for removing the deposits; they wished to see a currency of gold and silver take the place of a currency of depreciated paper, but none of them, except perhaps Benton, would have hazarded so bru-tal a measure as the specie circular. The principles of this new party were simple and consistent; and Van Buren's

administration showed with how much courage they were prepared to insist upon them and carry them into execution. These principles embraced a conservative construction of the Constitution and a scrupulous regard for the limitations of the powers of Congress. They therefore excluded the policy of internal improvements, the policy of interference with the business development of the country by means of protective tariffs, the policy of chartering a national bank, and everything that looked like a trespass on the reserved rights of the States This party wished to see the Treasury divorced from all connection with banks; it believed specie to be the "constitutional currency" of the country; it desired to see as much economy and as little governing as possible.

Until 1834, when it had assumed its new name, Whig, of conveniently ambiguous significance, the National Republican party of Clay and Adams had been too heterogeneous, too little united upon common principles, too little prepared to concert common measures, to be able to make any headway against the popularity of Jackson and the efficient organization of Jackson's followers. But by the middle of Jackson's second term it had fairly pulled itself together. By that time it had drawn several powerful factions to itself in the South, and had brought its other adherents to something like a common understanding and mutual confidence upon several important questions of public policy. It seemed to speak again with the voice of the old Federalists; for it leaned as a whole towards a liberal construction of the constitutional powers of Congress; it believed in the efficacy of legislation to effect reforms and check disorders in the economic life of the people. Its most conspicuous leaders were committed to the policy of large expenditures for internal improvements and to the policy of protective tariffs; and it contained,

The Whigs.

8

and for the most part sympathized with, the men who had fought for the renewal of the charter of the Bank of the United States.

The only thing that seemed now to imperil the integrity of parties was the anti-slavery movement. This Anti-slavery movement originated just as Jackson came movement. into power, had gathered head slowly, and had as yet little organic influence in politics. But it was steadily gaining a hold upon the minds of individuals and upon certain sections of the country; and it threatened the Democratic strength more than it threatened the Whig, simply because the Union between the Democrats and the South was of longer standing and of greater intimacy than the alliance between the southerners and the Whigs. Moreover, the anti-slavery feeling very early became conspicuous in politics by means of petitions poured in upon Congress praying against the slave-trade and slavery itself in the District of Columbia, and against the slave-trade between the States. The Democrats, under the leadership of the southern members, committed the fatal strategic blunder of refusing to allow these petitions to be read, printed, or referred. This of course gave the Abolitionists an important moral advantage. John Quincy Adams, too, was now spokesman for them in Congress. He had been sent to the House of Representatives in 1831 by the Anti-Masons, and remained there, an irrepressible champion of his own convictions, until 1848. Immediately after shutting off anti-slavery petitions Congress passed an Act in still further defiance of the anti-slavery feeling. June 7, 1836, the area of the State of Missouri, and therefore of slavery, was considerably increased to the westward, in direct contravention of the Missouri compromise, by adding to it the territory between its old western frontier and the Missouri.

58. Character of the Jacksonian Period (1829-1841).

It is not easy to judge justly the political character of this singular period as a whole. That the spoils system
Political or- of appointment to office permanently demoral-
ganization.   ized our politics, and that the financial policy of Jackson temporarily ruined the business of the country, no one can fail to see; but who can say that these movements of reaction against the older scheme of our national politics were not inevitable at some point in the
Disturbance   growth of our restless, raw, and suspicious democracy? Jackson certainly embodied the spirit of the new democratic doctrines. His presidency was a time of riot and of industrial revolt, of brawling turbulence in many quarters, and of disregard for law; and it has been said that the mob took its cue from the example of arbitrary temperament set it by the President. It is, however, more just to see, both in the President himself and in the mobs of his time of power, symptoms of one and the same thing; namely, a great democratic upheaval, the wilful self-assertion of a masterful people, and
The will of   of a man who was their true representative.
the people   The organic popular force in the nation came to full self-consciousness while Jackson was President. Whatever harm it may have done to put this man into the presidency, it did the incalculable good of giving to the national spirit its first self-reliant expression of resolution and of consentaneous power.

III.

THE SLAVERY QUESTION

(1842-1856).

59. References.

Bibliographies. — Lalor's Cyclopædia, Alexander Johnston's articles, "Slavery," "Whig Party," "Democrat Party," "Annexations," "Wars," "Wilmot Proviso," "Compromises," "Fugitive Slave Laws," "Territories," "Republican Party," Justin Winsor's Narrative and Critical History, vii pp. 297-310, 323-326, 353-356, 413 ff, 550 ff., W. E Foster's References to the History of Presidential Administrations, 26-40; C. K. Adams's Manual of Historical Literature. 566-581, 602 ff. 652-654, 657-659, 663-666.

Historical Maps. — Nos. 1, 2, this volume; Epoch Maps, Nos. 8, 11, 12; MacCoun's Historical Geography of the United States, series "National Growth," 1845-1848, 1848-1853, and series "Development of the Commonwealth," 1840, 1850, 1854, Labberton's Historical Atlas, plates lxix., lxx.; Scribner's Statistical Atlas, plates 15, 16.

General Accounts. — James F. Rhodes, History of the United States from the Compromise of 1850, i., ii. 1-236; Schouler's History of the United States, iv. pp. 359 ff., v. to p. 370; H. Von Holst's Constitutional History of the United States, ii. 371 ff, iii., iv., v, vi. 96; Carl Schurz's Henry Clay, chaps. xxii.-xxvii.; Johnston's American Politics, chaps. xv.-xviii.; J. H. Patton's Concise History of the American People, chaps. l.-lvii.; Bryant and Gay's Popular History of the United States, iv., chaps. xiii.-xvi.; Ridpath's Popular History of the United States, chaps. lvi.-lix.

Special Histories. — Nebel's War between the United States and Mexico; Stanwood's History of Presidential Elections, chaps. xvi.-xix.; Colton's Life and Speeches of Henry Clay; Stephen's Constitutional View of the War between the States; Greeley's American Conflict, i , chaps. xi.-xx.; W. Goodell's Slavery and Antislavery, pp. 143-219, 272 ff ; G. T. Curtis's Life of James Buchanan, i. pp. 458-619, ii. pp. 1-186; Tyler's Lives of the Tylers; F. W. Seward's Seward at Washington, 1846-1861, chaps. i.-xxxviii. ; Hodgson's Cradle of the Confederacy, chaps. x.-xiii ; P. Stovall's Life of Toombs, pp. 1-139; Merriam's Life and Times of Samuel

Bowles, i pp. 56–178; Olmstead's Cotton Kingdom; Draper's History of the Civil War, i., chaps. xxii.–xxv.; E. A. Pollard's Lost Cause, chaps. i.–iv.; T. N. Page's The Old South, Sato's Land Question in the United States (Johns Hopkins University Studies), pp. 61–69; Taussig's Tariff History of the United States, pp. 109–154, Garrison's (W. P. and F. J.) Life of William Lloyd Garrison.

Contemporary Accounts. — Benton's Thirty Years' View, ii. 209 ff. (to 1850); Sargent's Public Men and Events, ii., chaps. vi.–ix. (to 1853); Frederick L. Olmsted's Seaboard Slave States, Back Country, and Texas Journey (Condensed reprint as Cotton Kingdom); Clay's Private Correspondence; Webster's Private Correspondence; McCulloch's Men and Measures of Half a Century; G. W. Curtis's Correspondence of J. L. Motley; F. W. Seward's Seward: An Autobiography, chaps. xxxiii.–lxvi.; Chevalier de Bacourt's Souvenirs of a Diplomat (temp. Van Buren, Harrison, and Tyler), Herndon's Life of Lincoln, chaps. ix.–xii.; Thurlow Weed's Autobiography, chaps. xlviii.–lxi.

CHAPTER V.

THE SLAVERY SYSTEM.

60. Conditions favorable to Agitation.

So many and so various were the forces which were operative during the period of Jackson's presidency, and
Agitation and change. so much did a single issue, the financial, dominate all others during the administration of Van Buren, that it is difficult, if not impossible, to take accurately the measure of the times, to determine its principal forces, or to separate what is accidental in it from what is permanent and characteristic. During Jackson's eight years everything is changing; both society and politics are undergoing revolution; deep organic processes are in progress; significant atmospheric changes are setting in. The agitation has by no means ceased when Van Buren becomes President, but it manifests itself for the time being almost exclusively in profound

financial disorders, from which there is slow and painful recuperation. It is only after the first stages of the revolutionary ferment of this initial decade of the new democracy are passed that the permanent effects begin to show themselves. Then it is that the old phrases and costumes of our politics disappear, and the stage is cleared for the tragedy of the slavery question.

No one can contemplate the incidents of the presidential campaign of 1840 without becoming aware how much the whole atmosphere of national politics has changed since the old line of Presidents was broken, and a masterful frontiersman, type of a rough and ready democracy, put at the head of affairs   The Whigs, the party of conservative tradition and constructive pur-

New campaign methods. poses in legislation, put General Harrison forward as their candidate because he is a plain man of the people; they play to the commonalty by means of picturesque processions and hilarious barbecues, proposing the while no policy, but only the resolve to put out the pygmy Van Buren and bring the country back to safe and simple principles of government, such as a great and free people must always desire. They accept the change which Jackson has wrought in the methods of politics.

Parties emerge from the decade 1830–1840, in short, with methods and standards of action radically changed, and with a new internal organization intended to make of them effective machines for controlling multitudes of votes. The franchise has everywhere throughout the country been made practically universal, and the organization of parties must be correspondingly wide and general, their united exertions correspondingly concerted and active. There is a nation to be served, a vast vote to be controlled, a multitude of common men to be attracted. Hosts must be marshalled by a system of discipline.

There is something much more momentous than all this, however, in the creation of such a vast and generalized human force as had now been introduced into our national politics   The decade 1830–1840 possesses the deepest possible political significance, because it brings a great national democracy, now at length possessed in no slight degree of a common organic consciousness and purpose, into the presence of the slavery controversy.   Upon questions which seem simple and based upon obvious grounds of moral judgment, such a democracy, when once aroused, cannot be manipulated by the politician, or even restrained by the constitutional lawyer.   The institution of slavery, however deeply rooted in the habits of one portion of the country, and however solemnly guaranteed under the arrangements of the federal system, had in reality but a single stable foundation, — the acquiescence of national opinion.   Every social institution must abide by the issue of the two questions, logically distinct but practically inseparable: Is it expedient? Is it just? Let these questions once seriously take hold of the public thought in any case which may be made to seem simple and devoid of all confusing elements, and the issue cannot long remain doubtful.   That is what took place when a body of enthusiasts, possessed with the reforming spirit, took hold of the question of slavery in that momentous decade.   It was not really a simple question, but it could be made to seem so.

Slavery and the new national democracy.

61.   Antecedents of the Anti-Slavery Movement.

The Abolitionists by no means discovered the slavery question, but they succeeded in giving it a practical importance such as it had never had before.   A mild anti-slavery sentiment, born of the philanthropic spirit, had

existed in all parts of the country from the first. Nowhere were there to be found clearer or more plainly
spoken condemnations of its evil influence at once upon
masters and slaves and upon the whole structure and
spirit of society than representative southern men had

uttered. "Slavery," said George Mason of
Virginia, "discourages arts and manufactures.
The poor despise labor when performed by

Early anti-
slavery feel-
ing.

slaves.   They prevent the immigration of whites, . . .
they produce a pernicious effect on manners.   Every
master of slaves is born a petty tyrant.   They bring the
judgment of Heaven on a country."   In the northern
States, where slaves were comparatively few in number,
such sentiments had early led to emancipation (Formation of the Union, § 55); the system had, therefore, already become almost entirely confined to the southern
States, where slavery seemed more suitable to the climate.
There, too, the sentiment which had once existed in favor
of emancipation had given way before grave doubts as to
the safety of setting free a body of men so large, so ignorant, so unskilled in the moderate use of freedom; and
had yielded also to paramount considerations of interest, in the profitable use of slave labor for the production
of the immense cotton and tobacco crops which made the
South rich.   An African Colonization Society had been
organized in 1816 for the purpose of assisting free
negroes to form colonies in Africa, and this society had
been joined by both friends and opponents of the system
of slavery (Formation of the Union, § 126).   There had
been plans and promises of gradual emancipation even
in the South; and there were doubtless some who still
hoped to see such purposes some day carried out.

But these earlier movements, which had kept quietly
within the limits of law and of tolerant opinion, were
radically different from the movement which came to

a head in the formation of the American Anti-Slavery
Society in 1833; they can hardly be called even the
American
Anti-Slavery
Society precursors of that movement It was born
of another spirit. Garrison's " Liberator "
demanded the immediate and total abolition
of slavery throughout the country, laws and constitutions to the contrary notwithstanding; and this, with
some temporary abatements for policy's sake, became
the programme of the Anti-Slavery Society. The immediate effects of such a programme were anything but
favorable to its originators. Many who shared the
fashion of the age for reform eagerly subscribed to it;
but it powerfully repelled the mass of the people, ren-
Opposition dered deeply conservative by the inheritance
and practice of self-government, deeply im-
bued, like all of their race, with the spirit of political
compromise, patient of anomalies, good-natured too,
after the manner of large democracies, and desirous
always of peace. The responsible classes condemned
the leaders of the anti-slavery movement as fanatics
and stirrers up of sedition; the irresponsible classes
destroyed their printing-presses, and thought no violence
too grievous for them.

62. Occasion of the Anti-Slavery Movement.

But slowly, almost insensibly, the whole aspect of the
matter was altered. It is impossible to say what would
have happened had our system of law been then already
worked out in all its parts, the full number of States made
Question of
slavery ex-
tension up and closed, our framework of local government completed. If instead of a vast national
territory threatened with invasion by the aggressive slave interest, there had everywhere throughout
the continent been States with their own fully developed

systems of law, and their common pride of independence, possibly our national institutional structure would have been of too stiff a frame to succumb to revolution. But as it was, there were great issues of choice constantly thrusting themselves forward in national politics with reference to this very question of slavery. And the southern leaders were masterful and aggressive, ruthlessly pressing these issues and making them critical party tests. Safely intrenched though they were behind the guarantees of

Southern apprehensions.
federal law with regard to the autonomy of their own States, in this, as in all other questions of domestic policy, they had shown from the first an instinctive dread of being left in a minority in the Senate, where the States were equal. Their actions were dictated by an unformulated fear of what legislation might do should those who were of their interest fail of a decisive influence in Congress. They therefore fought for new slave territory, out of which to make new slave States; they insisted that anti-slavery petitions should not be so much as discussed in Congress ; and they forced northern members to accept the most stringent possible legislation with regard to the return of fugitive slaves. At every point they forced the fighting, exasperating, instead of soothing, the rising spirit of opposition in the North, choosing to lose rather by boldness in attack than by too great caution in defence.

These were circumstances extremely favorable to the anti-slavery party. The Missouri compromise of 1820

Anti-slavery advantage
showed that they could count upon a strong sentiment in favor of keeping the major part of the national territories free from slavery ; and it was to their advantage that the southern leaders should be always stirring this sentiment up by their attacks upon the Missouri arrangement. The practical denial of the right of petition in their case by Congress, moreover, gave them

an advantageous standing as martyrs in a cause as old and as sacred as English liberty. They were pressing a question upon the public conscience which could be made universally intelligible and universally powerful, if not irresistible, in its appeal to one of the broadest and most obvious of the moral judgments. Their own intense and persistent devotion, the hot and indiscreet aggressiveness of their opponents, and the intimate connection of the question of slavery with every step of national growth, gave them an increasing influence, and finally an over-whelming victory.

63. Establishment of the System of Slavery.

The general merits of the question of slavery in the United States, its establishment, its development, its social, political, and economic effects, it is now possible to discuss without passion. The vast economic changes which have taken place in all sections of the country since the close of the war have hurried us almost as far away from the United States in which slavery existed as any previous century could have carried us. It is but a single generation since the war ended, and we retain very intensely our sympathies with the men who were the principal actors on the one side or the other in that awful struggle; but doubtless for all of us the larger aspects of the matter are now beyond reasonable question. It would seem plain, for one thing, that the charges of moral guilt for the establishment and perpetuation of slavery which the more extreme leaders of the anti-slavery party made against the slave-holders of the southern States must be very greatly abated, if they are to be rendered in any sense just. Unquestionably most of the colonies would have excluded negro slaves from their territory, had the policy of England suffered them to do so. The selfish commer-

(marginal notes: Original responsibility; Moral question.)

cial policy of the mother-country denied them all choice in the matter; they were obliged to permit the slave-trade and to receive the slaves. Jefferson's original draft of the Declaration of Independence made it one of the chief articles of indictment against George the Third that he had " prostituted his negative for suppressing every legislative attempt to prohibit or to restrain this execrable commerce." The non-importation covenant which the Continental Congress had proposed in October, 1774, included slaves, and had been unanimously adopted by all the colonies, thus checking the slave-trade until the formation of the Confederation; and after the formation of the new government of the Union, the leading southern States of their own accord abolished the slave-trade before the year 1808, which the Constitution had fixed as the earliest date at which Congress could act in the matter.

The agricultural system of the South and its climatic conditions naturally drew a larger number of slaves to that Localization section than to the other parts of the country. of slavery. In 1775, upon the eve of the Revolution, there were 455,000 slaves in the South, to 46,102 in the North. While the Revolution was in progress, a series of inventions brought the whole modern machinery of cotton manufacture into existence. Following immediately upon the heels of this great industrial change, came Eli Whitney's invention of the cotton-gin (1793), which enabled even the unskilful slave to cleanse a thousand pounds of cotton of its seeds in a single day, instead of five or six pounds, as formerly. At once, almost at a single bound, the South became the chief cotton field of the world. In 1792, the year before Whitney's invention, the export of cotton from Cotton the United States amounted to only 138,328 pounds; by 1804 it had swelled to 38,118,041; and at the time of the first struggle touching the extension of slavery (the Missouri compromise), it had risen to

127,860,152, and its value from seven and a half to more than twenty-two millions of dollars. Before this tremendous development of cotton culture had taken place, slavery had hardly had more than habit and the perils of emancipation to support it in the South: southern life and industry had shaped themselves to it, and the slaves were too numerous and too ignorant to be safely set free. But when the cotton-gin supplied the means of indefinitely expanding the production of marketable cotton by the use of slave labor, another and even more powerful argument for its retention was furnished. After that, slavery seemed nothing less than the indispensable economic instrument of southern society.

64. Conditions of Slave Life.

Of the conditions of slave life it is exceedingly difficult to speak in general terms with confidence or with accuracy. Scarcely any generalization that could be formed would be true for the whole South, or even for all periods alike in any one section of it. Slavery showed at its worst where it was most seen by observers from the North, — upon its edges. In the border States slaves were constantly either escaping or attempting escape, and being pursued and recaptured, and a quite rigorous treatment of them seemed necessary. There was a slave mart even in the District of Columbia itself, where Congress sat and northern members observed. But in the heart of the South conditions were different, were more normal. Domestic slaves were almost uniformly dealt with indulgently and even affectionately by their masters. Among those masters who had the sensibility and breeding of gentlemen, the dignity and responsibility of ownership were apt to produce a noble and gracious type of manhood, and

Diversities

Domestic slaves

relationships really patriarchal. " On principle, in habit, and even on grounds of self-interest, the greater part of the slave-owners were humane in the treatment of their slaves, — kind, indulgent, not over-exacting, and sincerely interested in the physical well-being of their dependents," — is the judgment of an eminently competent northern observer who visited the South in 1844. " Field hands " "Field hands" on the ordinary plantation came constantly under their master's eye, were comfortably quartered, and were kept from overwork both by their own laziness and by the slack discipline to which they were subjected. They were often commanded in brutal language, but they were not often compelled to obey by brutal treatment.

The negroes suffered most upon the larger properties, where they were under the sole direction of hired over-seers. It was probably in some of the great Treatment. rice fields of the southern coast, where the malarious atmosphere prevented the master from living the year around in daily association with his slaves, and where, consequently, the negroes were massed in isolation and in almost inevitable misery, that their lot was hardest, their condition most deplorable. The more numerous the slaves upon any single property, as a rule, the smaller their chance of considerate treatment; for when they mustered by the hundreds it was necessary to group them in separate villages of their own, and to devise a discipline whereby to deal with them impersonally and in the mass, rather than individually and with discrimination. They had to be driven, they could not be individually directed. The rigorous drill of an army had to be preserved. Books like Mrs Stowe's " Uncle Tom's Cabin," which stirred the pity and deep indignation of northern readers, certainly depicted possible cases of inhuman conduct towards slaves. Such cases there may have been;

they may even have been frequent; but they were in every sense exceptional, showing what the system could produce, rather than what it did produce as its character-
Humane pub- istic spirit and method. For public opinion
lic opinion in the South, while it recognized the necessity for maintaining the discipline of subordination among the hosts of slaves, was as intolerant of the graver forms of cruelty as was the opinion of the best people in the North. The punishment of the negroes, when severe, was in most cases for offences which were in effect petty crimes, like the smaller sorts of theft. Each master was in practice really a magistrate, possessing a sort of domestic jurisdiction upon his plantation.

Probably the most demoralizing feature of the system taken as a whole was its effect upon the marriage rela-
Sale of tion among the negroes. It sometimes hap-
slaves. pened that husbands were sold away from their wives, children away from their parents; but even this evil was in most instances checked by the wisdom and moral feeling of the slave-owners   Even in the ruder communities public opinion demanded that when negroes were sold, families should be kept together, particularly mothers and their children. Slave-dealers were universally detested, and even ostracised; and the domestic slave-trade was tolerated only because it was deemed necessary for the economic distribution of the slave population.

65. Economic and Political Effects of Slavery.

The economic effects of slavery it is not so difficult to estimate; and these told not so much upon the slaves as
upon the masters. The system of slave-labor
Agriculture condemned the South not only to remain agricultural, but also to prosecute agriculture at the cost of a tremendous waste of resources. It was impossible in cul

tivating the soil by the work of slaves to employ the best processes, or any economical process at all. The system almost necessitated large "plantations," for with the sloth-

Waste. ful and negligent slave it was not possible to adopt intensive modes of farming. When the surface of one piece of land had been exhausted, a new piece was taken up, and the first left to recuperate its powers For all the South was agricultural, it contained within it a very much larger proportion of unimproved land than did any other section. Its system of labor steadily tended to exhaust one of the richest and most fertile regions of the continent.

The system produced, too, one of the most singular non-productive classes that any country has ever seen;

"Poor whites." this was the class known in the South as "poor whites." Free, but on that very account shut out from laboring for others, both because of the pride of freedom and because of the absence of any system of hired free labor; devoid also of the energy and initiative necessary to support themselves decently, these people subsisted partly by charity, partly by cultivating for themselves small patches of waste land. They belonged neither to the ruling class nor to the slave class, but were despised by both.

The political effects of slavery upon the South are no less marked. Judging from statistics taken about

The slave- the middle of the century, only one out of owning class every six of the white men of the South, or, at the most, one out of every five, was a slaveholder. Of course there were many white men engaged in the subordinate functions of commerce or in professional pursuits; there were many also, doubtless, who had the service of slaves without owning or hiring them in any numbers. Statistics of the actual number who owned slaves or hired them from their owners cannot furnish us with any exact statement of the number of those who enjoyed social position and influence such as to entitle them to be reckoned, in any careful characterization of the elements of southern society, as belonging to the slave-holding class. But upon whatever basis the estimate be made, it is safe to say that less than half the white people of the southern States should be classed among those who determined the tone and methods of southern politics. The ruling class in each State was small, compact,

Its power. and on the whole homogeneous. It was intelligent, alert, and self-conscious. It became more and more self-conscious as the anti-slavery agitation proceeded. Its feeling of separateness from the other sections of the country grew more and more intense, its sense of dependence for the preservation of its character upon a single fateful institution more and more keen and apprehensive. It had, besides, more political power and clearer notions of how it meant to use that power than any other class in the country. For the Constitution of the United States provided that three-fifths of the slaves should be added to the whole number of whites in reckoning the population upon which representation in Congress should be proportioned ; and the influence of the ruling class in the South was rendered by that provision still more disproportionate to its numerical strength Still another motive was thus added for the preservation of slavery and the social power which it conferred.

66. Legal Status of Slavery.

The existence of slavery within the respective States depended entirely upon their own independent choice. Statutory It had come into existence by custom merely. recognition It had, however, received statutory and judicial recognition, and no one pretended to think either that

Congress could interfere with it under the federal Constitution as it stood, or that there was the slightest prospect of the passage of a constitutional amendment giving Congress any powers concerning it. It was not the question of its continued existence in the States where it was already established, but the question of its extension into the Territories of the United States, or the admission into the Union of States like Texas, which already possessed slaves, that was the live question of national politics. It was upon this territorial question that the southern leaders thought it to their interest to be aggressive, in order that the slave States might not be left in a perilous minority when new States came to be added to the Union in the future; and it was here that their aggressiveness stirred alarm and provoked resistance.

This was the field of feverish anxiety and doubtful struggle. Many ominous things were occurring. In Disturbing 1831 Nat Turner's rebellion, the most formievents. dable and terrible of the outbreaks among the southern negroes, had taken place in Virginia, and had seemed to the startled southerners to have some connection with the anti-slavery movement. In 1833 the British Parliament passed a bill abolishing slavery throughout the British Empire, by purchase; and the example of abolition was brought uncomfortably near to our shores in the British West Indies. The Seminole War had dragged on from 1832 to 1839, and had had its immediate bearing upon the question of slavery; for more than a thousand slaves had fled into Florida, while it was a Spanish possession, and had taken refuge among the Indians, with whom they had in many cases intermarried, and it was known that the war was prosecuted largely for the recapture of these fugitives, whom the Seminoles refused to surrender. Last, and most important of all, the question of the admission of Texas, with her slave

system and her vast territory, arose to become the first
of a series of questions of free soil or slave soil which
were to transform parties and lead directly to civil war.
It was not the question of abolition that gained ground,
but the question of the territorial limitation of slavery.

As yet but two formal statutes had been passed
touching the question of slavery in the Territories, — the
Ordinance   first the celebrated Ordinance of 1787, which
of 1787.   had been adopted by the Congress of the
Confederation, and which had excluded slavery from the
"Northwest Territory," the region lying north of the
Ohio River and east of the Mississippi (Formation of the
Union, § 52). This Ordinance had been confirmed by an
Act passed by the Congress of the new government in
August, 1789, although it was generally admitted that the
Congress of the Confederation had had no constitutional
power either to acquire or to govern this territory. It
was taken for granted that the power was sufficiently
secured to the Congress of the Union by that article
of the Constitution which confers upon Congress the
power "to make all needful rules and regulations respecting the territory or other property belonging to the
United States." The second Act was that which con-
Missouri   cerned the admission of the State of Missouri
compromise.   to the Union, by which it had been determined that, with the exception of Missouri, slavery
should be wholly excluded from that portion of the Louisiana purchase which lay north of the southern boundary
of Missouri extended (Formation of the Union, § 127).
Although the greater part of the territory then belonging
to the United States had been thus barred against the
extension of slavery, not a little of it was left open. The
principle of compromise had been adopted, and the
southern leaders given to understand that, within a certain space, they had the sanction of the general govern-

ment in the prosecution of their efforts to extend their system and their political influence. It was, however, open to any successful party that chose to disregard this compromise in the future to break it and re-open the whole question.

CHAPTER VI.

TEXAS AND THE MEXICAN WAR (1836-1848).

67. The Whig Programme (1841).

THE Whig party fought and won the campaign of 1840 in one character, and then proceeded to make use of their victory in quite another character. They sought the election of Harrison as an opposition party, whose only programme of measures was that the erring Democrats should be ousted and rebuked; and then, when Harrison had been elected, forthwith interpreted the result to mean that they had been commissioned to carry out an elaborate programme of constructive legislation. The party had not been homogeneous enough to venture upon a formulation of active principles before they won the elections; but the elections once gained, they were found ready with a series of reforms.

The Whig transformation.

The campaign of 1840 had been one of unparalleled excitement and enthusiasm, and, when reckoned by electoral votes, the defeat of Van Buren had seemed overwhelming. Nineteen of the twenty-six States had given majorities for Harrison, only seven for Van Buren. But in most of the States the vote had been very close, and Harrison's popular majority was only 145,914 out of a total vote of almost two millions and a half. It was the noisy demonstrations of the campaign, still ringing in the ears of the Whigs, that made them deem the recent elections a popular revolution in their favor. A dispassionate examination of

Significance of Whig success.

the vote shows that nothing extraordinary had taken place, but only a moderate and equable, though singularly widespread and uniform, re-action from the drastic, and for the time distressing, policy of the Democratic administration. The Congressional elections were a much truer index of the result. In the preceding Congress the two parties had been almost equally matched in the House. In the next House the Whigs were to have a majority of twenty-five, and in the Senate a majority of six.

The recent financial troubles had brought real distress upon the government as well as upon the people, and it was deemed necessary to call an extraordinary session of Congress to devise measures of relief as speedily as possible. The Houses were summoned for the last day of May, and Mr. Clay was ready with a list of the measures which ought to be passed. That list included the repeal of the Independent Treasury Act, the establishment of a new national bank, the raising of a temporary loan, the laying of permanent tariff duties to supply the government with funds, and the distribution among the States of the proceeds of the sales of public lands. General Harrison was an earnest, straightforward, ingenuous man of the people; he enjoyed some military renown, and he had had some training in civil office. He was a sincere Whig, too, and thought that he had been elected to preside over Whig reforms. Mr. Clay's programme would probably have won his approval and support. But a sore disappointment was in store for the party. General Harrison was an old man, nearing his seventieth year; the campaign had been full of excitement and fatigue for him; and when he came to the presidency he shielded neither his strength nor his privacy, but gave up both to the horde of office seekers and advisers who

Whig programme

Death of General Harrison.

crowded about him.   Even his vigorous and toughened frame could not endure what he undertook; he suddenly sickened, and exactly one month after his inauguration he died.

68. The Vice-President succeeds (1841).

For the first time in the history of the government the Vice-President succeeded to the office of President. John Tyler. This was a contingency of which the party leaders had never dreamed when they chose John Tyler of Virginia for the vice-presidential chair. General Harrison was a Whig by principle; Mr. Tyler was a Whig only by accident.   He belonged to the southern group of public men, was a strict constructionist, and a friend of the system of slavery   He had opposed the re-charter of the Bank of the United States at the same time that he had also opposed Jackson's removal of the deposits.   He had maintained during the Missouri debates that Congress had no constitutional right to prohibit slavery in the Territories.   He had voted against the "Force Bill" during the nullification troubles of the winter of 1832-1833.   He had come to be reckoned among Whigs only because he had refused to submit in all things to the dictation of the Democratic majority; and he had received the second place on the presidential ticket of 1840 only because they desired to make sure of the somewhat doubtful allegiance of the southern group that were opposing the Democrats.   Now that he was President, therefore, the Whigs found themselves in a novel and most embarrassing situation.   Instead of a President who was their own man and a real Whig, they had a President who was at best only an eclectic Democrat.

The historian finds it extremely difficult to judge the character and conduct of Tyler as he appears during his

presidency. As gentle and courteous in manner as Van
Buren, he seemed to those who had had no experience of
his abilities, much less astute, much less a
master of policy. It was his instinct, when
brought into contact with opponents, to placate antagonisms. There was, moreover, in the general make-up of
his faculties, a tendency towards compromise which often
wore the unpleasing appearance of vacillation. Those
whom he thwarted and offended accused him of duplicity;
although his action was not the result of a dishonest spirit
so much as of a constitutional habit of trimming. His
past record in Congress furnished abundant evidence that
he was not without courage in acting upon his convictions, and that he held his convictions upon individual
questions with no slight degree of tenacity. But in his
mind political questions were separate, not members of a
systematic body of doctrine, and the aspects of each question changed with changes of circumstance. His mind,
without being weak, was sensitive to changes of influence;
it was a mind that balanced considerations, that picked
and chose among measures.

His unexpected elevation to the presidency, moreover,
brought new and subtle influences to bear upon him,
which rendered his course of action still more
incalculable. He was prompted, doubtless by
a small coterie of personal friends and advisers, to believe
that by a little shrewdness and a little boldness he could
transform himself from an accidental into a regular President, make himself the real leader of a party, and become
his own successor The Whigs were not united, and
projects for forming new parties amongst them seemed
feasible enough. Why might not the President, by making his own choice of measures, commend himself to the
country and supersede others in its confidence? Mr
Tyler at once showed himself determined to be a real

(marginal notes: Tyler as President. ... Tyler's policy)*

President; and in the end marred the whole programme of the Whigs. For a time, however, General Harrison's cabinet was retained; and it was made up of safe Whigs, led by the great Whig champion, Daniel Webster, as Secretary of State.

69. The Programme miscarries (1842).

Clay had serious misgivings concerning the new President, but he did not withhold his programme when Congress assembled. The first step was taken without difficulty: a bill repealing the Independent Treasury Act of the previous year was passed, and signed by the President. This was the negative part of the new policy; its necessary complement, according to Whig doctrine, was the creation of a new national bank. It was here that Tyler proved himself no Whig. The situation was one of great embarrassment for him His votes in Congress had distinctly committed him as an opponent of a national bank, and yet he had been elected Vice-President as the representative of a party whose record committed it to a national bank more unequivocally than to anything else. Apparently he had either to desert his party or his principles. He attempted to follow a middle course which would deliver him from so unpleasant a dilemma: he necessarily failed, and in failing he compromised himself most seriously.

Clay would have pressed for a bank of the old pattern, with its central offices in Wall Street, and its branches throughout the country. Tyler, however, it was found, could not smother his constitutional scruples on this subject. Like the Jacksonian Democrats, he doubted the power of Congress to establish such a bank. It was given out, however, that he would not oppose a central bank in the District of Columbia, the national government's own home-plot, or the establishment of branches of this central institution, upon assent being given to their establishment by the States in which they were to be placed.   Clay prepared a bill which yielded the point of the location of the central offices of the bank, but which did not provide for state assent to the establishment of branches.   The bill passed both houses;

Veto.   the President, after some hesitation, vetoed it, August 16, 1842; and the majority in favor of it in Congress was not large enough to pass it over the veto

Startled, and deeply solicitous to prevent the miscarriage of their cherished plans, the Congressional leaders "Fiscal Cor- sought to ascertain what sort of a bank bill the poration." President would sign.   After frank conferences with him, it came to be understood on both sides that President Tyler would accept a bill which established a "Fiscal Corporation" (so he preferred to call it), with its central offices in the federal District, and local agencies whose operations should not extend to the full banking functions of deposit and discount, but should be confined to interstate and international exchange.   Such a bill, after having first been considered and approved in cabinet meeting, passed both houses without alteration or amendment, and was sent to the President for his signature.   But Second he vetoed it (September 9).   It seemed a delibveto. erate act of bad faith.   Opposed to the creation of a bank by Congress, as to every other latitudinarian use of the powers granted by the Constitution, Mr. Tyler had yet suffered himself to become in some sort pledged to assist in carrying out a Whig programme.   Though he sought a compromise, his ambition to lead had prompted him to suggest its terms.   Possibly he had hoped that the measure he suggested would not prove acceptable to the friends of a national bank.   By the time the measure came to him for his signature, moreover, he was deeply exasperated by the outrageous reproaches that had been heaped upon him by the Whigs in Congress. He had involved himself in a very awkward position, and had extricated himself by force, rather than with honor.

His vetoes severed entirely his connection with the Whig party   Beyond measure disappointed and exasperated, and imprudently hasty in their expressions of resentment, the Whig members of Congress publicly repudiated the President, declaring that "all political connection between them and John Tyler was at an end from that day forth;" and every member of the cabinet at once resigned, except Webster, who was in the midst of delicate diplomatic business which could not be suddenly abandoned. The President had to fill the empty offices as best he could, with men of somewhat looser party ties.

Tyler discarded.

70. Some Whig Measures saved (1842).

The rest of the Whig programme went through without much difficulty. The immediate needs of the Treasury were provided for by a loan and a temporary Tariff Act. A law was passed providing for an annual division of the proceeds of the sales of public lands among the States, though a proviso was attached to it by the friends of low tariff, which in the end prevented it from going into effect. An amendment was incorporated which directed the suspension of the law whenever the tariff duties should exceed twenty per cent   Nevertheless, without the bank measure, the Whig policy was sadly mutilated. The Independent Treasury law had been repealed, but no other fiscal agency was provided for the use of the government: for the remainder of Tyler's term the handling and safe keeping of the revenues of the government remained unprovided for by law, to be managed at the discretion of

Distribution.

Deposit of balances

the Treasury. Fortunately the management of the administration was in this respect both wise and prudent, and the funds were handled without loss   In the regular session of 1841–1842 Congress passed a permanent Tariff Act. The twenty per cent duty which had been reached July 1, 1842, under the provisions of the compromise tariff of 1833, remained in force only two Tariff of   months. The new Tariff Act, which went into 1842   effect on the 1st of September, 1842, again considerably increased the duties to be levied. It had been only after a third trial that this Act had become law. Twice it had been passed with a provision for the distribution of surplus revenue among the States, and twice the President had vetoed it because of that provision; the third time it was passed without the obnoxious clause, and received his signature.

The diplomatic matters which kept Webster at his post when his colleagues were resigning, concerned the long-The Ashbur- standing dispute with Great Britain touching ton Treaty. the boundary line between the northeastern States of the Union and the British North American Provinces. The treaty of peace of 1783 had not distinctly fixed the boundary line in that quarter, and it had long been in dispute. The dispute was now complicated, moreover, by other subjects of irritation between the two countries, connected with certain attempts on the part of American citizens to assist rebellion in Canada, and with the liberation of certain mutinous slaves by the British authorities in the ports of the British West Indies. The northeastern States, too, were interested in getting as much territory as possible, and were not disposed to agree to moderate terms of accommodation. In August, 1842, by agreement between Mr. Webster and Lord Ashburton, a treaty was signed which accommodated the boundary dispute by running a compromise line across the district in controversy, and which also effected a satisfactory settlement of the other questions at issue After seeing this treaty safely through the Senate and past the dangers of adverse criticism in England, Mr. Webster also retired from the cabinet.

71. The Independent State of Texas (1819–1836).

Signs were not wanting that the people, as well as the President, were out of sympathy with the Whig policy, and were beginning to repent of the re-action against the Democrats. So early as the autumn of 1841 many state elections went against the Whigs, in States in which they had but recently been suc-cessful; and when the mid-term Congressional elections came around, the Whig majority in the House was swept utterly away, supplanted by a Democratic majority of sixty-one. The President, however, reaped no benefit from the change; he had ruined himself by being unfaith-ful to the party which had elected him. His Democratic opinions, however genuine, did not commend him to the Democrats, though they were of course glad to avail themselves of the advantages which his defeat of the Whig plans afforded them.

Whig losses

The Senate remaining Whig, the second Congress of Tyler's administration groped about amidst counsellings more confused and ineffectual than ever. The want of harmony between the two houses was added to the lack of concert between the President and both parties alike. The legislation effected was there-fore of little consequence, except in regard to a question which had so far been in no party programme at all. This was the question of the admission of Texas to the Union.

Lack of harmony

Texas had originally been part of the Spanish posses-sions in America, and when the United States acquired

Florida from Spain by the treaty of 1819, Texas had, upon much disputed grounds, indeed, been claimed as
Texas and Mexico. part of the Louisiana purchase This claim had, however, been given up, and a boundary line agreed upon which excluded her (Formation of the Union, § 124). In 1821, before this treaty had been finally ratified by Spain, the Spanish colonists in Mexico broke away from their allegiance, and established themselves in independence. In 1824 they adopted a federal form of government, and of this government the "State of Coahuila and Texas" became a constituent member, under a constitution, framed in 1827, which provided for
Emancipation. gradual abolition of slavery and prohibited the importation of slaves. But presently immigration transformed Texas from a Spanish into an American community. More and more rapidly, and in constantly augmenting numbers, settlers came in from the southern States of the Union, bringing their slaves with them, in despite of the Texan constitution. By 1833 the Americans had become so numerous that they made bold to take things in their own hands, and form a new constitution upon their own pattern. This constitution was never recognized by the Mexican government; but that mattered little, for the American settlers were presently to have a government of their own. In 1835 Santa Anna, the Mexican President, undertook to overthrow
Secession. the federal constitution, and reduce the States to the status of provinces under a centralized government. Texas at once seceded (March 2, 1836); Santa Anna, with five thousand men, was defeated by seven or eight hundred Texans, under General Sam Houston, in the battle of San Jacinto (April 21, 1836); and an independent republic was formed, with a constitution establishing slavery. It was almost ten years before Mexico could make up her mind to recognize the

independence of the revolted State; but the commercial
States of Europe, who wanted the Texas trade, and those
Indepen-   politicians in the United States who wanted
dence.   her territory, were not so long about it. The
United States, England, France, and Belgium recognized
her independence in 1837. Her recognition by the United
States had been brought about by her friends through
Jackson, without the consent of Congress.

72. First Steps towards Annexation (1837-1844).

It was no part of the ambition of Texas to remain an
independent State. The American settlers within her bor-
Purpose of   ders had practically effected a great conquest
annexation. of territory, and it was their ardent desire to
add this territory which they had won to the United
States. Hardly had they achieved separation from
Mexico when they made overtures to be admitted into
the Union. But this was by no means easily to be accomplished. To admit Texas would be to add to the area
of slavery an enormous territory, big enough for the
formation of eight or ten States of the ordinary size, and
thus to increase tremendously the political influence of
the southern States and the slave-holding class. For
this the northern members of Congress were not pre-
Opposition   pared. While public opinion in the North
             had no taste for any policy in derogation of
the compromises of the Constitution, it had, ever since
the debates on the Missouri Compromise, been steadily
making in favor of a limitation of the area of slavery,
its exclusion from as large a portion as possible of the
national domain. John Quincy Adams, now grown old
in his advocacy of the right of the anti-slavery men to be
heard in Congress, was looking about for some successor,
and had been joined in the House by Joshua R. Giddings,

a sturdy young pioneer from the Western Reserve of Ohio. Giddings had out-Adams'd Adams in offering obnox-

Giddings

ious petitions and resolutions, had been censured by the House; had thereupon resigned his seat, and been triumphantly re-elected by his constituents, — sent back to do the like again. There was too much feeling, too keen an anxiety about the slavery question, to make additions to slave territory just now easy, even if they should ever prove to be possible.

Van Buren, after seeming to dally with the question a little, had read the signs of the times, and declined the

Tyler's policy.

overtures of the Texans for annexation. Tyler was naturally more favorable to the project. By birth, training, and sympathy every inch a southerner, he shared to the full the principles, if not the courage, of the southern men of the stronger and sterner type, like Calhoun. He suffered himself to be led into negotiations with Texas. These negotiations were throughout the whole of their progress kept secret; Congress heard not a word of them until they were completed. Secrecy agreed well with the secretive, managing nature of the man, and favored the negotiations; open discussion would almost certainly have defeated them   Foreign nations

Arguments for annexation

were courting Texas for the sake of commercial advantage. Calhoun believed that England was seeking by every means to attach Texas to herself, if not actually to take possession of her. Mexico, it now appeared, at last despairing of recovering the territory, was straining every nerve to separate Texas from the United States, offering recognition of her independence in exchange for a promise from her to remain separate and independent. The slave interest was clamorous for the territory; so also were the speculators who held Texas land-scrip. To annex this great slave State might be too great a concession to slavery; but would it

not be worse to allow her to remain separate, a rival at
our doors, and a rival free, and likely, to ally herself with
European powers? Since our own people had taken possession of her, must not our government do so also?

Fostered and advanced by whatever motives, the secret
negotiations prospered, and in April, 1844, the President
A treaty   startled the politicians by submitting to the
defeated   Senate a treaty of annexation which he had
negotiated with the Texan authorities. It was rejected
by a decisive vote (16 to 35). Many even of those who
approved of the proposal did not like this way of spring-
ing it suddenly upon the country after clandestine negotiations, — particularly when it proceeded from a President
who belonged to neither party. But the President had,
at any rate, made the annexation of Texas a leading issue
of politics, concerning which party platforms must speak,
in reference to which party candidates must be questioned
and judged, by which votes must be determined.

73. Presidential Campaign of 1844

The treaty had been held in committee till the national
conventions of the two parties should declare themselves
Both conventions met in Baltimore, in May, to name candidates and avow policies. The Whigs were unanimous
as to who should be their candidate: it could be no one
but Henry Clay. Among the Democrats there was a very
strong feeling in favor of the renomination of Van Buren.
But both Clay and Van Buren had been asked their opinion about the annexation of Texas, both had declared
themselves opposed to any immediate step in that direction, and Van Buren's declaration cost him the Democratic nomination. He could have commanded a very considerable majority in the Democratic convention, but he
did not command the two-thirds majority required by

its rules, and James K. Polk of Tennessee became the nominee of the party. The convention having now committed itself, the Senate was allowed, June 8, to vote on the treaty, and rejected it.

Henry Clay was well known to have spent his life in advocating the lines of policy now clearly avowed by the Whigs; James K. Polk, though as yet little known by the country, proved an excellent embodiment of the principles of the Democrats. He had been well known in the House of Representatives, over which he had presided as Speaker, and where he had served most honorably, if without distinction. He was a southerner, and fully committed in favor of annexation. Though in no sense a man of brilliant parts, he may be said to have been a thoroughly representative man of his class, a sturdy, upright, straightforward party man. He believed in the policy for which his party had declared, and he meant, if elected, to carry it out.

The two party " platforms " were both of them for the most part old, embodying the things which everybody understood Whigs and Democrats to stand for. The only new matter was contained in the Democratic platform, in a resolution which demanded " the re-occupation of Oregon, and the re-annexation of Texas, at the earliest practicable period; " and this proved the make-weight in the campaign. It was clear what Polk meant to do; it presently became less clear what Clay meant to do. Clay had fatal facility in writing letters and making explanations. Again and again did he explain his position upon the question of annexation, in a vain endeavor to please both sides. Many, the Abolitionists among the number, concluded that an open enemy was more easily to be handled than an unstable friend. The "Liberty Party," the political organization of the Abolitionists, commanded now, as it turned out,

more than sixty thousand votes; and it was made up of
men who had much more in common with Whigs than
with Democrats. It put a candidate in the field, and
attracted many votes which Mr. Clay needed for his election. Fifteen States were carried for Polk, only eleven
for Clay. Polk's majority in the electoral college was
sixty-five. Almost everywhere the majorities had been
narrow. Had the "Liberty" men in New York voted for
Clay, he would have been elected. Many things had entered into the determination of the result, but the question
of the admission of Texas into the Union was undoubtedly
the decisive issue of the campaign.

Tyler hastened to be beforehand with the new administration. A joint resolution in favor of the annexation of
Texas ad-   Texas was urged in both houses, was passed,
mitted.   and was signed by the President, March 3,
1845. This resolution adopted the Missouri Compromise
line (36° 30' north latitude) with regard to the extension
of slavery within the new territory; for it was assumed
that the territory of Texas included all of the Mexican
country lying to the north between the Rio Grande and
the boundary lines fixed by the Spanish treaty of 1819.

74. The Oregon Question (1844-1846).

For a short time it looked as if the Democratic policy
of territorial aggrandizement would cost the country two
Rival claims. wars; but fortunately one of these wars was
            avoided, and that the one most to be dreaded.
The Democrats had coupled Oregon with Texas in the
resolution passed by their convention, in order to please
the Northwest as well as the South. They had succeeded
only too well : a strong feeling had been created in favor
of pressing a very doubtful claim. The boundaries of
the "Oregon country," as well as the right to the posses-

sion of it, were very inconclusively established. Russian

Russia. fur-traders had occupied a part of the region to the north, but Russia, by treaties with the United States and England in 1824 and 1825, had relinquished all claim to any part of the territory south of 54° 40′ north latitude. The claims of the United States rested in part upon a shadowy title which it was alleged

Spain she had derived from Spain through France upon purchasing Louisiana, in part upon exploration and settlement. The treaty of 1819, by which Spain ceded Florida to the United States, had fixed latitude 42° as the northern limit of the Spanish possessions. The region lying between 42° and 54° 40′ was the special

England. "Oregon country" claimed by both England and the United States. English fur-traders had occupied this region to some extent, and had even passed to the south of 49°, so that the British government was inclined to the last to insist upon the English right to everything north of the Columbia River. The United States had made official surveys south of 49°, and emigrants from the United States were slowly settling that district. The too-spirited policy of the Democrats in 1844 induced the hot-headed among them to start the cry " Fifty-four Forty or fight " (54° 40′) ; and for a time a war seemed scarcely avoidable, such was the

Settlement with England. feeling aroused in the country. But more prudent counsels in the end prevailed, and sensible concessions by both sides led (1846) to the conclusion of a treaty whereby 49° north latitude was finally fixed upon as the boundary between the United States and the British possessions. At last the northern boundary line of the Union, hitherto vague beyond the Rocky Mountains, was completed to the Pacific.

75. The Texan Boundary Dispute (1845-1846).

Our difficulties with Mexico with regard to the territory to be absorbed into the United States along with
Texan claim Texas were not so easily settled With England, which was strong, we were ready to compound differences; from Mexico, which was weak, we were disposed to snatch everything, conceding nothing. Texas had been a member of the federal republic of Mexico as part of the compound "State of Coahuila and Texas," but it was only Texas, not Coahuila, that had seceded from Mexico, and Texas extended to the southwest only so far as the Nueces River. Texas did indeed claim the territory of Coahuila, at least as far as the river Rio Grande; but she had not been successful in establishing that claim. She also claimed that on the north and west her territory extended from the sources of the Rio Grande due north to latitude 42°; but on this side, too, her claims were asserted rather than established. After having admitted Texas to the Union, the United States government was bound to make up its own mind as to the legitimate extent of Texan territory. President Polk very promptly decided what should be done. After Texas had accepted the proposition to enter the Union,
Troops sent under the joint resolution passed by Congress
forward. during the last days of Tyler's term, but before her entrance was formally complete, President Polk ordered General Zachary Taylor to cross the Nueces River and occupy its western bank with a force of United States troops. Taylor obeyed; and his force, which at first consisted of only about fifteen hundred men, was, in the course of the summer of 1845, increased to nearly four thousand. For six months nothing was done; the Mexicans made no hostile movement.

In December, 1845, Texas became a State of the Union.

Early in the following year the President, without con-
sultation with Congress, which was then in session, took
Taylor's   the responsibility of ordering General Taylor
advance.   to advance to the Rio Grande, to a point
threatening the Mexican town of Matamoras, on the opposite side of the river. Again, of course, Taylor obeyed
orders without question. Arista, the Mexican general,
demanded his retirement to the Nueces: Taylor refused
to withdraw; the Mexicans crossed the river, and on
April 23, 1846, ambushed a small body of American dra-
goons. A few days later an army of six thousand men
Palo Alto   met Taylor's force of twenty-three hundred
and Resaca   at Palo Alto, attacked it, and were repulsed.
de la Palma. The next day Taylor attacked Arista at
Resaca de la Palma and drove him in disastrous defeat
back across the river, and, himself passing the Rio
Grande, captured Matamoras. "Mexico," declared the
President's message of May 11, 1846, "has passed the
boundary of the United States, . . . and shed American
blood upon American soil. War exists, and exists by
the act of Mexico herself."

Upon the eve of these affairs Mexico had been filled
with civil disorders, and possibly it had not been ex-
Santa Anna's pected that she would resist the aggressions
intrigue.   of the United States to the point of actual
war. Our government tried to weaken her still further
by assisting her to another revolution; but that provident
intrigue miscarried. It only substituted the able and
astute Santa Anna, an old and implacable enemy of the
United States, for the much less capable Paredes as head
of the Mexican power.

76. War with Mexico (1846-1848).

Congress accepted the assertion that Mexico had begun the war, as convenient, whether true or not, and pro-

vided for the expenses of the conflict as for any necessity   A formal declaration of war was resolved upon on
Declaration   May 13, 1846, before the news of Palo Alto and
of war.   Resaca de la Palma had reached Washington; and the President was authorized to call for fifty
thousand volunteers for one year.   September 19-23, the
Americans, by slow and stubborn fighting, took the
strongly placed and heavily fortified city of Monterey,
some nineteen miles south of the Rio Grande.
Monterey.   February 22 and 23, 1847, Santa Anna, with a
force probably numbering at least twelve thousand men,
attacked Taylor's force, which then numbered fifty-two
Buena Vista.   hundred, on the broken plain of Buena Vista,
but, failing to gain any advantage, withdrew
to the defence of his capital, the City of Mexico.   He
had thought to destroy Taylor while he was weak; for in
November, 1846, General Winfield Scott had been appointed to the chief command in Mexico, to which his
military rank entitled him, and January had brought a
call for the greater part of Taylor's troops to assist the
commander-in-chief in an invasion of Mexico from Vera
Cruz on the coast.   The operations in the north ended
with the battle of Buena Vista.

General Scott began his operations with a force of
about twelve thousand men.   He had chosen a hard road
General Scott.   to the Mexican capital, but the dogged valor
and alert sagacity of his men made every-
thing possible.   The fleet which carried his troops came
to anchor near Vera Cruz on the 7th of March, 1847, and
Vera Cruz.   on the 27th of the same month Vera Cruz had
surrendered, having been taken without great
difficulty.   In the middle of April began the march of
Cerro Gordo.   two hundred miles northwestward to the City
of Mexico.   On the 18th Scott forced the rough
mountain pass of Cerro Gordo.   On the 10th of August,

after a delay caused by fruitless negotiations for peace, the City of Mexico was in sight from the heights of the Rio Frio Mountains. Selecting the weaker side of the city, which lay amid a network of defences and surrounded on all sides by marshy ground which could be crossed only upon causeways, the Americans slowly, by dint of heroic courage and patience, drove the Mexicans from one position of defence to another until Chapultepec finally the great fortress of Chapultepec was taken by storm (September 13) and the city captured. The occupation was complete by the 15th, and there was no further resistance anywhere by the Mexicans. At every point the American troops had fought against heavy odds. They were most of them only volunteers, and they had fought against a race full of courage, spirit, and subtlety. Their success was due to their moral qualities, — to their steady pluck and self-confidence, their cool intelligence, their indomitable purpose, their equal endowments of patience and dash.

77. The Wilmot Proviso (1846).

Not satisfied with seizing all that Texas claimed on the south and west, Mr. Polk and his advisers had turned covetous eyes towards Mexico's undisputed possessions on the northwest. During the spring and summer of 1846 New Mexico small military expeditions were sent out against and Califor- New Mexico and California, which they occunia pied without difficulty, being assisted in the seizure of California by a fleet under Commodores Sloat and Stockton. The end of the war, consequently, found the United States in possession of all the territory that Treaty of Texas had ever claimed, and of as much more Guadalupe besides. The treaty which ended this war Hidalgo of ruthless aggrandizement was signed at Guadalupe Hidalgo, Feb. 2, 1848. The United States agreed to pay Mexico fifteen million dollars for the provinces of New Mexico and California, which Mexico ceded; Mexico gave up all claim to Texas; and the Rio Grande was established as the southwestern boundary of the United States.

The northern boundary of Texas was still unsettled; the State still claimed all the territory that lay directly north of her as far as the forty-second parallel of north latitude, and the federal government could not in consistency deny the claim after it had served as a pretext for the seizure of the Mexican provinces. The purchase of her title became one of the features of the compromise legislation of 1850.

The ultimate outcome of the war had not been deemed doubtful at any time, and the opponents of slavery had The "Pro- very early determined to make every effort to viso" exclude that institution from any territory that the United States might acquire outside of Texas. In the North, Whigs and Democrats alike were anxious that all new territories should be kept free. Accordingly, early in August, 1846, when Congress was considering a money vote of two millions "for the settlement of the boundary question with Mexico" (which was understood to mean the acquirement of additional territory), David Wilmot, a Democratic member of the House from Pennsylvania, offered an amendment which became famous as the "Wilmot Proviso." Following the language of the Ordinance of 1787 for the government of the Northwest Territory, it provided that in any territories that might be acquired from Mexico, neither slavery nor involuntary servitude should exist, except for judicially determined crime. It passed the House, but reached the Senate late, and was lost by the dilatory speech of a senator who probably favored it.

The question which it involved was to come up again

and again, and was destined speedily to break both of the
Political old national parties in pieces. The slavery
effect. question had at last brought politics into a
period of critical change. It had forced upon the Democrats, the party of strict construction, a war of conquest
hardly consistent with any possible construction of the
Constitution. It was presently to bring utter destruction
upon them.

78. The Rest of the Democratic Programme (1846–1847).

In all other points of policy the Democrats had acted
quite resolutely in accordance with their avowed princi-
Tariff of ples. In July, 1846, Congress, which was Dem-
1846. ocratic in both branches, passed a Tariff Act
which may be said substantially to have conformed to the
professed Democratic ideal of a tariff of which the purpose was revenue rather than protection. It by no means
established free trade, but, grouping dutiable articles
under four several classes (known as schedules A, B, C,
and D), it put all those articles which usually claimed protection under a duty of only thirty per cent. Cottons were
put in class D, subject to a duty of twenty-five per cent;
while tea and coffee, which would naturally have been
chosen for taxation, had this been a tariff "for revenue
only," and not also incidentally for protection, were put
upon the free list. The new law was to go into effect
on December 1. August 6, 1846, another step was taken
towards the accomplishment of the full Democratic pro-
Independent gramme. On that day a new Independent
Treasury. Treasury Act, corresponding in all essential
points with that of July, 1840, became law. The measure
for which Van Buren had struggled so long, and on account of which he had sacrificed his chance for another
term of office, was at last made a permanent part of the

financial policy of the government. It has never since been altered in any essential feature.

The tariff was not again tampered with until 1857. Not even the expenses of the Mexican War could drive Revenue Congress either into increasing the tariff duties policy. for the sake of a larger revenue, or into connecting the government again with the banks for the sake of a serviceable currency. Both objects were thought to be sufficiently accomplished by large issues of interest-bearing treasury notes, and no further banking experiments were tried.

In the second Congress of Polk's administration, chosen in the autumn of 1846, with the Mexican War Elections coming on, the Democratic majority in the of 1846 House had disappeared ; there were 117 Whigs to 108 Democrats. But the Senate was still strongly Democratic, and the only result of the elections was that it became harder than ever to hit upon any policy for the government of the territories acquired from Mexico.

79. Slavery and the Mexican Cession (1846-1848).

The "Wilmot Proviso" was at once a symptom and a cause of profound political changes. It would seem that Arguments at first there was no serious opposition to the for the principle which it involved. It was objected Proviso. to, rather, as unnecessary, and as imprudent, because provocative of dangerous controversy. Slavery was already prohibited by Mexican law within the territories affected : why raise the question, therefore ; why take any steps concerning it ? The bill to which the proviso was attached had passed the House promptly and without difficulty, and it was the action of a minority only that prevented the Senate from accepting it also. But delay changed everything. The more the party leaders thought about the question involved, the less they relished the idea of taking any decisive step with regard to it.

During the session of 1846–1847, independent bills were passed by the two houses, appropriating three millions for Oregon question the settlement of the boundary disputes, instead of the two millions which had failed of appropriation in the previous session because of the proviso. In the Senate a bill passed without the proviso; in the House a bill which included it. The Senate bill finally prevailed. At the same time Oregon was dragged into the controversy. A bill providing for the organization of that Territory without slavery, originated in the House, failed in the Senate. Before the war of measures could be renewed, the Mexican struggle was over, and the treaty of Guadalupe Hidalgo had given us the vast territory then known as New Mexico and California, but covering not only the California and New Mexico of the present map, but also Nevada, Utah, Arizona, and portions of Colorado and Wyoming. Some government was imperatively necessary for these new possessions.

Meantime a few Democrats had invented a new doctrine, which promised a way of escape from the calamity "Squatter sovereignty" of party division. This was the doctrine of "squatter sovereignty." "Leave the question in abeyance; let the settlers in the new territory decide the question as between slavery or no slavery for themselves. It is a question of internal, not of national policy, to be determined by new States, as by the old, upon the principles of independent local self-government." The Whigs had no such doctrinal escape; neither could they keep together on the question. Southern Whigs would vote one way, northern Whigs another, along with the small body of Democrats who stood by Mr. Wilmot and his proviso.

August 12, 1848, after debates which had raged ever
since May around the question of the organization of
Oregon   Oregon and the new Mexican territories, a bill
organized.   at last became law which gave Oregon a regular territorial government, and which extended to her that
provision of the ordinance of 1787 which prohibited
slavery; but California and New Mexico were still left
without a permanent organization.

80. Presidential Campaign of 1848.

Thereupon ensued the presidential election of 1848,
which made the effects of this question upon politics very
Democratic   painfully evident.   Significant things hap-
convention.   pened during the months of preparation for
the campaign.   In the first place, the two regular parties
refused to commit themselves upon the real question of
the day.   The Democratic national convention met first
in Baltimore, May 22, 1848; nominated for President
Lewis Cass of Michigan, one of the safest and most intelligent of its more conservative leaders; and adopted
a platform which simply repeated its declarations of principle of 1840 and 1844.   A resolution to the effect that
non-interference with property in slaves, whether in the
States or in the Territories, was "true republican doctrine," the convention rejected by the overwhelming vote
of 216 to 36.   It would not commit itself in favor of sla-
The Whigs.   very in the Territories.   The Whig convention
              would commit itself to nothing.   Falling back
upon the policy which they had so successfully pursued in
1840, the Whigs nominated a plain man who had gained
distinction as a soldier, and made no declaration of
principles whatever.   Their candidates were, for President, General Zachary Taylor of Louisiana (a native of
Virginia); for Vice-President a Mr. Millard Fillmore of
New York.

But it was not alone the timid, non-committal policy of the two great parties which was significant. There had come from New York to the Democratic convention Democratic two delegations. One of these represented factions. the non-committal wing of the party, dubbed "Hunkers" in New York. The other represented the numerous Democrats in that State known as "Barnburners," who stood with Van Buren in holding explicit opinions as to what ought to be done. The nickname "Barnburners" is said to have been bestowed upon this radical wing of the Democrats by way of reference to a story, much told upon political platforms at that time, of the Dutchman who burned his barn to rid it of rats. Were they willing to destroy the party to get rid of slavery in the Territories? When the convention, with characteristic weakness, voted to admit both these delegations and to divide the vote of the State between them, both withdrew.

Nor was this the end of the matter. The withdrawal of these delegations from the Democratic convention was a signal for independent action, a revolt against the regular party nominations. In June the "Barnburners" held Bolt of the a convention of their own, in which they were " Barnburn- joined by delegates from Massachusetts, Con-ers " necticut, Ohio, and Wisconsin, and nominated Mr. Van Buren for the presidency. In August Mr. Van Buren was again nominated, by a new party, born in a convention composed of four hundred and sixty-five delegates, representing eighteen States, which met at Buffalo, at the call of citizens of Ohio. The resolutions adopted by this convention admirably formulated the issues of the future struggle. They declared for "free soil for a The "Free- free people." They proposed "no interference Soilers." by Congress with slavery within the limits of any State," for there it rested, they acknowledged, "upon state laws which could not be repealed or modified by the federal government ; " but they maintained that Congress had "no more power to make a slave than to make a king, to establish slavery than to establish a monarchy," and that the existence of slavery ought to be specifically forbidden in the Territories. Other resolutions declared for principles, such as internal improvements, which sounded much more Whig than Democratic   The Liberty, or Abolitionist, party had held its third convention the preceding November, and had nominated John P. Hale of New Hampshire ; but upon the nomination of Van Buren by the "Barnburners," Mr. Hale withdrew. The Free Soil party absorbed the Liberty party, henceforth they are practically one and the same, and the more radical programme of abolition is replaced by the more practicable programme of the exclusion of slavery from the Territories. The final contest is taking shape.

The split in the Democratic party in New York was decisive of the result of the presidential election. Outside of New York the Free-Soil vote drew strength away from the Whigs rather than from the Democrats : it was New York that decided the choice. The Democratic vote being divided between Cass and Van Buren, her thirty-six electoral votes went to Taylor and Fillmore; and thirty-six was exactly the Whig majority in the electoral college, where the vote stood 163 for Taylor, 127 for Cass. The popular vote was very close, neither candidate having a majority, because of the 291,263 votes cast for Van Buren. In the slowly changing Senate there was still to be a large Democratic majority, but in the House nine Free-Soilers were to hold the balance of power. The disintegration of parties was presaged by the vote of the South in the election. Six southern States (South Carolina, Georgia, Florida, Kentucky, Tennessee, and Louisiana) had voted for Taylor, a southerner and slave-holder, rather than go with the Democrats for Cass and a declaration of principles from which their own doctrine of non-interference with slavery in the Territories had been pointedly excluded.

The new feelings and purposes aroused by the campaign and election showed themselves at once, in the short session of Congress, during the closing months of Polk's term of office. The House now instructed a committee to prepare measures for the organization of New Mexico and California, upon the principle of the exclusion of slavery, and a bill for California was framed and passed But the Senate would have nothing to do with it, and the session closed without action upon the issue now so rapidly coming to a head.

Territorial dispute.

CHAPTER VII.

THE TERRITORIES OPENED TO SLAVERY (1848-1856).

81. Political and Economic Changes (1840-1850).

THERE were many symptoms of the coming in of new events and forces. The so-called Dorr Rebellion in Rhode Island marked the imperative force of the agen-

The Dorr Rebellion. cies that were operative throughout the country in the direction of a broad, democratic structure of government. The constitution of Rhode Island very narrowly restricted the suffrage, excluding from the elective franchise quite two-thirds of the men of voting age in the State, and the state authorities stubbornly resisted all liberal change. In the winter of 1841-1842, accordingly, revolutionary methods of reform were resorted to by the popular party, under the leadership of one Thomas W. Dorr. And though revolution was prevented, the reforms demanded were forced upon the party of order.

The same period witnessed serious troubles of another kind in New York. There the heirs of certain of the

Rent troubles in New York. old Dutch patroons, who held title to large portions of several of the counties lying along the Hudson River, still insisted upon the payment of rents in kind. They were at last obliged to consent to the extinguishment of their rights by sale, because of the absolute refusal of the tenants to pay for anything but a fee-simple. The affair as a whole was as significant of

11

economic tendencies as the Dorr Rebellion of the tendencies of politics. Manhood suffrage and freehold
titles were to be the permanent bases of our social
system.

Almost simultaneously with the conclusion of the
treaty of Guadalupe Hidalgo, gold was discovered in
Discovery   California, and before the census of Septem-
of gold   ber, 1850, more than eighty thousand settlers
had gone thither in search of treasure. California had
a great population and was ready to become a State before the politicians had gotten ready to organize her as
a Territory.

Meantime change and development were proceeding,
everywhere but in the South, with increasing rapidity and
momentum. In 1844 Morse's electric telegraph was put
into successful operation between Baltimore and Washington, just in season to keep the Democratic members
Invention   of Congress apprised of what their party con-
and expan-   vention was doing in Baltimore. During the
sion.   decade 1840-1850 more than six thousand miles
of railway were built, — an increase of more than two
hundred per cent over the preceding decade; and now,
with the assistance of the electric telegraph, systems of
communication could be both safely extended and readily
diversified. The population of the country increased
during the period from seventeen to twenty-three millions, and the steady advance of settlement is shown by
the admission of three States besides Texas. Florida
entered the Union March 3, 1845, Iowa December 28,
1846, Wisconsin May 29, 1848, — two free States offset-
ting two slave States.

82. Immigration (1845-1850).

Now at length, moreover, immigration was beginning
to tell decisively upon the composition of the population.

Until the year 1842 the total number of immigrants in
any one year had never reached one hundred thousand,
Causes of   and in 1844 it had fallen to seventy-eight
immigration. thousand.   But in 1845 a notable increase
began: the number of immigrants exceeded 114,000; in
1846 it was more than 154,000; and in 1847 it was
234,968.   Almost the whole decade was a period of dis-
quietude and crisis in Europe.   1846 and 1847 were the
years of the terrible famine in Ireland, and much of the
immigration of the time came from that unhappy country.
1848 brought a season of universal political disturbance
throughout Europe; and by 1849, the number of immigrants had risen to 297,024.   But the causes which
brought foreigners in vast numbers to our shores proved
not to be temporary.   The huge stream of immigrants
continued to flow in steady volume until checked by war.
And it had its deep significance as a preparation for the
Distribution. war which was at hand.   These new comers
swelled the national, not the sectional, forces
of our politics; they avoided the South, where labor was
in servitude, for they were laborers; they crowded into
the northern cities, or pressed on into the great agricultural region of the Northwest, hastening that development
and creating those resources which were to be the really
decisive elements in the coming struggle between the
slave section and the free section.
   The infusion of so large a foreign element, moreover,
quickened the universal movement and re-settlement of
the population which the railways were contributing to
make easy and rapid, and added stimulation to the spirit
Movement of of enterprise in new undertakings which the
population prevalent prosperity was everywhere encouraging   It tended, too, to deepen that habit of change, of
experiment, of radical policies and bold proposals, which
was bringing the people into a frame of mind to welcome

even civil war for the sake of a reform.   So long, too, as
a vast growth and movement of population continued
to be one of the chief features of the national life, the
question of free soil would continue to be a question of
pre-eminent importance, of immediate and practical interest, which could not be compromised without being
subsequently again and again re-opened.

Invention still kept pace with industrial needs.   The
power-loom was invented in 1846, as well as a fully practicable sewing machine.   The rotary printing press was
invented in 1847.   Piece by piece the whole mechanical apparatus of quick, prolific work, and of the rapid communication of thought and impulse, was being perfected.   The
The South.   South felt these forces, of course; it felt, too,
with genuine enthusiasm, the inspiration of
the national spirit and idea.   Southern politicians, indeed,
were busy debating sectional issues; but southern merchants presently fell to holding conventions in the interest
of the new industrial development.   These conventions
spoke very heartily the language of nationality; they
planned railways to the Pacific; they invited the co-
operation of the western States in devising means for
linking the two sections industrially together, they
hoped to be able to run upon an equality with the other
sections of the country in the race for industrial wealth.
But in all that they said there was an undertone of disappointment and of apprehension.   They wished to take
part, but could not, in what was going forward in the
rest of the country.   They spoke hopefully of national
enterprise, but it was evident that the nation of which
they were thinking when they spoke was not the same
nation that the northern man had in mind when he
thought of the future of industry.

83. Issue joined upon the Slavery Question (1849).

During the year 1849 a deep excitement settled upon the country. The difficulty experienced by Congress in fixing upon a policy with regard to the admission of slavery into the new Territories, the serious disintegration of parties shown by the presidential campaign of 1848, the rising free-soil spirit in the North, and the increasing pro-slavery aggressiveness of the South, were evidently Sectional bringing the whole matter to a critical issue. division. The sectional lines of the contest had been given their first sharp indication during the discussion upon the admission of Texas to the Union. "Texas or disunion" was the threat which the hotter headed among the southern annexationists had ventured to utter; and some of the northern Whigs had not hesitated to join John Quincy Adams, early in 1843, in declaring to their constituents that in their opinion the annexation of Texas would bring about and fully justify a dissolution of the Union; while later, in 1845, William Lloyd Garrison had won hearty bursts of applause from an anti-annexation convention, held in Boston, by the proposal that Massachusetts should lead in a movement to withdraw from the Union. Upon the first defeat of the Wilmot Proviso in the Senate in 1846, the legislatures of most of the northern States, and even the legislature of Delaware, had adopted resolutions in favor of the proviso, members of both the national parties concurring in the votes; while with even greater unanimity and emphasis, the southern legislatures had ranged themselves on the other side.

In February, 1847, Calhoun had presented in the Senate a set of resolutions which affirmed that, inasmuch as Calhoun's the Territories were the common property of position. all the States, Congress had no constitutional right whatever to exclude slaves from them, the legal

property of citizens of so many of the States of the
Union. Privately he had gone even further, and suggested to his friends in the South the co-operation of the
southern States, acting in formal convention, in closing
their ports and railways against commerce with the
northeastern States, while encouraging intercourse and
trade with the northwestern, until justice should be done
in the matter of the Territories   It might be possible
thus to divide the opposing section upon grounds of in-
Demands of   terest   The only just course, it came to be
the South.   thought in the South, was one of complete
non-intervention by Congress. The southern men asked
"simply not to be denied equal rights in settling and
colonizing the common public domain;" and that, when
States came to be made out of the Territories, their people "might be permitted to act as they pleased upon the
subject of the status of the negro race amongst them, as
upon all other subjects of internal policy, when they came
to form their constitutions." Before the final compromise of 1850 was reached, the legislatures of most of the
southern States had, in one manner or another, directed
their governors to call state conventions, should the Proviso be adopted by Congress, in order to take, if necessary, concerted action against a common danger. It was
ominous of the worst that the chief questions of politics
should have become thus sectionalized. It was the first
challenge to the final struggle between the radically di-
verse institutions of the two sections, — the section which
commerce, industry, migration, and immigration had expanded and nationalized, and the section which slavery
and its attendant social institutions had kept unchanged
and separate.

As yet the real purposes of parties, however, had not
reached their radical stage. As yet the Abolitionists,
with their bitter contempt for the compromises of the Con-

stitution, their ruthless programme of abolition whether
with or without constitutional warrant, and their readiness for separation from the southern States
Abolitionists
and Free-   should abolition prove impossible, had won but
Soilers.   scant sympathy from the masses of the people,
or from any wise leaders of opinion.   The Free Soilers
were as widely separated from them as possible both in
spirit and in opinion.   They had no relish for revolution, no tolerance for revolutionary doctrine, as their impressive declaration of principles in 1848 conclusively
attested.   The issue was not yet the existence of slavery
within the States, but the admission of slavery into the
Territories.   The object of the extreme southern men
was to gain territory for slavery; the object of the men
now drawing together into new parties in the North was to
exclude slavery altogether from the new national domain
in the West.

84. Independent Action by the Territories (1848-1850).

The controversy was hurried on apace by the discovery
of gold in California in January, 1848.   From every
quarter of the country, across the continent
California.
by caravan, around the coasts and across the
Isthmus of Panama, around both continents and the Cape,
a great population of pioneers, — a population made up
almost exclusively of strong, adventurous, aggressive men,
— poured into the new Territory, establishing camping
settlements destined to become great cities, improvising
laws and their administration, almost unconsciously creating a great frontier State.   To General Taylor, the new
Taylor's   President, as he witnessed this great develop-
policy   ment, it seemed the simplest way out of the difficulty of organizing governments in the new possessions
to arrange that the several communities of settlers there
should form state constitutions for themselves, and come

into the Union with institutions of their own choosing.
Accordingly, he sent a confidential agent to California to
act with General Riley, the provisional military governor,
in organizing such a movement among the settlers, and to
encourage them to make immediate application to Congress for admission into the Union. In the autumn of
1849 a constitution was framed which prohibited slavery;
a state government was formed at once under the new
instrument; and General Riley withdrew. The people of
New Mexico, under similar direct stimulation from the
President, adopted a state constitution early in the following year. The Mormons of Utah so long ago as
March, 1848, had framed a form of government for a
State of their own, which they desired to call " Deseret."
Apparently the Territories were to be beforehand with
Congress in determining their institutions and forms of
government.

When Congress met, December 3, 1849, its first difficulty was to organize. So nice was the balance of par-
Congress   ties, so strong the disposition to independent
perplexed.   action, that nearly three weeks were consumed
in the effort to elect a Speaker. The President very
frankly avowed his views to the houses in regard to the
principal question of the day. He said that he had himself advised the new Territories to form state governments; that California had already done so; and that he
thought that she ought to be admitted at once. He advised Congress, too, to wait upon the action of New
Mexico in framing a constitution before taking any resolution with regard to that portion of the new domain.
But the party leaders, lacking the President's soldierly
definiteness of purpose and directness of action, were
only made uneasy, they were not guided, by his outspoken
opinions. During all the autumn, southern governors had
been talking plainly to their legislatures of secession;

and although the legislatures held back from every extreme policy, they were uttering opinions in response
which made politicians anxious   What between the ex-
tremists of the North who urged disunion, and the ex-
tremists of the South who threatened it, the politician's
life was rendered very hard to live.

85. Compromise debated (1850).

It was under these circumstances that Henry Clay came
forward, with the dignity of age upon him, to urge meas-
Clay's pro- ures of compromise.   He proposed, Jan. 29,
posal.   1850, that Congress should admit California
with her free constitution; should organize the rest of the
Mexican cession without any provision at all concerning
slavery, leaving its establishment or exclusion to the
course of events and the ultimate choice of the settlers;
should purchase from Texas her claim upon a portion of
New Mexico; should abolish the slave trade in the District of Columbia, but promise, for the rest, non-interference elsewhere with slavery or the interstate slave
trade; and should concede to the South an effective fugitive slave law.   The programme was too various to hold
together.   There were majorities, perhaps, for each of its
proposals separately, but there was no possibility of making up a single majority for all of them taken in a body.
After an ineffectual debate, which ran through two months,
direct action upon Mr. Clay's resolutions was avoided by
their reference to a select committee of thirteen, of which
Mr. Clay was made chairman.   On May 8 this committee
reported a series of measures, which it proposed should
be grouped in three distinct bills.   The first of these, —
Omnibus   afterwards dubbed the "Omnibus Bill," be-
Bill.   cause of the number of things it was made to
carry, — proposed the admission of California as a State,
and the organization of Utah and New Mexico as Terri

tories, without any restriction as to slavery, the adjustment of the Texas boundary line, and the payment to Texas of ten million dollars by way of indemnity for her claims on a portion of New Mexico. The second measure was a stringent Fugitive Slave Law. The third prohibited the slave trade in the District of Columbia.

This group of bills of course experienced the same difficulties of passage that had threatened Mr. Clay's Significant group of resolutions. The "Omnibus Bill," debate. when taken up, was so stripped by amendment in tne Senate that it was reduced, before its passage, to a few provisions for the organization of the Territory of Utah, with or without slavery as events should determine ; and Clay withdrew, disheartened, to the sea-shore, to regain his strength and spirits. Both what was said in debate and what was done out of doors seemed for a time to make agreement hopeless. Clay, although he abated nothing of his conviction that the federal government must be obeyed in its supremacy, although bolder and more courageous than ever, indeed, in his avowal of a determination to stand by the Union and the Constitution in any event, nevertheless put away his old-time imperiousness, and pleaded as he had never pleaded before for mutual accommodation and agreement. Even Webster, slackened a little in his constitutional convictions by profound anxiety for the life of the Constitution itself, urged compromise and concession. Calhoun, equally anxious to preserve the Constitution, but convinced of the uselessness to the South of even the Constitution itself, should the institutions of southern society be seriously jeoparded by the action of Congress in the Southern pro- matter of the Territories, put forth the programme. gramme of the southern party with all that cold explicitness of which he was so consummate a master. The maintenance of the Union, he solemnly

declared, depended upon the permanent preservation of a
perfect equilibrium between the slave holding and the
free States: that equilibrium could be maintained only
by some policy which would render possible the creation
of as many new slave States as free States; concessions
of territory had already been made by the South, in the
establishment of the Missouri compromise line, which
rendered it extremely doubtful whether that equilibrium
could be preserved; the equilibrium must be restored, or
the Union must go to pieces; and the action of Congress
in the admission of California must determine which
alternative was to be chosen.   He privately advised that
the fighting be forced now to a conclusive issue; because, he said, "we are stronger now than we shall be
hereafter, politically and morally."

Still more significant, if possible, — for they spoke the
aggressive purposes of a new party, — were the speeches
Seward and   of Senator Seward of New York, and Senator
Chase.   Chase of Ohio, spokesmen respectively of the
Free-soil Whigs and Free-soil Democrats.   Seward demanded the prompt admission of California, repudiated
all compromise, and, denying the possibility of any equilibrium between the sections, declared the common domain of the country to be devoted to justice and liberty
by the Constitution not only, but also by "a higher law
than the Constitution."   While deprecating violence or
any illegal action, he avowed his conviction that slavery
must give way "to the salutary instructions of economy
and to the ripening influences of humanity;" that "all
measures which fortify slavery or extend it, tend to the
consummation of violence, — all that check its extension
and abate its strength, tend to its peaceful extirpation."
Chase spoke with equal boldness to the same effect.

Seward was the President's confidential adviser.   General Taylor had surrounded himself in his cabinet, not

with the recognized masters of Whig policy, but with men who would counsel instead of dictating to him. Several of these advisers were Seward's friends; and the President, like Seward, insisted that California be admitted without condition or counterbalancing compromise.

The Texan authorities, when they learned of the action of New Mexico in framing a constitution at the President's suggestion, prepared to assert their claims upon a portion of the New Mexican Territory by military force; the governor of Mississippi promised assistance; and southern members of Congress who called upon the President expressed the fear that southern officers in the federal army would decline to obey the orders, which he had promptly issued, to meet Texan force with the force of the general government. "Then," exclaimed Taylor, "I will command the army in person, and any man who is taken in treason against the Union I will hang as I did the deserters and spies at Monterey." The spirited old man had a soldier's instinctive regard for law, and unhesitating impulse to execute it. There was a ring as of Jackson in this utterance.

Southern feeling.

86. Compromise effected (1850).

But the spirit of compromise ultimately triumphed. A state convention in Mississippi, held the previous year, had issued an address to the southern people, proposing that a popular convention of the southern States should meet at Nashville, Tennessee, on the first Monday in June, 1850. The proposition met with favor, and at the appointed time the Nashville convention came together; but instead of threatening disunion, it expressed a confident hope of accommodation Within a few weeks thereafter General Taylor was dead. He had imprudently exposed

Nashville convention

Taylor's death.

himself to the sun on the fourth of July; the fever which ensued was at first too little heeded; and on the ninth of July he died, — the type of a brave officer whose work was unfinished.

Once more the Whigs had to accept the second man upon their presidential ticket as President; but Mr. Fillmore did not thwart them, as Tyler had done.
Fillmore. He was more docile than the dead President would have been. The cabinet was immediately reconstructed, with Webster as Secretary of State, and the compromise measures prospered in Congress. The new President followed his party leaders. By September 20 the Senate had accepted all the measures that Mr. Clay had proposed. The House followed suit, passing the bills in such order and combination as it chose, and the Compromise of 1850 was complete.

The result was to leave the Missouri compromise line untouched, — for the line still ran all its original length across the Louisiana purchase of 1803, — but
Results of the compromise. to open the region of the Mexican cession of 1848 to slavery, should the course of events not prevent its introduction. The slave trade was abolished in .he District of Columbia, but the North was exasperated by the Fugitive Slave Law, which devoted the whole executive power of the general government within the free States to the recapture of fugitive slaves. This part of the compromise made it certain that antagonisms would be hotly excited, not soothingly allayed. Habits of accommodation and the mercantile spirit, which dreaded any disturbance of the great prosperity which had already followed on the heels of the discovery of gold in California, had induced compromise; but other forces were to render it ineffectual against the coming crisis.

While Mr. Clay's compromise committee was deliberating, Mr. Clayton, President Taylor's Secretary of State, had concluded with the British authorities, acting through their American minister, Sir Henry Lytton Bulwer, the Clayton-Bul- treaty which was to be known in the United wer Treaty States as the Clayton-Bulwer Treaty (April 19, 1850), establishing a joint Anglo-American protectorate over any ship canal that might be cut through the Isthmus of Panama. The quick movement of population and trade between the Atlantic and Pacific coasts of the continent which had followed upon the discovery of gold in California had called into existence many projects for opening an easy passage from ocean to ocean through the Isthmus; and England had competed with the United States for the control of this new route of trade by seeking to gain a commanding influence among the petty Central American States. The treaty very fortunately effected an amicable adjustment of the questions of right which might have followed upon further rivalry. But, although a railway was opened across the Isthmus in January, 1855, more than thirty years were to elapse before a ship canal should be seriously attempted.

Six months before the passage of the compromise measures John C. Calhoun was dead, and one of the Death of leading parts in the culminating drama of Calhoun. politics was vacant. He died March 31, 1850, the central month of the great compromise debate. The final turning point had been reached; he had seen the end that must come; and it had broken his heart to see it. A new generation was about to rush upon the stage and play the tragedy out.

87. The Fugitive Slave Law (1850-1852).

For a short time after the passage of the compromise measures the country was tranquil. But the quiet was not a healthful quiet: it was simply the lethargy of re-

action. There was on all hands an anxious determination to be satisfied, — to keep still, and not arouse again
the terrible forces of disruption which had so
startled the country in the recent legislative
struggle, — but nobody was really satisfied.
That the leaders who had made themselves responsible
for the compromise were still profoundly uneasy was soon
made abundantly evident to every one. Mr. Webster
went about anxiously reproving agitation. These measures of accommodation between the two sections, he insisted, were a new compact, a new stay and support for the
Constitution ; and no one who loved the Constitution and
the Union ought to dare to touch them. Mr. Clay took
similar ground. Good resolutions were everywhere devoted to keeping down agitation. Party magnates sought
to allay excitement by declaring that there was none.

But the Fugitive Slave Law steadily defeated these
purposes of peace. The same section of the Constitution which commanded the rendering up by
the States to each other of fugitives from justice had provided also that persons " held to
service or labor in one State under the laws thereof,
escaping into another," should be delivered up on the
claim of the party to whom such service might be due ;
and so early as 1793 Congress had passed a law intended
to secure the execution of this section with regard to both
classes of fugitives (Formation of the Union, § 79). Apparently it had been meant to lay the duty of returning
both fugitives from justice and fugitives from service upon
the state authorities; but while considerations of mutual
advantage had made it easy to secure the interstate ren-
dition of criminals, there had been a growing
slackness in the matter of rendering up fugitive slaves. The Supreme Court of the United States,
moreover, had somewhat complicated the matter by de-

Uneasiness after the compromise.

Constitutional provisions

The old law ineffective.

ciding, in the case of *Prigg* vs. *Pennsylvania* (1842), that
the federal government could not impose upon state officials the duty of executing a law of the United States,
as it had sought to do in the legislation of 1793. Local
magistrates, therefore, might decline to issue warrants for
the arrest or removal of fugitive slaves. In view of the
increasing unwillingness of the free States to take any part
in the process, the southern members of Congress insisted that the federal government should itself make
more effective provision for the execution of the Constitution in this particular; and it was part of the compromise accommodation of 1850 that this demand should be
complied with.

Doubtless it would have been impossible to frame any
law which would have been palatable to the people of
Provisions   the free States. But the Fugitive Slave Act
of the Act.   of 1850 seemed to embrace as many irritat-
ing provisions as possible. In order to meet the views
of the Supreme Court, the whole duty of enforcing the
Act was put upon officers of the United States. Warrant
for the arrest or removal of a fugitive slave was to proceed in every case from a judge or commissioner of the
United States; this warrant was to be executed by a
marshal of the United States, who could not decline to execute it under a penalty of one thousand dollars, and who
would be held responsible under his official bond for the
full value of any slave who should escape from his custody;
all good citizens were required to assist in the execution
of the law when called upon to do so, and a heavy fine,
besides civil damages to the owner of the slave, was to
be added to six months imprisonment for any assistance
given the fugitive or any attempt to effect his rescue;
the simple affidavit of the person who claimed the negro
was to be sufficient evidence of ownership, sufficient
basis for the certificate of the court or commissioner:

and this certificate was to be conclusive as against the operation of the writ of *habeas corpus.*

The law, moreover, was energetically and immediately put into operation by slave owners. In some cases ne-

Resistance to groes who had long since escaped into the
its execution. northern States, and who had settled and married there, were seized upon the affidavit of their former owners, and by force of the federal government carried away into slavery again. Riots and rescues became frequent in connection with the execution of process under the law. One of the most notable cases occurred in Boston, where, in February, 1851, a negro named Shadrach was rescued from the United States marshal by a mob composed for the most part of negroes, and enabled to escape into Canada.

It was impossible to quiet feeling and establish the compromise measures in the esteem of the people while such

Mutual a law, a part of that compromise, was being
misunder- pressed to execution in such a way. Neither
standing. section, moreover, understood or esteemed the purpose or spirit of the other. "Many of the slave holding States," Clay warned his fellow Whigs in the North, when they showed signs of restlessness under the operation of the Fugitive Slave Law, "and many public meetings of the people in them, have deliberately declared that their adherence to the Union depends upon the preservation of that law, and that its abandonment would be the signal of the dissolution of the Union." But most northern men thought that the South had threatened chiefly for effect, and would not venture to carry out half her professed purpose, should she be defeated. Southern men, on their part, esteemed very slightingly the fighting spirit of the North. They regarded it disdainfully as a section given over to a self-seeking struggle for wealth, and they knew commercial

12

wealth to be pusillanimous to a degree when it came to meeting threats of war and disastrous disturbances of trade.

88. Presidential Campaign of 1852.

It was under such circumstances that the presidential campaign of 1852 occurred. The Democratic convention met in Baltimore on June 1, 1852. The leading candidates for the nomination were Lewis Cass of Michigan, James Buchanan of Pennsylvania, and Stephen A. Douglas of Illinois; but the rule of Democratic conventions which made a two thirds vote necessary for the choice of a candidate, rendered it impossible, as it turned out, to nominate any one of these gentlemen. The convention, therefore, turned by a sudden impulse to a younger and comparatively unknown man, and nominated Franklin Pierce of New Hampshire. Mr. Pierce was a handsome and prepossessing man of forty-eight, who had served his State both in her own legislature and in Congress, and who had engaged in the Mexican War, with the rank of brigadier general; but in none of these positions had he won distinction for anything so much as for a certain grace and candor of bearing. The Whig delegates, who met in convention in the same city on June 16, put aside the statesmen of their party, as so often before, and nominated General Winfield Scott.

Nominations

The platforms were significant of the critical state of politics. Both Whigs and Democrats added to their usual declaration of principles anxious asseverations of their entire satisfaction with the compromise measures. The Democrats went even further. They declared that they would "faithfully abide by and uphold the principles laid down in the Kentucky and Virginia Resolutions of 1798 and 1799, and the Report

Platforms

of Mr. Madison to the Virginia Legislature in 1799," — adopting those principles "as constituting one of the main foundations of their political creed," and resolving "to carry them out in their obvious meaning and import." But the principles of opposition which the two great national parties so much dreaded were spoken with great plainness by the Free Soil convention, which met at Pittsburg, August 11. This party repeated its utterances of 1848, pronounced the Fugitive Slave Law repugnant both to the principles of law and the spirit of Christianity, and announced its programme to be: "No more slave States, no more slave Territories, no nationalized slavery, and no national legislation for the extradition of slaves." The Free Soilers did not command the same strength that they had mustered in 1848, for the country was trying to rest; but scores of Whigs, not yet prepared to vote with this third party, were greatly repelled both by the military candidate of their party and by its slavish acquiescence in the distasteful compromise of 1850. The Democrats, on the other hand, were satisfied both with their party and their candidate, and the election was to bring them an overwhelming triumph.

The Free Soil convention

Before the end of the campaign both Mr. Clay and Mr. Webster were dead. Mr. Clay was on his death-bed when the Whig convention met. He died on the 29th of June, 1852. Mr. Webster followed him on the 23d of October. The great leaders of the past were gone: the future was for new men and new parties.

Deaths of Clay and Webster.

Although his popular majority was small in the aggregate vote, Mr. Pierce carried every State except four (Vermont, Massachusetts, Tennessee, and Kentucky), and received two hundred and fifty-four electoral votes, to General Scott's forty-two. At the same time the Democratic majority in the House of Representatives was increased by thirty-seven, in the Senate by six. Before another presidential election came around, the Whig party had practically been ousted from its place of national importance by the Republicans, — the great fusion party of the opponents of the extension of slavery.

89. Symptoms of Change (1851-1863).

In the mean time a most singular party pressed forward as a candidate for the vacant place. This was the party Anti-foreign which called itself "American," but which its movement. opponents dubbed the "Know Nothing" party. Once and again there had been strong efforts made in various parts of the country against the influence of foreigners in our politics. As immigration increased, these movements naturally become more frequent and more pronounced. They were most pronounced, too, in the cities of the eastern seaboard, into which immigration poured its first streams, and where it left its most unsavory deposits, — where, consequently, municipal misrule was constantly threatening its worst consequences of corruption and disorder. In 1844 "native" majorities had carried the cities of New York and Philadelphia, and had sent from those cities several representatives to Congress. For a short time after that date the feeling disappeared again; but about 1852 it was revived, for its final run of success. The revolutionary movements "Know of 1848-1850 in Europe caused a sudden increase in the immigration of disappointed and organization. turbulent men, apt and ambitious in political agitation. A secret order was formed, whose motto was: "Americans must rule America." From it emanated counsels which, commanding the votes in many places of active and united minorities, not infrequently determined

the results of local elections. The order had its hierarchy; only those who attained to its highest ranks were
inducted into its most sacred mysteries; and it was the
constant profession of entire ignorance of its secrets by
members of the order that gave them their popular name
of " Know Nothings." A singular opportunity for political importance was presently to come to this party.

In the summer of 1852 appeared a new engine of anti-
slavery sentiment, Mrs. Harriet Beecher Stowe's powerfully written novel, "Uncle Tom's Cabin,"
"Uncle   with its moving imaginative portrayal of the
Tom's   pathos, the humor, the tragedy, the terror of
Cabin"
the slavery system. While it unquestionably showed what
might come out of the system, it was built upon wholly
exceptional incidents. It was a product of the sympa-
thetic imagination, which the historian must reject as
quite misleading, but it nevertheless stirred to their profoundest depths thousands of minds in the North which
the politician might never have reached with his protests
against the extension of slavery. It was a subtle instrument of power, and played no small part in creating the
anti-slavery party, which was presently to show its strength
upon so great a scale in national politics.

All the while the industrial development of the country
went on as if there were no politics From May to October, 1851, the world attended England's
Industry.   great international industrial Exhibition, which
the noble Prince Consort had so humanely planned in the
interest of universal peace. The foreign trade of the
United States steadily grew in volume, receiving its impulse in part, of course, from the great gold discoveries
in California. A transcontinental railway was spoken of.
Population   The population, while it became more and
more dense, grew also more and more heterogeneous. It was at this time that Chinese first appeared

in strong numbers upon the Pacific coast, bringing with
them a new and agitating social problem.   The year
1851 saw the first state law prohibiting the manufacture
and sale of intoxicating liquors come into operation in
Maine, — a provocation to similar experiments elsewhere.
In the autumn of 1851 the country welcomed Louis Kos-
suth, the exiled Hungarian patriot, heard his engaging
eloquence with a novel rapture, and accorded him the
hearty sympathies of a free people.

90. Repeal of the Missouri Compromise (1854).

The Democratic Congress elected along with Franklin
Pierce met Dec. 5, 1853, and easily effected an organization.   The President's message assured the country of Mr.
Pierce's loyal adherence to the compromise of 1850, and of
the continued reign throughout the country of that peace
and tranquillity which had marked the quiet close of his
predecessor's term.   But immediately after Christmas, on
Jan. 4, 1854, Mr. Stephen A. Douglas introduced into the
Senate, as chairman of its Committee on Territories, a
bill, providing for the organization of the Territory of Nebraska, which was destined to destroy at once all hope
of tranquillity.   The region stretching beyond Missouri
"Platte   to the Rocky Mountains, then called the
country."   " Platte country," which this bill proposed to
organize as a Territory, was crossed by the direct over-
land route to the Pacific.   Mr. Douglas had been trying
ever since 1843, when he was a member of the House,
to secure the consent of Congress to its erection into a
Territory, in order to prevent its being closed to settlement and travel by treaties with the Indian tribes,
which might otherwise convert it into an Indian reserve.
The bill which Mr. Douglas now introduced into the
Senate from the Committee on Territories differed, how-

ever, in one radical feature from all former proposals.
The Platte country lay wholly within the Louisiana purchase, and all of it that was to be affected by this legislation lay north of the Missouri compromise line, 36° 30′,
which had been run across that purchase in 1820. All
previous proposals, therefore, for the erection of a Territory there had taken it for granted that slavery had once
for all been excluded by the action taken when Missouri
The Ne-   was admitted. This latest bill, however, ex-
braska bill. pressly provided that any State or States subsequently made up out of the new Territory should
exercise their own choice in the matter. This was simply following the precedent set in the organization of the
Territories of Utah and New Mexico four years before;
and in the opinion of Mr. Douglas a strict adherence to
the principles of that precedent was dictated by "a proper
sense of patriotic duty." The measure was at once attacked by amendment; and in order to avoid a tinkering
of their bill in open Senate, the committee secured its
recommitment. On January 23 they produced a substi-
Kansas-Ne- tute measure, which proposed the creation, not
braska bill of a single Territory, but of two Territories,
one of which should embrace the lands lying between latitudes 37° and 40°, and be known as Kansas; the other,
those lying between latitudes 40° and 43° 30′, and be
known as Nebraska. The bill further provided that all
            laws of the United States should be extended
Popular sov-
ereignty   to these Territories, "except the eighth sec-
clause.   tion of the Act preparatory to the admission
of Missouri into the Union, approved March 6, 1820
[the "compromise" section], which, being inconsistent
with the principles of non-intervention by Congress
with slavery in the States and Territories, as recognized
by the legislation of 1850, commonly called the compromise measures, is hereby declared inoperative and void.'

It was declared to be the "true intent and meaning" of the Act, "not to legislate slavery into any Territory or State, nor to exclude it therefrom, but to leave the people thereof perfectly free to form and regulate their domestic institutions in their own way, subject only to the Constitution of the United States." Finally, it was provided that the Fugitive Slave Law should extend to the Territories.

No bolder or more extraordinary measure had ever been proposed in Congress; and it came upon the country like a thief in the night, without warning or expectation, when parties were trying to sleep off the excitement of former debates about the extension of slavery. Southern members had never dreamed of demanding a measure like this, expressly repealing the Missouri compromise, and opening all the Territories to slavery; and no one but Douglas would have dared to offer it to them, — Douglas, with his strong, coarse grained, unsensitive nature, his western audacity, his love of leading, and leading boldly, in the direction whither, as it seemed to him, there lay party strength. Mr. Pierce, it seems, had been consulted about the measure beforehand, and had given it his approbation, saying that he deemed it founded "upon a sound principle, which the compromise of 1820 infringed upon," and to which such a bill would enable the country to return. Not a few able and aggressive opponents of the extension of slavery had of late been added to Seward and Chase in the Senate. Hamilton Fish had been sent from New York, Solomon Foote from Vermont, Benjamin Wade from Ohio, and from Massachusetts Charles Sumner, who had declared very boldly his distaste for the Fugitive Slave Law, and his determination to oppose every attempt either to carry freedom to the slave States or the sectional evil of slavery into the free States. These men made every effort, of course, to prevent the passage of

Audacity of the bill.

the bill; but they were overwhelmingly outvoted. The southern members gladly accepted what they had not asked for, and the northern Democrats reck-lessly followed Douglas. The Senate passed the bill by a vote of 37 to 14. Similar influences carried it through the House by a vote of 113 to 100. Douglas commanded the votes of forty-four northern Democrats, — just half the Democratic delegation from that section, — and nearly the whole southern vote. Nine southern members voted with the northern Whigs, and forty-four northern Democrats in the negative. On May 30 the President signed the bill, and it became law.

Passage of the bill

91. The Kansas Struggle (1854–1857).

The Act sowed the wind; the whirlwind was not long in coming. The compromise measures of 1850 had, of course, affected only the Territories acquired from Mexico; no one till now had dreamed that they re-acted to the destruction of the compromise of 1820, — a meas-ure which applied to a region quite distinct, and which was now more than thirty years deep in our politics. To the North, the Kansas-Nebraska Act seemed the very extravagance of aggression on the part of the slave in-terest, the very refinement of bad faith, and a violation of the most solemn guarantees of policy. The bill, moreover, contained a fatal ambiguity. When and in what manner were the squatter sovereigns of Kansas and Nebraska to make their choice with regard to slavery? Now, during the period of settle-ment, and while the districts were still Territories? or afterwards, when ready for statehood and about to frame their constitutions? No prohibition was put upon the territorial legislatures of Kansas and Nebraska: were they at liberty to proceed to make their choice at once?

The law's ambiguity

Whatever may have been the intention of the framers of the law, purposeful action in the matter did begin at once and fiercely, hurrying presently to the length of civil war. Organized Both from the North and from the South movement an organized movement was made to secure into Kansas. the Territory of Kansas by immediate settlement. The settlers who were in the slave interest came first, pouring in from Missouri. Then came bands of settlers from the free States, sent or assisted by emigration aid societies. The Missouri men hastened to effect a territorial organization; carried the elections to the territorial legislature, — when necessary by the open use of voters from Missouri at the polls; and the pro-slavery legislature which they chose met and adopted, in addition to the laws of Missouri in bulk, a stringent penal code directed against all interferences with the institution of slavery. The free settlers attempted to ignore the government thus organized, on the ground of Topeka con- its fraudulent nature. They met in convention stitution. at Topeka, October, 1855, adopted a free constitution for themselves, and ventured in January, 1856, to set up a government of their own. But the legal advantage was with the other side; whether fraudulently established or not, the pro-slavery government had at any rate been set up under the forms of law, and the federal government interfered in its behalf. As the struggle advanced, free settlers came in greater and greater numbers, and came armed, after the example of their Missouri rivals. Actual warfare ensued, and the interposition of federal troops became necessary. At last, in October, Free settlers 1857, the free settlers gained control at the gain control. polls of the legitimate legislature of the Territory, and the game was lost for slavery. A constitution was adopted without slavery, and with that constitution the Territory sought admission to the Union as a State.

In July, 1856, the House of Representatives had passed a bill for the admission of Kansas as a State, under the constitution adopted by the free settlers at Topeka, but the Senate had rejected it.

92. The Republican Party (1854-1856).

The majority which put the Kansas-Nebraska bill through the House in 1854 was destroyed in the elections "Anti-Ne- of the same year. All "Anti-Nebraska" men braska" men. drew away from the old parties. Most of these, however, were Whigs, and had no taste for the companionships which would be thrust upon them should they enter the Free Soil party. In this dilemma they took refuge with the "Know Nothings," who volunteered, with reference to the slavery question, to be Do Nothings. A desperate attempt was made to create a diversion, and by sheer dint of will to forget the slavery question altogether. Southern Whigs for a time retained their party name, and tried to maintain also their party organization; but even in the South the Know Nothings were numerously joined, and for a brief space it looked as if they were about to become in fact a national party. Know   In the elections of 1854 they succeeded in Nothing   electing, not only a considerable number of successes.   Congressmen, but also their candidates for the governorship in Massachusetts and Delaware. Before the new House met, in December, 1855, the Know Nothings had carried New Hampshire, Massachusetts, Rhode Island, Connecticut, New York, Kentucky, and California, and had polled handsome votes, which fell very little short of being majorities, in six of the southern States.

What with Anti-Nebraska men and Free Soilers, Democrats, southern pro-slavery Whigs, and Know Nothings, the House of Representatives which met Dec. 3, 1855, presented an almost hopeless mixture and confu- sion of party names and purposes. It spent two months "Republi- in electing a Speaker. Within a year, how- can" party. ever, the fusion party temporarily known in Congress as Anti-Nebraska men drew together in cohe- rent organization under the name "Republican." Groups of its adherents had adopted that name in the spring of 1854, when first concerting opposition to the policy of the Kansas-Nebraska bill. It was no sooner organized than it grew apace. Within the first year of its existence it obtained popular majorities in fifteen States, elected, or won over to itself, one hundred and seventeen members of the House of Representatives, and secured eleven adherents in the Senate. Representatives of all the older parties came together in its ranks, in novel agree- ment, their purposes mastered and brought into impera- tive concert by the signal crisis which had been precipitated upon the country by the repeal of the Missouri compromise. It got its programme from the Free Soilers, whom it bodily absorbed; its radical and aggressive spirit from the Abolitionists, whom it received without liking; its liberal views upon constitutional ques- tions from the Whigs, who constituted both in numbers and in influence its commanding element; and its popular impulses from the Democrats, who did not leave behind them, when they joined it, their faith in their old party ideals.

93. Territorial Aggrandizement (1853-1854).

Every sign of the times was calculated to quicken the energy and form the purposes of this new party. Not only did the struggle in Kansas constantly add fuel to the flame of excitement about the extension of slavery into the Territories, but it seemed that an end had not

yet been made of adding new Territories to those already acquired. Only four or five months before the adoption of the Kansas-Nebraska Act a new region had been The Gads- purchased from Mexico. The treaty of Gua-
den purchase. dalupe-Hidalgo (§ 77) had not satisfied Mexico with regard to the definition of the southern boundaries of the territories which she had surrendered to the United States on the Pacific coast. She still claimed a consider-able region south of the Gila River, which crosses the southern portion of the present Territory of Arizona. Santa Anna even led an army into the disputed district, and made threat of a renewal of war. Hostilities were averted, however, by a new purchase. Acting through Mr. Gadsden, the federal government agreed, Dec. 30, 1853, to pay Mexico ten million dollars for the something more than forty-five thousand square miles of territory in controversy, and the southwestern boundary was at last finally fixed.

This was the addition also of new territory in the re-gion most likely to be occupied by slavery; and appar-ently annexations in the interest of slavery were not to end there. There seemed to be a growing desire on the part of the South to see Cuba wrested from Spain, and added as new slave territory to the United States. Some of the more indiscreet and daring of the southern politicians even became involved in attempts to seize Cuba and effect a revolutionary expulsion of the Spanish power. In 1854, under pressure of the southern party, Mr. Pierce directed the American ministers to Great Britain, France, and Spain (James Buchanan, John Y. Mason, and Pierre Soulé) to meet and discuss the Cuban "Ostend question. The result was the "Ostend Mani-
Manifesto" festo" of October 18, 1854, which gave deep offence to the Free Soil party. Meeting at Ostend, these gentlemen agreed to report to their government that in

their opinion the acquisition of Cuba would be advantageous to the United States; and that if Spain refused to sell it, the United States would be justified in wresting it from her, rather than see it Africanized, as San Domingo had been. Expeditions, too, were organized by a few southern men against Central America, and repeated, though futile, attempts made to gain new territory to the south of Texas. The men who engaged in these mad attempts at conquest acted without organized support or responsible recognition by any southern government; but the North regarded their actions, nevertheless, as symptomatic of the most alarming tendencies, the most revolutionary purposes. The South, on its part, presently saw the contest for supremacy in Kansas turn overwhelmingly against the slave owners; saw free Territories rapidly preparing to become free States; saw fast approaching the destruction of the sectional equilibrium in the Senate. Parties formed and planned accordingly.

Crisis.

94. Presidential Campaign of 1856.

The Presidential campaign of 1856 was a four-cornered contest. The first party to prepare a platform and put forward candidates was the American, or Know Nothing, whose convention assembled Feb. 22, 1856, in Philadelphia. It nominated for President Mr. Fillmore, and in its platform it repeated those declarations in favor of restricting the privileges of foreigners, and of respecting the Constitution and the reserved rights of the States, by which it thought to divert attention from slavery and secure peace. But a minority of the members withdrew even from this peace loving convention, because they could not obtain a satisfactory utterance on the slavery question.

Know Nothing convention

The Democratic convention met in Cincinnati on the 2d of June. The party, in spite of some serious breaks ~Democrats.~ in its ranks, still substantially preserved its integrity. The southern delegates wished the renomination of Mr. Pierce ; moderate northern men preferred Mr. Buchanan, who, because of his absence on a foreign mission, had not been obliged to take public ground on the territorial question ; some desired the nomination of Mr. Douglas. On the seventeenth ballot Mr. Buchanan was nominated. Mr. John C. Breckenridge of Kentucky, who represented the slaveholding southern element, was named for the vice-presidency. To the usual Democratic platform were added a strong reiteration of the party's devotion to the principles of the compromise of 1850 and a formal indorsement of the theory of non-intervention with slavery in the Territories embodied in the Kansas-Nebraska Act of 1854. Finally, there came an almost pathetic insistence that there were "questions connected with the foreign policy of this country which are inferior to no domestic questions whatever," as preamble to the hope that the United States might control the means of communication between the two oceans, and might by some means assure its ascendency in the Gulf of Mexico.

The Republican party held its first national convention in Philadelphia on the 17th of June. All the northern ~Republicans~ States were represented, but no others except Maryland, Delaware, and Kentucky. The party was as yet too young to have produced tried and accredited leaders. It therefore put forward as its candidate for the presidency John C. Frémont, a young officer who had aided in the conquest of California (§ 77). The platform was brief and emphatic. It declared that neither Congress, nor a territorial legislature, nor any in-

dividual or association of individuals, had any authority
"to give legal existence to slavery in any Territory while
the present Constitution shall be maintained." It denounced the whole action of the government with regard
to Kansas, and demanded the immediate admission of
that Territory as a free State. It pronounced the argument of the Ostend circular to be "the highwayman's
plea, that might makes right." Finally, it urged a railway to the Pacific, as well as such appropriations by Congress for the improvement of rivers and harbors as might
be "required for the accommodation and security of our
existing commerce." Such was its Free-Soil-Anti-Ne-
braska-Whig creed. Its nomination of Frémont, who
had been reckoned a Democrat, was its recognition of
the Democracy.

A remnant of the Whig party met in Baltimore on
September 17 and accepted Mr Fillmore, the nominee of

Whigs

the Know Nothings, as their own candidate,
declaring that they saw in such a choice the
only refuge for those who loved the Constitution as it
was, and the compromises by which it had recently been
bolstered up.

The Democratic candidates were elected. They received one hundred and seventy-four of the electoral

The vote

votes, as against one hundred and fourteen
for Frémont, and eight (those of Maryland)
for Fillmore But the strength displayed by the Republicans was beyond measure startling. Their popular
vote had been 1,341,264, while that for Buchanan was
only 1,838,169. They carried every northern State but
Pennsylvania, New Jersey, Indiana, and Illinois, and had
gained portentous strength even in those States. In the
West they were practically the only party which disputed
supremacy with the Democrats; and hereafter they were
to be the only powerful party standing face to face with

the Democrats in the East. The Know Nothings and the Whigs vanished from the field of national politics. Parties were to be henceforth both compact and sectionalized. One more administration, and then the wind sown in 1854 shall have sprung into a whirlwind.

13

IV.

SECESSION AND CIVIL WAR

(1856-1865).

95. References.

Bibliographies. — Lalor's Cyclopædia (Johnston's articles on "Secession," "Dred Scott Case," "Rebellion," "Confederate States "); W. E. Foster's References to the History of Presidential Administrations, 40-49; C. K. Adams's Manual of Historical Literature, 566-581, 602 ff., 663-666, Bartlett's Literature of the Rebellion; T. O. Sumner, in Papers of American Historical Association, iv. 332-345; A. B. Hart's Federal Government, § 40.

Historical Maps. — Nos. 3, 4, this volume (Epoch Maps, Nos. 12, 13); MacCoun's Historical Geography, series "National Growth," 1848-1853, 1853-1889; series "Development of the Commonwealth," 1861, 1863; Labberton's Historical Atlas, pl. lxxi.; Scribner's Statistical Atlas, pl. 16 ; Comte de Paris's History of the Civil War in America, Atlas ; Scudder's History of the United States, 375, 378, 386, 396, 401, 403, 411 ; Theodore A Dodge's Bird's-Eye View of the Civil War, *passim*, Johnston's School History of the United States, 293.

General Accounts. — Johnston's American Politics, chaps. xix., xx.; Patton's Concise History of the United States, chaps. lvii.-lxv. (to p. 963); Bryant and Gay's History of the United States, iv., chaps. xvi.-xxiii. ; Ridpath's Popular History of the United States, chaps. lx.-lxvi.; H. von Holst's Constitutional History of the United States, vi., vii. (to 1861); J. F. Rhodes's History of the United States, ii. (1854-1860) ; James Schouler's History of the United States, v. 370-512 (to 1861); Jefferson Davis's Rise and Fall of the Confederate Government, vol. i. (parts i., iii.), vol. ii. ; Henry Wilson's Rise and Fall of the Slave Power in America, ii. (chaps xxv.-lv.), iii. (chaps. i.-xxxi.) James G. Blaine's Twenty Years of Congress, i. (chaps. vii.-xxvi.) J. G. Nicolay and John Hay's Abraham Lincoln, a History, vols. ii.-x.

Special Histories. — Edward Stanwood's History of Presidential Elections, chaps. xx., xxi.; Horace Greeley's American Conflict, i. (chaps. xxi.-xxxviii.) ; E. A. Pollard's Lost Cause (chap. v. to end) ; Joseph Hodgson's Cradle of the Confederacy (chaps. xiv. *et seq.*); G. T.

Curtis's Buchanan, ii. 187–630; Henry J. Raymond's Life of Lincoln; F. W. Seward's Seward at Washington, i., xxxix.-lxvii., ii., i.-xl ; L. G. Tyler's Lives of the Tylers; G. S. Merriam's Samuel Bowles, i. 179–419, P. Stovall's Toombs, 140–285; John W. Draper's Civil War, i., chap. xxvi. *et seq.*, ii., iii.; Edward McPherson's Political History of the Rebellion; Comte de Paris's Military History of the Civil War, William H. Seward's Diplomatic History of the Civil War; F. W. Taussig's Tariff History of the United States, 155–170; J. J. Knox's United States Notes; A. S. Bolles's Financial History of the United States, ii., chaps. xv., iii. book i.; Theodore A. Dodge's Bird's-Eye View of the Civil War; John C. Ropes's History of the Civil War (in preparation); Leverett W. Spring's Kansas; N. S. Shaler's Kentucky; C. F. Adams, Jr.'s Charles Francis Adams (in preparation); John T. Morse, Jr.'s Abraham Lincoln (in preparation); J. K. Lothrop's William H. Seward (in preparation), F. L. Olmsted's Seaboard Slave States, Texas Journey, and Back Country (or Cotton Kingdom); Marion G. McDougall's Fugitive Slaves; Mary Tremain's Slavery in the District of Columbia.

Contemporary Accounts. — Appleton's Annual Cyclopædia for the several years (particularly under the titles "Congress of the United States," "Congress, Confederate," "Confederate States," "United States," "Army," "Navy"); Horace Greeley's American Conflict, ii., and History of the Great Rebellion; Herndon's Life of Lincoln (chaps. xii. *et seq.*), L. E. Chittenden's Recollections of President Lincoln and his Administration, O. A. Brownson's American Republic (chap. xii); Alexander Stephens's War between the States, ii. 241–631, and appendices; George W. Julian's Reminiscences; George Cary Eggleston's A Rebel's Recollections; Jones's A Rebel War Clerk's Diary; J. H. Gilmer's Southern Politics; Thurlow Weed's Autobiography (chaps. lxi.-lxv.); G. W. Curtis's Correspondence of J. L. Motley, i. (chaps. xiii.), ii. (chaps. i.-vi.); Hugh McCulloch's Men and Measures of Half a Century (chaps. xiv.-xviii., xxi., xxii.), U S. Grant's Personal Memoirs; W. T. Sherman's Memoirs; S. S. Cox's Three Decades of Federal Legislation, 1855–1885 (chaps. i.-xvi.); Ben: Perley Poore's Perley's Reminiscences, ii. (chaps. i.-xvi.); Henry A. Wise's Seven Decades of the Union (chap. xiv.); James S. Pike's First Blows of the Civil War, 355–526 (to 1861); Alexander Johnston's Representative American Orations, iii. (parts v. vi.); William H. Seward's Autobiography.

CHAPTER VIII.

SECESSION (1856-1861).

96   Financial Stringency (1857).

A WIDESPREAD financial stringency distressed the country during the first year of Mr. Buchanan's administration. Commercial (Ever since 1846 there had been very great development. prosperity in almost all branches of trade and manufacture. ⁄ Great advances had been made in the mechanic arts, and easy channels both of domestic and of international trade had been multiplied in every direction by the rapid extension of railways and of steam navigation; so that the stimulus of enterprise, along with the quickening influences of the great gold discoveries, had been transmitted in all directions (But this period of prosperity and expansion, like all others of its kind, brought its own risks and penalties. Sound business methods presently gave way to reckless speculation. There was an excessive expansion of business ;) many enterprises were started which did not fulfil their first promise; there were heavy losses as well as great gains ; and at last there came uneasiness, the contraction of loans, failures, and panic.)

(The revenue laws, it was thought, contributed to increase the difficulties of the business situation, by drawing the circulating medium of the country into the Treasury, chiefly through the tariff duties, and keeping it there in the shape of an augmenting surplus.) With a view, therefore, to relieving the stringency of the money market, Congress undertook a revision of the tariff. The

other, more critical, questions of the day seem to have
absorbed partisan purpose, and this revision differed
Tariff   from previous tariff legislation in the temper-
of 1857.   ateness of view and equity of purpose with
which it was executed. In the short session of the
thirty-fourth Congress (1856–1857) all parties united in
reducing the duties on the protected articles of the existing tariff to twenty-four per cent, and in putting on the
free list many of the raw materials of manufacture. It
was hoped thus to get money out of the Treasury and
into trade again.) Financial crisis, however, was not prevented, but disturbed the whole of the year 1857.

97. The Dred Scott Decision (1857).

A brief struggle brought the business of the country
out of its difficulties; but the strain of politics was not so
The facts.   soon removed, and a decision of the Supreme
Court now hurried the country forward towards
the infinitely greater crisis of civil war. (Dred Scott was
the negro slave of an army surgeon. His master had
taken him, in the regular course of military service, from
Missouri, his home, first into the State of Illinois, and
then, in May, 1836, to Fort Snelling, on the west side of
the Mississippi, in what is now Minnesota; after which,
in 1838, he had returned with him to Missouri. Slavery
was prohibited by state law in Illinois, and by the Missouri
Compromise Act of 1820 in the territory west of the Mississippi; and after returning to Missouri the negro endeavored to obtain his liberty by an appeal to the courts,
on the ground that his residence in a free State had operated to destroy his master's rights over him. In course of
appeal the case reached the Supreme Court of the United
States. The chief, if not the only, question at issue was
a question of jurisdiction. Was Dred Scott a citizen

within the meaning of the Constitution; had he had any
rightful standing in the lower courts? To this question
the court returned a decided negative. The
Jurisdiction. temporary residence of the negro's master in
Illinois and Minnesota, in the course of his official duty
and without any intention to change his domicile, could
not affect the status of the slave, at any rate after his
return to Missouri. He was not a citizen of Missouri
in the constitutional sense, and could have therefore no
standing in the federal courts. But, this question decided, the majority of the judges did not think it *obiter
dicens* to go further, and argue to the merits of the case
regarding the status of slaves and the authority of Congress over slavery in the Territories. They were of the
opinion that, notwithstanding the fact that the Constitution spoke of slaves as "*persons* held to service and
Status of labor," men of the African race, in view of
the negro. the fact of their bondage from the first in
this country, were not regarded as persons, but only as
property, by the Constitution of the United States; that,
as property, they were protected from hostile legislation
on the part of Congress by the express guarantees of
the Constitution itself; and that Congress could no more
legislate this form of property out of the Territories than
it could exclude property of any other kind, but must
guarantee to every citizen the right to carry this, as he
might carry all other forms of property, where he would,
within the territory subject to Congress. The legislation,
therefore, known as the Missouri compromise was, in
their judgment, unconstitutional and void.)

The opinion of the court sustained the whole southern
claim. Not even the exercise of squatter sovereignty
Scope of the could have the countenance of law; Congress
decision. must protect every citizen of the country in
carrying with him into the Territories property of what-

ever kind, until such time as the Territory in which he settled should become a State, and pass beyond the direct jurisdiction of the federal government. Those who were seeking to prevent the extension of slavery into the Territories were thus stigmatized as seeking an illegal object, and acting in despite of the Constitution.

98. The Kansas Question again (1857–1858).

For the Republicans the decision was like a blow in the face. And their uneasiness and alarm were the greater because the new administration seemed wholly committed to the southern party. Mr. Buchanan had called into his cabinet both northern and southern men; the list was headed by Lewis Cass of Michigan as Secretary of State, a sturdy Democrat of the old Jacksonian type. But the President was guided for the most part by the counsel of the southern members, — men like Howell Cobb of Georgia, and Jacob Thompson of Mississippi. It was natural that he should be. Only two northern States, Pennsylvania and New Jersey, had been carried for Buchanan in 1856, and only two States of the Northwest, Indiana and Illinois. The chief strength of the Democrats was in the South; and apparently it was upon the South that they must depend in the immediate future. The course of the administration, as an inevitable consequence, was one of constant exasperation to its opponents, particularly in connection with the affairs of Kansas.

Buchanan's policy.

The free settlers of Kansas gained control of the territorial legislature, as we have seen, in the October of this first year of Mr. Buchanan's term; but before resigning its power, the expiring pro-slavery majority had called a convention, to meet at Lecompton in September, to frame a state constitution.

Lecompton constitution.

The convention met accordingly, and adopted (October 7) a constitution which provided for the establishment and perpetuation of slavery. The convention determined not to submit this constitution as a whole to the popular vote, but only the question of its adoption "with slavery" or "without slavery," — a process which would not touch any other feature of the instrument nor affect the various safeguards which it sought to throw around slave property so far as it already existed. The free settlers refrained from voting, and the constitution was, in December, adopted "with slavery" by a large majority. The new territorial legislature, with its free-state majority, directed the submission of the whole constitution to the vote of the people; and on Jan. 4, 1858, it was defeated by more than ten thousand majority, the pro-slavery voters, in their turn, staying away from the polls.

The whole influence of the administration was brought to bear upon Congress to secure the admission of Kansas to the Union under the Lecompton constitution; but although there were Democratic majorities in both Houses, the measure could not be gotten through the House of Representatives. The opposition in the Democratic ranks was led by Senator Douglas, who adhered so consistently to his principle of popular sovereignty that he would not consent to force any constitution upon the people of Kansas. Compromise was tried, but failed. Kansas was obliged to wait upon the fortunes of parties. While she waited, the free State of Minnesota entered the Union, May 11, 1858, under an enabling Act passed by the previous Congress in February, 1857.

Democratic dissensions.

99. The Lincoln-Douglas Debate (1858).

The elections of 1858 showed a formidable gain in strength by the Republicans, and bore an ominous warn-

Republican ing for the Democrats. Everywhere the Re-
gains publicans gained ground; even Pennsylvania, the President's own State, went against the administration by a heavy vote. The number of Republicans in the Senate was increased from twenty to twenty-five, from ninety-two to a hundred and nine in the House; and in the latter chamber they were to be able to play the leading part, since there were still twenty-two Know Nothings in the House, and thirteen "Anti-Lecompton" Democrats, the followers of Senator Douglas. Douglas himself was returned with difficulty to his seat in the Senate, and his canvass for re-election had arrested the attention of the whole country. The Republicans of Illinois had formally

Lincoln's announced that their candidate for the Senate
attitude. would be Abraham Lincoln, a man whose extraordinary native sagacity, insight, and capacity for debate had slowly won for him great prominence in the State, first as a Whig, afterwards as an Anti-Nebraska man and Republican. Lincoln and Douglas "took the stump" together, and the great debates between them which ensued, both won for Lincoln a national reputation and defined the issues of the party struggle as perhaps nothing less dramatic could have defined them. In Lincoln's mind those issues were clear cut enough. "A house divided against itself," he declared, "cannot stand. I believe this government cannot endure half slave and half free. I do not expect the house to fall, but I expect it will cease to be divided. It will become all one thing

Douglas's or all the other." He forced Douglas upon
dilemma the dilemma created for him by the Dred Scott
decision. What became of the doctrine of popular sover-

eignty if the people of the Territories could not interfere
with slavery until they came to frame a state constitution ?   Slavery could not exist, replied Douglas, without local legislation to sustain it ; unfriendly legislation
would hamper and kill it almost as effectually as positive
prohibition.   An inferior legislature certainly cannot do
what it is not within the power of Congress to accomplish, was Lincoln's rejoinder.   The state elections went
for the Democrats, and Mr. Douglas was returned to the
Senate ; but Lincoln had made him an impossible presidential candidate for the southern Democrats in 1860 by
forcing him to deny to the South the full benefits of the
Dred Scott decision.

The disclosures of policy made by the Executive to
Congress during the next winter still further intensified
party issues.   Mr. Buchanan's message of
December 6 urged territorial expansion in
good set terms : the country ought by some means to
obtain possession of Cuba ; ought to assume a protectorate over those pieces of the dissolving Mexican republic
which lay nearest her own borders ; ought to make good
her rights upon the Isthmus against Nicaragua and Costa
Rica.   The impression gained ground that the South was
urging the President on towards great acquisitions of
slave territory.   Again and again, until the very eve of
the assembling of the Democratic nominating convention
in 1860, did the President urge this extraordinary policy
upon Congress, greatly deepening, the while, the alarm
and repugnance of the North.

Territorial expansion. (margin note)

100. John Brown's Raid (1859).

The year 1859 witnessed a perilous incident in the
struggle against slavery, which stirred the South with a
profound agitation.   In 1855 John Brown, a native of
Connecticut, moved from Ohio into Kansas, accompanied

by his four sons. Brown possessed a nature at once rugged and intense, acknowledging no authority but that of
Brown in his own obstinate will, following no guidance
Kansas but that of his own conceptions of right, — conceptions fanatical almost to the point of madness. His only intention in entering Kansas was to throw himself and his sons into the struggle going forward there against slavery ; and he was quick to take a foremost part in the most lawless and bloody enterprises of his party, going even to the length of massacre and the forcible liberation of slaves. It was not long before he had earned outlawry and had had a price set upon his head by the govern-
Harper's ment. In January, 1859, he left Kansas, and in
Ferry. July settled near Harper's Ferry, Virginia, with the mad purpose of effecting, if possible, a forcible liberation of the slaves of the South, by provoking a general insurrection. On the night of Sunday, October 17, at the head of less than twenty followers, he seized the United States arsenal at Harper's Ferry, and hastened to free as many negroes and arrest as many white men as possible before making good his retreat, with an augmented following, as he hoped, to the mountains. Caught, before he could withdraw, by the arrival of a large force of militia, he was taken, with such of his little band as had survived the attempt to stand siege in the arsenal. A speedy trial followed, and the inevitable death penalty on December 2. His plan had been one of the maddest folly, but his end was one of singular dignity. He endured trial and execution with manly, even with Christian, fortitude.

The South was shaken by the profoundest emotion. A slave insurrection was the most hideous danger that
Effect in southern homes had to fear. It meant mas-
the South sacre and arson, and for the women a fate worse than any form of death or desolation. Southerners did not discriminate carefully between the different

classes of anti-slavery men in the North; to the southern thought they were all practically Abolitionists, and
Abolitionists had uttered hot words which could surely
have no other purpose than to incite the slaves to insurrection. It was found, upon investigation, that Brown
had obtained arms and money in the North; and although it was proved also that those who had aided him
had no intimation of his designs against the South, but
supposed that he was to use what they gave him in Kansas, the impression was deepened at the South that this
worst form of violence had at any rate the virtual moral
countenance of the northern opponents of slavery. It
was not easy, after this, for the South to judge dispas-
sionately any movement of politics. Already some
southern men had made bold to demand that Congress,
in obedience to the Dred Scott decision, should afford
positive statutory protection to slavery wherever it might
have entered the Territories; there was even talk in some
quarters of insisting upon a repeal of the laws forbidding
the slave trade; and proposals of territorial expansion
were becoming more and more explicit and persistent.
The exasperation of the incident at Harper's Ferry only
rendered the extreme men of the South the more determined to achieve their purposes at every point.

101. Presidential Campaign of 1860.

When the new Congress assembled, in December,
1859, disclosures came which brought the administration
into painful discredit. A committee of the
House, constituted to investigate the charge
made by two members, that they had been
offered bribes by the administration to vote for the admission of Kansas with the Lecompton Constitution,
brought to light many things which cast a grave suspicion
of corruption upon those highest in authority, and hast-

Investigation of the admin-istration.

ened the already evident decline of confidence in the President and his counsellors.

Meantime, the country turned to watch the party conventions.   The Democratic convention met in Charleston, South Carolina, on April 23, 1860.   Its proceedings at once disclosed a fatal difficulty about the adoption Disintegra- of a platform.   A strong southern minority tion of the wished explicitly to insist upon carrying out Democratic party to the full the doctrine of the Dred Scott decision; but the majority would join them only in favoring the acquisition of Cuba "on terms honorable to ourselves and just to Spain," and in condemning the adoption by northern States of legislation hostile to the execution of the Fugitive Slave Law.   When defeated on the resolutions, most of the southern members withdrew.) Without them, the convention found it impossible to get together a two-thirds majority for any candidate for the presidential nomination.   On the 3d of May, accordingly, it adjourned, to meet again in Baltimore on the 18th of June. (Meantime the southern members who had withdrawn got together in another hall in Charleston, and adopted their own resolutions.   The regular convention re-assembled in Baltimore on the appointed day; but, upon certain questions of re-organization being decided in favor of the friends of Mr. Douglas, most of the southern delegates who had remained with the convention upon the occasion of the former schism, in their turn withdrew, carrying with them the chairman of the convention and several northern delegates.   The rest of the body proceeded to the business of nomination, and named Stephen A. Douglas of Illinois for the presidency.   The second group of seceders from the convention, joined by delegates who had been refused admission, and even by some of the delegates who had withdrawn and acted separately in Charleston, met in Baltimore on the 28th of June, adopted the resolutions that had been adopted by the minority in Charleston, and nominated John C. Breckinridge of Kentucky for the presidency.

Breckinridge convention

A remnant of the minority convention in Charleston on the same day ratified these nominations in Richmond.

(Already, on the 9th of May, another convention had met and acted. This was the convention of a new party, the "Constitutional Union," made up for the most part of the more conservative men of all parties, who were repelled alike by Republican and by Democratic extremes of policy. The Know Nothing party was dead, but this was its heir. It contained, besides, some men who would not have been Know Nothings. It adopted a very brief platform, recognizing "no political principle other than the Constitution of the country, the union of the States, and the enforcement of the laws," and nominated John Bell of Tennessee for the presidency.

"Constitutional Union" party.

The Republican convention met in Chicago on May 16, full of an invigorating confidence of success. (The platform adopted denounced threats of disunion, but warmly disavowed all sympathy with any form of interference with the domestic institutions already established in any State. It demanded the immediate admission of Kansas as a free State. It repudiated the doctrine of the Dred Scott decision as a dangerous political heresy, claiming that the normal condition of all Territories of the United States was a condition of freedom, and that it was the plain duty of the government to maintain that condition by law. It favored a protective tariff, internal improvements, and a railway to the Pacific. William H. Seward of New York and Salmon P. Chase of Ohio, unquestionably the leading men of the party, were the most prominent

Republican convention.

candidates for the presidential nomination; but they had
made enemies in dangerous numbers. Mr. Seward, the
Nomination more prominent and powerful of the two, was
of Lincoln. regarded as a sort of philosophical radical,
whom careful men might distrust as a practical guide.
The party was, after all, a conglomerate party; and it
seemed best, under the circumstances, to take some less
conspicuous man, and to take him from some wavering
State. Although Mr. Seward led at first, therefore, in
the voting for candidates, Abraham Lincoln of Illinois
was nominated on the third ballot. Mr. Hannibal Hamlin of Maine was nominated for the vice-presidency.

The result of the campaign which ensued was hardly
doubtful from the first. (The presence of four candidates
Campaign. in the field, and the hopeless breach in the
Democratic ranks, made it possible for the
Republicans to win doubters over to themselves in every
quarter.) In only one northern State, New Jersey, were
Democratic electors chosen, and even in that State four
out of the seven electors chosen were Republicans.
Douglas received only the nine electoral votes of Missouri and those three from New Jersey. Virginia, Tennessee, and Kentucky cast their votes for. Bell. The
rest of the southern States went for Breckinridge. The
total reckoning showed one hundred and eighty electoral
votes for Lincoln and Hamlin, one hundred and three
for all the other candidates combined. The popular vote
The popu- was not so decisive. For Lincoln and Hamlin
lar vote. it was 1,866,452; for Douglas, 1,375,157, the
Douglas ticket having polled heavy minorities in the
States which had been carried for Lincoln; for Breckinridge, 847,953; for Bell, 590,631. The total opposition
vote to the Republicans was thus 2,823,741, — a majority
of almost a million, in a total vote of a little over four
millions and a half. In the North and West alone the

total opposition vote was 1,288,611. In Oregon and
California, whose electoral votes went to the Republicans, the aggregate popular opposition vote was almost
twice the vote for Lincoln and Hamlin. In Illinois itself,
Mr. Lincoln's own State, the opposition vote fell less
than three thousand short of that polled by the Republicans. It was a narrow victory, of which it behooved the
Republican leaders to make cautious use.

102. Significance of the Result.

The South had avowedly staked everything, even her
allegiance to the Union, upon this election. "The triumph
Southern ap- of Mr Lincoln was, in her eyes, nothing less
prehension.   than the establishment in power of a party
bent upon the destruction of the southern system and
the defeat of southern interests, even to the point of
countenancing and assisting servile insurrection." In the
metaphor of Senator Benjamin, the Republicans did not
mean, indeed, to cut down the tree of slavery, but they
meant to gird it about, and so cause it to die. It
seemed evident to the southern men, too, that the North
would not pause or hesitate because of constitutional
guarantees. For twenty years northern States had been
busy passing "personal liberty" laws, intended to bar
the operation of the federal statutes concerning fugitive
slaves, and to secure for all alleged fugitives legal privileges which the federal statutes withheld. More than
a score of States had passed laws with this object, and
such acts were as plainly attempts to nullify the constitutional action of Congress as if they had spoken the language of the South Carolina ordinance of 1832. Southern
Southern   pride, too, was stung to the quick by the po-
pride.   sition in which the South found itself. The
agitation against slavery had spoken in every quarter the
harshest moral censures of slavery and the slaveholders.

The whole course of the South had been described as one of systematic iniquity; southern society had been represented as built upon a wilful sin; the southern people had been held up to the world as those who deliberately despised the most righteous commands of religion. They knew that they did not deserve such reprobation. They knew that their lives were honorable, their relations with their slaves humane, their responsibility for the existence of slavery among them remote.'' National churches had already broken asunder because of this issue of morals. The Baptist Church had split into a northern and a southern branch as long ago as 1845: and 1844 had seen the same line of separation run through the great Methodist body.

The Republican party was made up of a score of elements, and the vast majority of its adherents were almost as much repelled by the violent temper and disunionist sentiments of the Abolitionists as were the southern leaders themselves. The abolitionist movement had had an exceedingly powerful and a steadily increasing influence in creating a strong feeling of antagonism towards slavery, but there was hardly more of an active abolitionist party in 1860 than there had been in 1840. The Republicans wished, and meant, to check the extension of slavery; but no one of influence in their counsels dreamed of interfering with its existence in the States. They explicitly acknowledged that its existence there was perfectly constitutional. But the South made no such distinctions. It knew only that the party which was hotly intolerant of the whole body of southern institutions and interests had triumphed in the elections and was about to take possession of the government, and that it was morally impossible to preserve the Union any longer. "If you who represent the stronger portion," Calhoun had said

Temper of the Republicans.

in 1850, in words which perfectly convey this feeling in their quiet cadences, "cannot agree to settle the great questions at issue on the broad principle of justice and duty, say so; and let the States we both represent agree to separate and depart in peace."

103. Secession (1860–1861).

South Carolina, alone among the States, still chose her presidential electors, not by popular vote, but through her legislature After having chosen Breck-inridge electors, Nov. 6, 1860, her legislature remained in session to learn the result of the election. The governor of the State had consulted other southern governors upon the course to be taken in the event of a Republican victory, and had received answers which encouraged South Carolina to expect support, should she determine to secede. When news came that Lincoln was elected, therefore, the South Carolina legislature called a state convention, made provision for the purchase of arms, and adjourned. In Charleston, on the 20th of December, the convention which it had called passed an ordinance which repealed the action taken in state convention on the 23d May, 1788, whereby the Constitution of the United States had been ratified, together with all subsequent Acts of Assembly ratifying amendments to that Constitution, and formally pronounced the dissolution of the union "subsisting between South Carolina and other States, under the name of the United States of America." It also made what provision was necessary for the government of the State as a separate sovereignty, and for such exigencies of defence as might arise in case of war. By the 1st of February, 1861, Georgia and four of the Gulf States—Florida, Alabama, Mississippi, Louisiana— had followed South Carolina and seceded from the Union; and Texas was on the point of joining them.

South Carolina.

Delegates, appointed by the several conventions in the
seceding States, met in Montgomery, Alabama, on the
Montgomery 4th of February, 1861, framed a provisional
Convention. constitution and government for the "Confederate States of America," and chose Jefferson Davis
of Mississippi provisional President, Alexander H. Stephens of Georgia provisional Vice-President. In March
a permanent constitution was adopted, to take effect the
next year.

The legal theory upon which this startling and extraordinary series of steps was taken was one which would
Legal theory hardly have been questioned in the early
of secession. years of the government, whatever resistance
might then have been offered to its practical execution.
It was for long found difficult to deny that a State could
withdraw from the federal arrangement, as she might
have declined to enter it. But constitutions are not mere
legal documents : they are the skeleton frame of a living
organism ; and in this case the course of events had
nationalized the government once deemed confederate.
Twenty States had been added to the original thirteen
since the formation of the government, and almost all
of these were actual creations of the federal government,
first as Territories, then as States. Their populations had
New States. no corporate individuality such as had been
possessed by the people of each of the colonies. They came from all parts of the Union, and had
formed communities which were arbitrary geographical
units rather than natural political units. Not only that,
but north of the Missouri compromise line the population of these new States had been swelled by immigration from abroad ; and there had played upon the whole
northern and northwestern section those great forces of
material development which made steadily for the unifi-
cation of interests and purposes. The "West" was the

great make-weight. It was the region into which the whole national force had been projected, stretched out, and energized, — a region, not a section; divided into States by reason of a form of government, but homogeneous, and proceeding forth from the Union.

These are not lawyer's facts: they are historian's facts. There had been nothing but a dim realization of them until the war came and awoke the national spirit into full consciousness. They have no bearing upon the legal intent of the Constitution as a document, to be interpreted by the intention of its framers; but they have everything to do with the Constitution as a vehicle of life. The South had not changed her ideas from the first, because she had not changed her condition. She had not experienced, except in a very slight degree, the economic forces which had created the great Northwest and nationalized the rest of the country; for they had been shut out from her life by slavery. The South withdrew from the Union because, she said, power had been given to a geographical, a sectional, party, ruthlessly hostile to her interests; but Dr. von Holst is certainly right when he says: "The Union was not broken up because sectional parties had been formed, but sectional parties were formed because the Union had actually become sectionalized." There had been nothing active on the part of the South in this process. She had stood still while the rest of the country had undergone profound changes; and, standing still, she retained the old principles which had once been universal Both she and her principles, it turned out, had been caught at last in the great national drift, and were to be overwhelmed. Her slender economic resources were no match for the mighty strength of the nation with which she had fallen out of sympathy.

Sectionalization of the Union

CHAPTER IX.

THE CIVIL WAR (1861-1865).

104. A Period of Hesitation (1861).

DURING the early months of 1861 the whole posture of affairs was most extraordinary. Nowhere was there de-
Southern cided purpose or action except in the South.
activity. The federal authorities seemed paralyzed. On all hands southern officers were withdrawing from the army, as their States seceded; in like rapid succession the representatives of the seceding States were withdrawing from the Senate and House of Representatives. The southern States, as they left the Union, took possession of the federal arsenals, custom houses, and post-offices within their jurisdiction. Presently only Fortress Monroe in Chesapeake Bay, Fort Sumter in Charleston harbor, Fort Pickens at Pensacola, and the fortifications near Key West remained in federal possession. Many civil officials of the federal government resigned their commissions. Commissioners from South Carolina had appeared in Washington before the year opened, to arrange for a division of the national debt and a formal transfer of the national property lying within the State. Military preparations were made everywhere in the South; and some northern governors ordered the purchase of arms and made ready to mobilize the militia of their States. But the federal authorities did nothing. Almost everywhere in the North and West the people were strangely lethargic, singularly disposed to wait and see the trouble blow over.

Buchanan's counsels had hitherto been guided by
southern influences; and when this crisis came, although
Buchanan's   the southern men withdrew from his cabinet,
course   or were displaced, to make room for firmer
adherents of the Union, he seemed incapable of deciding
upon any course of action against the South.   Mr.
Buchanan believed and declared that secession was illegal; but he agreed with his Attorney General that there
was no constitutional means or warrant for coercing a
State to do her duty under the law.   Such, indeed, for
the time, seemed to be the general opinion of the country.   Congress was hardly more capable of judgment or
action than the Executive.   On January 29, 1861, after
the withdrawal of the southern members had given the
Republicans a majority in the Senate, it passed the bill
which was to admit Kansas to the Union under her latest
free constitution; the Territories of Nevada, Colorado,
and Dakota were organized, without mention of slavery;
and a new Tariff Act, which had passed the House the
previous winter, passed the Senate, in aid of the now
Congression- embarrassed finances of the government.   But
al paralysis. on the subject of most pressing exigency every
proposal failed.   Compromise measures without number were brought forward, but nothing was agreed upon.
A Peace Congress, made up of delegates from all but
the seceding States, met, at the suggestion of Virginia,
and proposed acts of accommodation; a senatorial
committee joined it in advocating the extension of the
Missouri compromise line to the Pacific, the positive establishment of slavery by Congress to the south of that
line, and compensation from the federal Treasury for
fugitive slaves rescued after arrest.   Even Mr. Seward,
the Republican leader in Congress, was willing to concede some of the chief points of Republican policy with
regard to slavery in the Territories for the sake of con-

ciliation. But nothing was done; everything was left to the next administration.

The situation, singular and perilous as it seemed, was really due to causes which were, in the long view, sources of strength. The people of the country were doubtless bewildered for a time by being brought so unexpectedly into the presence of so great a crisis, but this trying pause before action was due very much more to their conservative temper and deep-rooted legal habit. Even after the crisis had been transformed into a civil war, and the struggle had actually begun for the preservation of the Union, every step taken which strained the laws caused a greater or less reaction in the popular mind against the party in power. Policy had to carry the people with it; had to await the awakening of the national idea into full consciousness; and this first pause of doubt and reflection did but render the ultimate outcome the more certain.

Conservative temper of the people

The feeling of experiment and uncertainty was not confined to the North. At first neither side expected an actual conflict of arms, — perhaps neither side expected a permanent dissolution of the Union. There was a strong party of opposition to secession in the South, notably in Georgia, where even Mr. Stephens, now Vice-President of the Confederacy, had opposed it. Secession had been in some sense a movement of political leaders rather than of the people. The object was to make terms with the North about slavery, and they thought that probably better terms could be made out of the Union than in it. The States which followed South Carolina felt bound to support their sister State in demands with which they sympathized. Border States like North Carolina and Virginia and Tennessee held off only until coercion should be attempted. Compromise was hoped for, even confidently expected. Some

First object of secession

dreamed, in the North as well as in the South, that the dissolution would be final and peaceful! Action was hurried forward too rapidly to be based upon careful calculation or any wise forecast.

105. President Lincoln (1861).

The successor to whom President Buchanan very willingly resigned the responsibility of guiding affairs at this Lincoln's critical juncture was one of the most singular character. and admirable figures in the history of modern times. Abraham Lincoln came of the most unpromising stock on the continent, the "poor white trash" of the South. His shiftless father had moved from place to place in the western country, failing where everybody else was succeeding in making a living; and the boy had spent the most susceptible years of his life under no discipline but that of degrading poverty. And yet a singular genius for getting and using knowledge manifested itself in him from the first, and was the more remarkable because free from morbid quality, and slow, patient, and equable in its development He was altogether like the rough frontiersmen with whom he lived, in his coarse, neglected dress, his broad and boisterous humor, his careless, unstrenuous ways of life; but he was vastly above them in intellectual and moral stature. He gained an easy mastery over them, too, by cultivating, as he did, the directer and more potent forms of speech. And his supremacy was the more assured because it was a moral as well as an intellectual supremacy To everybody who knew him he was "Honest Abe." When at length he undertook to meet Douglas in public debate (§ 99), he had come into the full maturity of his splendid power to understand and persuade. Having developed among the people, slowly, as if in their company, by mastering what they but partially comprehended, penetrated the while by their sentiments and aspirations, he came into the leadership of his party with an aptitude and equipment for affairs which no other man could rival.

His task as President was " more difficult than that of Washington himself had been," as he had said to his neighbors, with solemn solicitude for the future. There was a sentiment to create and a party to compact; and these things were to be done by a man comparatively unknown as yet. He meant to respect the Constitution in all things. It was in the oath that he took as President, he said, that he would to the best of his ability preserve, protect, and defend the Constitution; and he did not feel that he might " take an oath to get power, and break the oath in using that power." Neither did he feel, however, that he could be said even to have tried to preserve the Constitution if, " to save slavery or any minor matter," he should " permit the wreck of government, country, and Constitution all together." He sought to follow a course of policy in which firmness and conciliation should be equally prominent, and in which he could carry the plain people of the country with him.

His purpose.

He put both Mr. Seward and Mr. Chase into his cabinet, because they were recognized as the most conspicuous and representative men of his party; but he associated with them others less conspicuous, and also less radical, chosen from the other groups which had combined to make up the Republican strength. Then he addressed himself to the slowest and most cautious policy that the rapid movement of critical events would allow. When Mr. Seward proposed, with amazing weakness and fatuity, that the slavery question be eliminated in all dealings with the South, and the nation at once aroused and united by a vigorous and aggressive

The cabinet.

foreign policy, Lincoln's reproof showed him a master both in commanding others and in controlling himself When the ardent anti-slavery faction would have pushed him to the other extreme, they too were baffled by his prudent purpose and quiet reserve of strength. Events went swiftly enough of themselves. He was not afraid to take the initiative, but he would not take it rashly or too soon. He governed and succeeded by sympathy. He knew the mettle and temper of the people who had put him in charge of the government.

106. Opening of Hostilities (1861).

During the very month of his inauguration commissioners arrived from the confederate States. They were Southern refused official recognition; but Mr. Seward, commission. who believed himself to be the real head of the administration, kept them waiting a long time for his decision, unofficially holding out hopes of concession, the while, through Justice Campbell, of the Supreme Court, who wished, if possible, to mediate in the interest of peace. On April 8, while they waited, formal notice was sent from the federal authorities to Governor Pickens of South Carolina that the federal garrison in Fort Sumter, which the southern authorities had summoned to surrender, would be succored and provisioned.
Sumter. April 12, the confederate batteries opened fire upon that fort, and on the 14th the little garrison was forced to surrender. The next day, the 15th, the President, by proclamation, called for seventy-five thousand volunteers. The northern States promptly, even eagerly, responded. On the 19th of April a regiment of Massachusetts volunteers was attacked by a mob in the streets of Baltimore as it passed through on its way to Washington. Four of the southern border States, rather

than obey the call for volunteers and acquiesce in the use of coercive force, withdrew from the Union and joined the southern Confederacy: Arkansas on May 6, North Carolina on May 20, Virginia on May 23, and Tennessee on June 18. They had held off from the original movement of secession, but they were hotly opposed to the coercion of a State by the federal power, and had already formed "military leagues" with the seceding States, by which their territories were opened to the confederate armies.

Secession of four more States.

The confederate capital was moved from Montgomery to Richmond; President Davis also called for volunteers, and his call was obeyed as eagerly as President Lincoln's had been in the North. Regiments went blithely forth, oftentimes with gay pomp and laughter, from the southern towns, as if to holiday parade, little dreaming how awful a struggle was about to begin. Whatever doubts may have been entertained among the southern people about the wisdom or the policy of secession were dispelled upon the instant by threat of coercive force. It then seemed to them that they were asserting rights of self-government as plain and as sacred as any that lay at the heart of the history of English liberty. In the North, too, there were scruples about coercion, and Mr. Lincoln had to be the more careful because of them. But when Sumter was fired on, and the war begun, these scruples too were dispelled. Both sides were aroused.

Confederacy aroused.

107. The War Policy of Congress (1861-1862).

Having called for and obtained the military support demanded by the immediate exigency, Mr. Lincoln summoned Congress to convene in special session on July 4. A colossal task confronted it. The advantage of first preparation was with the South.

Confusion.

What with the resignations and surrenders which followed
the first actions of the seceding States, the army of the
United States had gone almost to pieces. The treasury
was practically empty. Even the civil service needed to
be reconstructed, because of the number of southern men
who had withdrawn from it. More than a year was to

Organization. elapse before the overwhelming material power
of the North could be brought to bear upon
the concentrated forces of the South. Congress devoted
itself very heartily to the financial and military measures
rendered necessary by the situation. It directed a blockade of the Southern ports; it authorized a loan and voted
large appropriations, increasing the tariff duties, August
5, to produce the necessary revenue; it provided for the
calling out of five hundred thousand volunteers; passed
Acts defining and punishing conspiracy against the government; and provided for the confiscation of all property
employed against the United States. During its regular
winter session it resumed the same policy of strengthen-
ing both the laws and the resources of the government
. against hostile attack. It then took the first steps of that

Financial financial policy which was unflinchingly car-
measures ried out until the close of the war: industries
were to be stimulated to the utmost possible extent by
protective duties, and then used by direct taxation for
the support of the war. By the middle of the summer
of 1862 this system of policy was virtually complete. In
February a great issue of irredeemable paper money was
voted, and the paper given full legal tender quality; in
July a Tariff Act was passed which very greatly increased
the duties on imports, and an internal revenue law adopted
which, besides imposing specific taxes on the production
of iron, steel, paper, coal oil, leather, etc, and a general
ad valorem tax on other manufactures, required licenses
for many callings, established a general income tax, and

mulcted railway, steam-boat, and express companies in taxes on their gross receipts. The same month saw the charter of the Union Pacific Railway pass Congress, with huge grants of land and money from the federal government. Public lands were granted also to the various States in aid of the establishment of agricultural colleges; and a "Homestead Bill" was adopted, which offered portions of the public domain to heads of families at a nominal fee. Wealth and taxes were to be made to grow together, the expansion of population and industry and the successful prosecution of the war.

108. Manassas and the "Trent" Affair (1861).

Meantime it was becoming evident that the struggle was to be both fierce and prolonged, taxing to the utmost even the superb resources of the North, whose ports were open, and whose material power had chance of augmentation even in the midst of war itself. The volunteers at first called out had been enlisted for only three months' service; it was expected that something would be done at once which should be decisive of the sectional issue. Towards the end of July, 1861, General McDowell moved with the federal forces upon Richmond, the confederate capital, and on the 21st met the confederate forces at Manassas, under Generals Joseph E. Johnston and Beauregard A stubborn and sanguinary battle ensued, which resulted in the utter rout of McDowell, whose troops fled back to Washington in hopeless confusion. Already there had been several engagements upon a small scale in western Virginia, where the sympathy of the people was with the Union. These had resulted in giving to federal troops under General McClellan control of the upper sources of both the Potomac and the Ohio rivers. Similar side campaigns during the autumn and winter secured also for the federal power the greater part of Missouri and Kentucky, and fixed sharply enough the geographical area of secession.

A significant international incident called attention in the autumn to the possible part that foreign govern-

Foreign re-
lations of the
Confederacy.

ments might play in the conflict as it grew more serious. The confederate government had from the first hoped for and even ex-pected foreign recognition and assistance. The southern States were the great cotton field of the world, and there were hundreds of factories in England which must stand idle, thousands of families who must starve, if the south-ern ports should be effectually closed against the expor-tation of the great staple. European powers, it was thought, would not be loath to see the great republic in America lose some of its formidable strength by divi-sion; and it was soon known that in England the most influential classes sympathized with the aims of the South. J. M. Mason and John Slidell, commissioners from the Confederate States to England and France respectively, ran the federal blockade at Charleston and

"Trent" affair

embarked at Havana on the English steamer "Trent" for England. On November 8 the steamer was overhauled by a United States man-of-war, and the commissioners were taken from her and carried prisoners to Fort Warren, in Boston harbor. At once Eng-land demanded their surrender, and an apology from the United States for so gross a breach of international right, accompanying her demand with open preparations for war. The international rights for which she contended were such as the United States herself had always insist-ed upon, and the commissioners were released; but the "'Trent' affair" made a very painful impression upon public opinion in both countries, — an impression of active hostility and bitterness of feeling which was slow to wear off. At the very beginning of the struggle, upon receipt of the news of President Lincoln's proclamation declaring the southern ports blockaded, and of President Davis's offer to provide vessels with letters of marque and reprisal against the commerce of the United States, both England and France had issued proclamations of neutrality which gave to the Confederate States international standing as belligerents. Apparently foreign governments were waiting only for some pronounced success of the southern armies to recognize the independence of the Confederacy.

109. Military Operations of 1862.

Early in 1862 the area and plan of the war began to be defined. On the one hand, the long sectional frontier Theatre was broken by the movement of federal of war. armies down the valley of the Mississippi. On the other hand, the fighting grew thick and fast in Virginia and Maryland, in the region lying round about and between the two capitals, Richmond and Washington. In the West the federal armies were almost uniformly successful; in the East almost uniformly unsuccessful. On the 6th of March, 1862, a severe engagement at Pea Ridge, in northwestern Arkansas, had given to the federal forces in that region the decisive advantage which finally secured to them the control of Missouri. A month earlier an actual invasion of the Western seceding States had been begun. A land campaign. force under Ulysses S. Grant moved up the Tennessee River, in co-operation with a fleet of gunboats under Commodore Foote, and on February 6 took Fort Henry. Immediately crossing to the Cumberland, Grant captured Fort Donelson on that river on the 16th. A federal force under General Pope, also supported by gunboats, then, with the greatest difficulty, cleared the Mississippi of the confederate blockades at New Madrid and Island Number Ten. Pushing forward, meanwhile, the plan of securing the Mississippi valley and opening the river, Grant advanced up the Tennessee, seeking to reach Corinth, a railway centre of northern Mississippi. On Sunday morning, April 6, he was suddenly checked by the overwhelming onset of a confederate force commanded by General Albert Sidney Johnston. The day's fighting drove Grant back to Pittsburg Landing. But federal reinforcements arrived under Buell; Johnston had been mortally wounded; and on Monday the confederates, under Beauregard, were forced to retire. Grant followed, and took Corinth, after a siege, on the 30th of May. The Mississippi was open as far as Vicksburg. It had been opened below Vicksburg, also, by the surrender of New Orleans. On the 18th of April Commodore Farragut had begun the bombardment of the forts below New Orleans; unable to take them at once, he had daringly run his ships past them on the 24th, and on the 28th had taken the city; after which the forts presently fell into his hands. Early in June Memphis was taken, after desperate fighting, by the river forces operating above.

Lower Mississippi campaign.

In the East the federal forces were suffering a series of defeats. General Joseph E. Johnston, the confederate commander, had not followed up his signal victory over McDowell at Manassas. The war was then young, and the troops on both sides were raw and inexperienced. A period of further preparation followed. McDowell was superseded by McClellan, who was fresh from his successes in western Virginia; and McClellan spent the winter organizing and disciplining his forces, the "Army of the Potomac." When he took the field in the spring of 1862, he chose the old revolutionary fighting ground. Transporting his army by water to Fortress Monroe, he moved upon Richmond by the

Peninsula campaign

peninsula that lies between the York and James rivers. A month was spent in the siege of Yorktown, which was evacuated on the 4th of May. Following his retreating opponents, McClellan again attacked them at Williamsburg, but did not prevent their crossing the Chickahominy. Johnston, in his turn, threw himself upon a portion of McClellan's army at Fair Oaks, before the rest of it had crossed this stream, and the federal forces were with difficulty saved from rout, after two days' fighting. Johnston was wounded in the conflict, and General Robert E. Lee succeeded him in the command. McClellan had expected to be joined by reinforcements under McDowell; but the brilliant manœuvres of another confederate commander had changed the plans of the authorities at Washington. This was Thomas J. Jackson, who had already won the sobriquet " Stonewall " by his steadfast gallantry in making stand against the charges of the enemy in the first battle of Manassas. By a series of sudden marches and surprises characteristic of his genius, he had cleared the Shenandoah valley of federal troops, and, seeming to threaten Washington, had kept McDowell there to defend the seat of government. Then he as suddenly turned about and carried his forces down by rail to assist Lee against McClellan. Together Lee and Jackson forced McClellan back to the James River, hammering at him irresistibly for seven days.

McClellan was withdrawn from the command, and General Pope called from his exploits at New Madrid and Island Number Ten on the Mississippi to take his place. But Pope fared even worse than McClellan. By a forced march through the mountains, Jackson turned his flank and defeated General Banks, in command of the western end of his line, at Cedar Mountain, August 9. August

Second Eastern campaign of 1862.

15

29 and 30 a combined force under Pope and McDowell
was routed at Manassas by Lee and Jackson. After
sending out a force which captured Harper's Ferry, with
its arsenal and supplies and eleven thousand federal
troops, Lee then crossed the upper Potomac with his main
body, entered Maryland, and fronted the federal army
again, now once more under McClellan's command, at
Antietam Creek. Here, on September 17, a battle was
fought, so undecisive of victory that Lee recrossed the
Potomac and retired towards his base of operations.
Still experimenting with commanders, the federal authorities put General Burnside at the head of the unhappy
Army of the Potomac. December 13, Burnside threw himself upon the confederate forces occupying Fredericksburg heights, and was repulsed with great loss. Then
there followed a pause until the spring.

110. The Emancipation Proclamation (1863).

For a year and a half now Lincoln had maintained,
against all radical suggestions, the conservative policy
with which he had set out. He knew that
Circumstances. the fighting force of the Union must come,
not from the leaders of parties, who were thinking fast
in these stirring times, but from the mass of unknown
men who were thinking more slowly and upon a narrower
scale. The rank and file of the nation, when the struggle
began, was opposed to an abolition war. Had the war
been short and immediately decisive for the Union, the
federal power would not have touched slavery in the States.
But it was not short. It was so long and so stubborn as
to provoke the sternest resolutions and test to the utmost
the strength and persistence of the purposes that sustained it. And as its strain continued, thought changed
and purpose expanded. At first Mr. Lincoln had promptly

checked all attempts to set free the negroes in the territory overrun by the federal armies. But by September,

Preliminary 1862, he had made up his mind that it would
proclamation. stimulate the forces of the North if the war
were made a war against slavery, as well as a war for the
Union; and that it would at the same time put the South
in the wrong before the opinion of the world, and imperatively prevent that foreign recognition of the southern
Confederacy which he dreaded. He waited only for
some victory in the field to furnish a dignified opportunity for the step he contemplated. Antietam served
his purpose sufficiently well; and on the 22d of September he issued a proclamation which gave formal notice
that unless the southern States yielded allegiance to the
Union within a hundred days thereafter, he should de-

Emancipation. clare the slaves within their limits free. On
the 1st of January, 1863, accordingly, he put
forth a formal proclamation of emancipation. The act
was of course without constitutional warrant; it carried no
other authority than that which the President exercised
as commander-in-chief of the military forces of the government. As an act of military power he could set free
the negroes within territory occupied by the federal
armies, but his proclamation could not abolish a legal
institution. It served its purpose, nevertheless, as an
announcement of policy.

111. Radical Measures (1862-1863).

Meantime Congress also was growing more radical in
policy. There had been a slight reaction in the country

Congress. against the President's abolition proclamation
of September, and there was a good deal of
dissatisfaction with the way in which the war had hitherto been conducted. The autumn elections of 1862 had

reduced the Republican majority somewhat in the House
of the Thirty-eighth Congress, which was to meet in December, 1863. But the existing House was not daunted,
and the party policy was pushed forward. December
31, 1862, a practically revolutionary step was
taken by admitting forty of the western
counties of Virginia to the Union as a separate State, under the name of West Virginia. These
counties had not shared the secession sentiment of the
rest of the State, and when they came to make their
choice between adhering to the State or adhering to the
Union, had chosen the latter alternative and set up a
revolutionary state government of their own. After Virginia seceded, Congress adopted the fiction which the
western Virginians had pressed for acceptance, that this
revolutionary government of the western counties was
the only legitimate government of Virginia; assumed the
consent of that government to a division of the State to
be a sufficient satisfaction of the provisions of the Constitution; and erected the State of West Virginia.

Creation of West Virginia.

By an Act approved March 3, 1863, the President was
authorized to suspend the operation of the writ of *habeas
corpus* in cases of persons suspected of disaffection towards the Union, as he had already
been doing by declaring martial law in district after
district ever since his first call for volunteers in April,
1861. The same day a stringent Draft Act
became law, which provided for conscription
by lot. The execution of this law caused intense excitement in some of the eastern States, and even provoked
resistance. In some cases the officers in charge of the
arrangements for the conscription acted in a grossly partisan manner, levying most heavily upon Democratic
counties and districts. The most formidable outbreak
against the execution of the Act took place in New York

Habeas corpus

Draft Act.

city, where there were terrible "draft riots," during which the city was for four days, July 13–16, 1863, practically at the mercy of mobs. But inequalities of administration were corrected, and the provisions of the Act everywhere carried out.

Such legislation was thought to be necessary by reason of the growing magnitude of the war. Both fleets and armies had to be created on the grand scale.

Blockade. A blockade of the southern ports had been proclaimed by President Lincoln on the 19th of April, 1861; but the southern coast stretched three thousand miles long; there were but forty-two vessels in commission; and the navy which was to make the blockade effective had to be created. The operations of the blockading squadrons were somewhat facilitated by the capture of Fort Hatteras, North Carolina, so early as August 29, 1861, and of Port Royal, South Carolina, November 7 of the same year; and the building and equipment of war ships of every pattern, old and new, was pushed forward with extraordinary rapidity; for the blockade was deemed as necessary as it proved difficult. Until the southern ports should be closed, southern cotton could be sent abroad, and arms and military supplies be brought back in exchange. It was expedient that the South should be shut in as speedily as possible to the rapid consumption of its own diminishing resources. Early in 1862 the confederates had nearly swept Hampton Roads of its federal squadron by the onset of the armored ram "Virginia," improvised out of the frigate "Merrimac;" but on March 9 the terrible successes of the "Virginia" were cut short by the arrival of Ericsson's turreted "Monitor," and it was evident to the world that a revolution had been effected in naval warfare.

Privateers. Confederate privateers, and cruisers fitted out in foreign ports, went everywhere capturing United

States merchantmen, for a time almost sweeping the seas of all commerce under the federal flag. But the privateers were one after another taken, and more and more effectually the blockade was drawn about the southern harbors; the southern wealth of cotton made useless.

112. Military Operations of 1863.

In the spring of 1863 military operations began again upon the fields of the previous year. After Fredericks-
Virginia   burg, General Hooker had taken Burnside's
campaign.   place in command of the Army of the Poto-
mac. Attempting a movement upon Richmond, Hooker met the forces of Lee and Jackson at Chancellorsville, on the second and third days of May, and was disastrously defeated. The confederates, however, suffered the irreparable loss of " Stonewall " Jackson, killed, by tragical mistake, by pickets of his own force. Following up his advantage, Lee again ventured upon a forward movement
              and invaded Pennsylvania. Here, at Gettys-
Gettysburg.   burg, he met General Meade, and was repulsed
with heavy losses. The federal troops were strongly posted and intrenched; for three days, — the first three of July, — Lee's army beat upon them, and the second day saw their lines partly driven in, their position partly taken. But on the third day the lost ground was recovered, and Lee withdrew, his army almost decimated.

Almost at the same time Vicksburg, on the Mississippi, fell before Grant's persistent attack. The defence of
The Mississip- Vicksburg had been stubborn, prolonged,
pi reopened.   heroic, and almost successful. Plan after plan of attack had been tried by General Grant, and had failed. Finally, occupying the country back of the stronghold, and taking Jackson, the capital of the State, he succeeded in shutting up the confederate forces, under

General Pemberton, in the fortress. His assaults upon
its works being always repulsed, he sat down to a regular
siege, and in that way forced the garrison to surrender
to him, half starved, on the 4th of July. July 9, Port
Hudson, below, the only remaining confederate stronghold on the river, yielded to General Banks and the
necessities of the situation, and the Mississippi was commanded throughout its entire length by the federal power:
Louisiana and Texas were cut off from the rest of the
Confederacy.

Presently the Union armies were pushed forward directly towards the heart of the Confederacy. After the
evacuation of Corinth, Mississippi, by General
Confederate
movement in- Beauregard in the preceding May, Gen. Brax-
to Kentucky. ton Bragg had taken some 35,000 of the confederate force by rail to Mobile, and thence northward again
to Chattanooga, which he occupied. From Chattanooga
as a base, he moved upon Louisville, Kentucky; but an
army under General Buell was too quick for him, checking him in a decisive action at Perryville, Oct. 8, 1862,
and necessitating his retirement to Chattanooga. General
Van Dorn had taken advantage of this diversion to lead
a confederate force against Corinth, and had almost possessed himself of the town when he was driven back by
General Rosecrans, on the second day of desperate fighting, Oct. 4, 1862. Step by step the operations of the
two armies were transferred to the central strongholds
Tennessee   of Tennessee and Georgia. Rosecrans suc-
campaign.   ceeded Buell in command of the federal forces
in Tennessee, and just as the year 1862 was closing and
the year 1863 opening (December 31 to January 2), he
encountered Bragg in three days' terrible fighting around
Murfreesboro. The federal force held its ground against
Bragg's terrific attacks, or, having lost it, regained it, and
Bragg withdrew. Forced back by the movements of the

federal armies during the summer and autumn of 1863,
Bragg felt obliged to leave even Chattanooga itself to
them; but at Chickamauga, Georgia, on the 19th and
20th of September, he made a stand against Rosecrans,
and inflicted upon him a defeat which nothing but the
extraordinary coolness and firmness of General Thomas,
who commanded the left federal wing, prevented from
becoming the most overwhelming federal disaster of the
war.

General Grant now came from his success at Vicksburg to take charge of the army which Bragg had shut
Grant in   up in Chattanooga.   Taking advantage of the
Tennessee   absence of a portion of Bragg's besieging
force, sent to meet Burnside in eastern Tennessee, Grant
attacked Bragg's positions upon Missionary Ridge and
Lookout Mountain, November 24 and 25, with such force
and success as to compel him to break up the siege and
retreat. Bragg fell back to Dalton. General Longstreet,
with the force which Bragg had sent into eastern Tennessee, crossed the mountains and joined Lee in Virginia.
Then came the winter's pause of arms.

113. The National Bank System (1863-1864).

The Thirty-eighth Congress convened Dec. 7, 1863,
with a large Republican majority in the Senate, and a
                sufficient working majority in the House, and
Finances   before its adjournment, July 2, 1864, had
pushed forward very vigorously the financial legislation
by which it was seeking to support the war. It authorized new loans, new direct taxes, new and heavier tariff
duties, and it revised and amended the National Bank
Banking   Act of the previous year. By a law of Feb.
system.   25, 1863, a national bank system had been created, at the suggestion of Mr. Chase, the Secretary of the
Treasury, based substantially upon the "free banking"

system originated in New York in 1838 (§ 49). June 4, 1864, a new Act was substituted for the legislation of the previous year, by way of a thorough revision of the measure first adopted. ⸤The immediate purpose of this legislation was to create a market for the bonds of the government. It helped the government very much while the war lasted, and it proved the foundation of an admirable financial system. It created a new Treasury bureau, under a "Comptroller of the Currency," whom it "authorized to permit the establishment, for a term not exceeding twenty years, of banking associations consisting of not less than five persons, with a minimum capital, except in small places, of one hundred thousand dollars. Such associations were required to deposit with the Treasury Department United States bonds to the extent of at least one-third their capital, for which there should be issued to them circulating notes in amount equal to ninety per cent of the market value of their bonds, but not be-

Currency. yond ninety per cent of the par value of such bonds ⸥ The issue of currency made in this manner was not to exceed three hundred millions, "that amount to be apportioned among the States according to population and banking capital." ⸤It was intended that state banks should take advantage of these Acts to obtain national issues ; but very few of them did so until after the passage of the Act of March 3, 1865, which put a tax of ten per cent on their circulation. After that, hundreds of state banks were at once converted into national banks, and national bank notes superseded all others. ⸥

114. Military Operations of 1864.

It was not Congress, however, but the fortunes of the armies in the field and the approach of another presidential election that principally engaged the attention of the

country. General Grant's steady successes in the West
made him the principal figure of the war on the federal
side, and in March, 1864, he was put in
command of all the armies of the United
States, with the rank of lieutenant-general.
Giving the western command to General Sherman, whom
he had learned to depend upon at Vicksburg and Chattanooga, he himself assumed direct control of the operations in the East against Lee. Then began the final
movements of the war. In May, Grant, with Meade, advanced from the Potomac upon Lee, who lay between
them and Richmond. The armies met in the
"Wilderness" of wood and thick undergrowth
that stretched south of Fredericksburg and the Rap-
pahannock to the York River. The federal army greatly
outnumbered Lee's force. but Lee operated on shorter
lines and behind intrenchments. Although forced slowly
back by the flank movements of his opponent, which
constantly threatened to cut him off from Richmond,
the great confederate commander held Grant in hand
for sixteen days of wellnigh continuous fighting, before
making a stand at Cold Harbor. There, on
the 2d of June, Grant stormed his position
along its whole line, but was decisively repulsed with
great loss within an hour. Failing thus upon Lee's
front, Grant threw his forces across the James River to
the left and advanced upon Petersburg, to cut off Richmond's supplies from the South; but here again he was
balked of his purpose, and had to content himself with
sitting down before Petersburg for a nine months' siege.
There were operations, meanwhile, in the valley of Virginia, from which the federal forces under General Hun-
ter had been driven earlier in the year. General Early,
with part of Lee's troops, operating there during the
summer and early autumn, defeated both General Lew

Margin notes:
General Grant commander-in-chief.

Battles in the "Wilderness."

Advance on Richmond.

Wallace and General Crook, and even, by a rapid movement, came upon the defences of Washington, when, with but a little more promptness, he might have taken them. But in the end he was driven back by Sheridan, and all forces concentrated about Richmond and Petersburg.

While Grant was forcing Lee back upon Richmond, Sherman was forcing Joseph E. Johnston, Bragg's successor in the confederate command, back upon Atlanta. As in the "Wilderness," so here, there was continuous fighting, but no set battle, Johnston not being strong enough to face Sherman in the open field, but only strong enough to effect a most handsome retreat. By July Johnston was in Atlanta, for a final stand upon the edge of the great tableland that stretched thence southward to the sea. Affecting dissatisfaction with Johnston's policy of retreat, President Davis removed him from the command and substituted General Hood. Sherman's chief difficulty was removed. Repulsing Hood's repeated rash attacks upon him, and moving around Atlanta, Sherman cut its lines of supply and took the place, September 2. Hood withdrew northward towards Tennessee, apparently hoping to draw Sherman after him. But Sherman left him to face Thomas, and himself prepared to march southward to the sea. Hood met and drove back a portion of Thomas's army at Franklin, Tennessee, and encamped before Thomas himself at Nashville. Here Thomas attacked him, December 15, and so utterly defeated him that his army was never brought together again as an effective force. Sherman meanwhile had moved as he pleased. He had left Atlanta in November. In December he reached and took Savannah. Turning northwards thence, he traversed South Carolina, in the opening months of 1865, ruthlessly destroying and burning as he went. No seaport of importance

Last operations in Georgia.

Sherman's march to the sea.

now remained in the hands of the confederates, for Mobile had been taken, August 5, 1864, by Admiral Farragut, in co-operation with land forces; Sherman's movements had forced the evacuation of Charleston; and before he left Savannah, Fort Fisher and Wilmington, North Carolina, had been taken by the naval and military forces operating there. Sherman had only to find employment for Joseph E. Johnston, who retreated before him in North Carolina, in order to leave Grant free to work his will upon Richmond and Petersburg.

115. Presidential Election of 1864.

The presidential election of 1864 had resulted in the easy choice of Lincoln for a second term. It

Dissatisfaction with Lincoln. had looked for a time, to those who watched the politicians only, as if it would be difficult to obtain a re-nomination for Mr. Lincoln. He had not satisfied the radical men at all; he had seemed to them much too conservative about some things, and much too arbitrary about others. The feeling against him found strong expression in the resolutions of a convention of some three hundred and fifty persons which met in Cleveland, Ohio, May 31, 1864, and by acclamation nominated General John C. Frémont for the presidency.

The convention which met in Baltimore on the 17th of June to nominate Mr. Lincoln was not a Republican con-

Republican convention. vention exclusively, but a convention of all the groups, Democrats included, who were in favor of the full maintenance of the Union It put upon the ticket with Mr. Lincoln, therefore, as its candidate for the vice-presidency, Andrew Johnson, a Union man, but a Democrat, of Tennessee.) Its platform strongly indorsed what the administration had done; favored the pensioning of the soldiers who had received "disabling

and honorable wounds; " approved " the speedy construction of a railroad to the Pacific coast ; " and pledged itself
to the full payment of the national debt, so enormously
swelled by the war.

The Democratic convention, which met in Chicago
on August 29, easily found strong grounds of complaint
Democratic against Mr. Lincoln's administration. In
convention very many cases he had unquestionably exceeded, oftentimes very greatly, his constitutional powers,
acting always in good conscience, no doubt, and certainly never with any purpose of usurpation, but doing
what only the supreme exigency of the situation could in
any wise warrant. But a supreme exigency did exist,
and protest from the Democrats was of no weight at such
a moment. They declared the war, moreover, to have
been " four years of failure," and then made themselves
ridiculous by nominating for the presidency General
McClellan, who hastened to say, in his letter of acceptance, that it had been nothing of the kind. The result
Result of the campaign was a foregone conclusion.
General Frémont withdrew, and Mr. Lincoln
carried every State that took part in the election, except
New Jersey, Delaware, and Kentucky. Almost immediately after his second inauguration came the end of
the war.

116. The End of the War (1865).

Assisted by Sheridan, Grant drew his overwhelming
forces round about Lee, forcing him, the while, to weaken
Lee's sur- himself by desperate efforts to keep open his
render lines of supply to the south   April 2, Lee
withdrew from Richmond, which was no longer tenable,
and sought to effect a junction with Johnston towards
Danville; but everywhere he was cut off and outnumbered, and on April 9 he surrendered to Grant at Appo-

mattox Court House, being granted the most honorable
terms by his generous antagonist. Both men and officers were to be released upon parole, and they were to
keep their horses, "because they would need them for the
spring ploughing and farm work."   On the 26th, Johnston
surrendered to Sherman upon similar terms, and the war
was over.

But the President was dead. He was shot while in
his box at Ford's Theatre, in Washington, on the evening
Lincoln's   of the 14th of April, by John Wilkes Booth, a
assassination distinguished actor, who was also a half crazed
enthusiast for the southern cause. Mr. Lincoln's death
took away the best assurance the country could have had
of a wise policy of reconstruction. The assassin lost his
life while trying to make good his escape.

CHAPTER X.

CONSTITUTION AND GOVERNMENT OF THE CONFEDERATE STATES (1861-1865).

117. Method of Secession.

STUPENDOUS as was the war struggle from every point of view, its deepest and most extraordinary qualities are
The two revealed only when it is viewed from the side
combatants. of the southern Confederacy.   On the part of the North it was a wonderful display of spirit and power, a splendid revelation of national strength and coherency, a capital proof of quick, organic vitality throughout a great democratic body politic.   A nation awoke into consciousness, shook its locks, and established its power.   But its material resources for the stupendous task never lacked or were doubted; they even increased while it spent them.   On the part of the South, on the other hand, the great struggle was maintained by sheer spirit and devotion, in spite of constantly diminishing resources and constantly waning hope.   Her whole strength was put forth, her resources spent, exhausted, annihilated; and yet with such concentration of energy that for more than three years she seemed as fully equal to the contest as did the North itself.   And all for a belated principle of government, an outgrown economy, an impossible purpose.   There is, in history, no devotion not religious, no constancy not meant for success, that can furnish a parallel to the devotion and constancy of the South in this extraordinary war.

The separateness of the South in character and develop-

ment we have several times spoken of. It had again and
again been manifested at critical moments in the history
Sovereign   of national politics : more and more emphat-
conventions. ically as the rest of the country expanded
and changed its character. But never had it been so
manifest as it became amidst the processes of secession
and war. The South then resumed, most naturally, the
political methods of 1788. The whole country had acted
then, in adopting the new government of the Union,
through conventions, as through sovereign bodies. The
Constitution had not been submitted to the vote of the
people. As the whole country acted then, so did South
Carolina and her companion States act now, in the momentous winter of 1860–1861. Again popular conventions became sovereign bodies. They repealed the Acts
of those elder conventions by which their States had
come into the Union ; they elected delegates to attend
a common convention at Montgomery for the formation
of a new confederation ; and when the Montgomery convention had framed a constitution and chosen temporary
officers for the new government, they ratified its acts.
Nothing went to the people until the year's term appointed
for the provisional government of the Confederacy had
expired. Then the people chose electors and elected
members to serve in the new Congress. The electors
confirmed the provisional choice of Mr. Davis and Mr.
Stephens as President and Vice-President.

  This was but carrying the old theory of the sovereignty
of the popular convention logically a little farther, using
it to serve the pressing exigencies of a critical stage of
Popular   transition, when concert and promptness of
feeling in   action counted for everything. It is impossi-
the South   ble to believe that what was thus done lacked
the substantial support of the people   That secession was
the project of the leading classes in the South, the men in

whom pride of race and of self-direction was most pronounced, is not to be doubted. Such a policy did not
spring from the impulse of the great body of the white
people in the South. In Georgia, at any rate, if nowhere
else in the group of cotton States, there was at first a
decided preponderance of opinion against any measures
so extreme and hazardous. But the voting population of
the southern States was in a sense the most political in
the world, — the least likely to follow blindly, because the
most deeply interested in politics, closely attentive to its
issues, and even to its personalities, sensitive to nothing
more keenly than to new aspects of public affairs. It
could be managed by its leaders only because it was so
thoroughly homogeneous, only because it so entirely
understood and sympathized with their points of view.
While the political leaders of the South, therefore, carried secession on their own initiative, they carried it by
persuasion, not by usurpation; by the domination of
argument rather than by mere domination of will. Men
who intimately knew the minds of their fellow-voters went
up and down the districts where there was doubt; convinced the majority that new terms should be made with
the Union, and that better terms could be made out of it
than in it; and gained, by appeal and the communication
of strong convictions, that popular support without which
they would have ventured to do nothing. If some were
moved against their judgment, very few were moved
against their principles.

The principles upon which secession was attempted
were, indeed, plain enough to everybody in the South,
Principle of   and needed no argument. The national idea
secession   had never supplanted in the South the original
theory of the Constitution. Southern opinion had stood
with Calhoun all along in regarding the Constitution as
an instrument of confederation, not of national consolida-

16

tion. Even in the North the national idea had been slow to grow. Webster's interpretation of the Constitution, in his reply to Hayne, had been a prophecy rather than a statement of accomplished fact. Even after the southern States had acted upon the old-time theory and seceded, the North for a moment was not sure that they had acted beyond their right. It required the terrible exercise of prolonged war to impart to the national idea diffused vitality and authentic power.

118. The Confederate Constitution (1862).

The Constitution framed by the Montgomery convention, although in most respects a reproduction of the Constitution of the United States, was made very explicit upon all points of controversy under the older instrument. The southern leaders were not dissatisfied with Constitution-the Constitution of the United States as they al changes. understood it; they were dissatisfied only with the meanings which they conceived to have been read into it by a too loose and radical interpretation. In the new constitution which they framed for themselves it was explicitly stated that in the adoption of the instrument each State acted "in its sovereign and independent character." Protective tariffs were specifically prohibited, as well as all internal improvements at the general charge. It embodied the principle of the recognition and protection of slavery in all the Territories of the new government. It added to the separate weight of the individual States by providing that in the Senate, when the question was the admission of a new State, the vote should be taken by a poll of the States; and by according to each of the several state legislatures the right to impeach confederate officers whose duties were confined to their own territory. The demand of three States was made sufficient to secure the calling of a convention for the amendment of the constitution. The States were denied, on the other hand, the privilege which they had enjoyed under the federal Constitution, of granting the franchise to persons not citizens under the general law of naturalization.

Such other changes of the federal Constitution as were introduced were changes, for the most part, only of
Details   detail, meant to improve the older instrument where experience was thought to have shown it susceptible of alteration for the better. (The presidential term was lengthened to six years, and the President was made ineligible for re-election. The President was given the right to veto individual items of appropriation bills,) and Congress was forbidden to make any appropriations not asked for and estimated by the heads of the executive departments, except by a two-thirds vote, unless such appropriations were for the legitimate expenses of Congress itself or for the payment of just claims, judicially determined, upon the government. (Congress was given the right to bring itself into closer co-operative relations with the Executive by granting seats, with the privileges of debate, to the heads of the executive departments) and it was granted a partial oversight of the President's relations with his subordinates by the provision that, except in the cases of the chief executive and diplomatic agents of the government, no official should be removed except for cause explicitly stated to the Senate   The power to emit bills of credit was withheld from Congress. The slave trade was prohibited, and Congress was empowered to prevent even the introduction of slaves from the States of the Union.

Much as there was among these changes that was thoroughly worth trying, it was of course impossible to test anything fairly amidst the furious storms of civil

war. One of the most interesting of them,—the per-
mission to introduce the heads of the executive depart-
Cabinet and Congress. ments into Congress,—had actually been
practised under the provisional government
of 1861; but under the formal constitution the houses, as
was to have been expected, never took any steps towards
putting it into practice. The Congress was inclined
from time to time to utter some very stinging criticisms
upon the executive conduct of affairs. It could have uttered them with much more dignity and effect in the
presence of the officers concerned, who were in direct
contact with the difficulties of administration. It might
then, perhaps, have hoped in some sort to assist in the
guidance of administration. As it was, it could only
criticise, and then yield without being satisfied.

119. Resources of the South (1861).

For it was inevitable in any case, in the presence of
a war of such exigency, that the suggestions of the Executive should be imperative, its power very little restrained. Almost every atom of force stored up in the
southern country had to be gathered into a single head
of strength in the stupendous struggle that ensued, and
only some central and unified authority could serve the
instant necessities of command. The population of the
Population country in 1860 was 31,443,321. The States
which seceded contained less than one third
of this population; and out of their 9,103,343 more than
three million and a half were slaves. The white male
population of the South, reckoning all ages, was only
2,799,818; and the North was to call more than two million and a half men into the field before the war ended.
The South, moreover, was an agricultural region, and
almost without material resources of any other kind. It

produced all the cotton, almost all the rice, and a very large proportion of the tobacco of the country. Nearly

Products.

one-third of the Indian corn came from the southern fields; hardly more than one-fifth of the wheat, however, and just one-tenth of the rye. Manufactures there were none, — except here and there an isolated cotton factory or flour mill. The principal markets for the great cotton and tobacco crops, moreover, lay beyond the borders of the Confederacy; the South bought what it needed in the shape of manufactured products in the North or abroad, where its own products were sold. The wealth of the southern States was not a money wealth: the planters had no money until their crops were sold, and most of what they received then had to be devoted to the payment of what they had borrowed in anticipation of the harvest. As the federal government increased its navy from month to month, and the blockade of the Southern ports became more and more effective, the crops, which usually sold for millions, only accumu-

Cotton and the blockade.

lated, useless for the present, and without value, and money there was none. The value of the cotton export in 1860 was $202,741,351; in 1861 it was but forty-two millions; in 1862 but four millions.

It was money and men and arms, of course, that the Confederacy most needed. The men were at first forthcoming in abundance: President Davis's call for volunteers was as heartily responded to as was President Lincoln's. But in the matter of money and arms it was different, and even men were presently hard to get. The federal arsenals in the South had been seized by the States as they seceded, and many thousand stand of arms and a great deal of ammunition had been seized with them; for their stores had been replenished as late as the spring of 1860, when General Scott was asking leave from the Secretary of War to station troops in the South to prevent secession. Secretary Floyd had sent arms, but no soldiers. What was thus seized, however, did not suffice to equip even the southern armies that first went into the field; and there were no manufactories of arms or ordnance in the South.

120. War Materials and Men (1861-1865).

Arms and military stores were sent for to England, and brought in through the blockade, or across Texas, after transportation through Mexico. Private
Supplies.
fowling pieces were purchased or contributed by their owners, and were actually used by the troops in the field. There were muskets in use and side-arms that had come down as heirlooms from the times of the Revolution. Preparations were begun to arm some regiments with pikes simply. Brass bells of all kinds and sizes were called for, to be melted down and cast into cannon; devoted housekeepers even contributed their brass preserving kettles, and everything else that they possessed that was made of brass, for the same purpose. Not until the war was more than half fought out, and almost decided, had the necessary factories been built and equipped for the manufacture of the arms and military supplies needed by the armies.

The supply of men, too, speedily proved inadequate as against the great levies of the North, and conscription was resorted to. In April, 1862, the Confederate Con-
Conscription.
gress passed an Act making all males between the ages of eighteen and thirty-five subject to military service, and in September of the same year the provisions of the Act were extended to all males between the ages of eighteen and forty-five. Before the war ended, the conscription was extended even to boys of sixteen and seventeen and to old men. Slaves served the armies from the first in labor upon fortifications, as

teamsters, hostlers, cooks, and body servants. Just before the close of the war, after much natural hesitation and debate, the Congress had, with something like the general consent, determined to enroll some of the slaves as troops. But this resolution was taken too late to be of any practical advantage, or disadvantage. The principal function of the slaves throughout was to cultivate the crops, which all the white men had been obliged to leave for service in the armies; and they proved both their docility and their contented faithfulness by keeping quietly and obediently to their tasks, with few but women to oversee them.

121. Financial Measures (1861-1865).

In its extraordinary straits for money, the government of the Confederacy had resort to every expedient known

Paper money. to finance, even the most desperate. It issued treasury notes by the million, payable "six months after the close of the war," but never undertook to make them legal tender; it asked and obtained from the planters loans from their crops, promises that, when their cotton was sold, the price of a certain number of the

Cotton loans. bales or of a certain proportion of the crop should be paid over to the government for the conduct of the war, eight per cent bonds being given in return. But as time went on, less and less of these crops could be sold, and the government was driven to make direct purchases of the products of the field, paying its eight per cent bonds therefor; for there was nothing else to pay. The States undertook to support their own quotas of troops so far as possible, and themselves began to make

Requisitions. paper issues for the purpose. In some cases supplies for the armies were taken from the people as required, and state certificates of indebtedness paid for them. The property of all alien enemies was

sequestrated. In 1863, not without exciting great indignation, the Congress authorized the seizure of food supplies at rates of payment fixed, not by the farmers, but
by state commissioners, who were to make their as-
sessments of prices every sixty days. At first both the
Depreciation. farmers and the government had lived on
credit, hoping for the sale of the crops ; but at
last, when credit was gone, it became necessary to live
directly upon the produce of the fields. Repeated, even
desperate, attempts were made by the Congress to prevent, by some legislative device, even by obligatory redemption, the rapid depreciation of the vast mass of
paper that had got into circulation; but of course all
attempts failed, and the circulating medium became almost worthless.

The crops did not fail. In 1864, the last and most disastrous year of the war, they were particularly abundant.
Inefficient means of transportation. There was no lack of corn or garden produce
or rich pasture. But the means of distribut-
ing what the fields produced, of bringing it
within reach of the armies, and of others who were almost starving, were wretchedly inadequate. The southern lines of railway were few in number and inferior in
equipment ; and as the war advanced, their efficiency steadily declined. So great was the demand for men in the
field that few were left to keep the roads in repair; so
great the scarcity of iron that there were no materials for
their repair. The rails wore out, and were not renewed ;
the running stock ran down, and could not be replaced.
The railways came to be controlled almost wholly by the
government, too, as means of military transportation, and
the main lines were extended or repaired by the use of
ties and rails taken from the shorter side lines. All provident management was out of the question.

122. Character of the Government (1861-1865).

Such trade as did make its way through the blockade was used, like everything else, to support the government. Foreign trade. An order of the confederate Treasury commanded that no vessel be granted a clearance unless at least one half of her cargo were shipped, on government account, from the otherwise unsalable stores which the government had been accumulating. The history of the Confederacy was the history of the absorption Centralization of all the resources of the southern country into the hands of the confederate authorities. Everything gave way, even law itself, before the inexorable exigencies of war. The executive *personnel* of the government was for the most part excellent; but excellence felt bound to approve itself in those days of trial and jeopardy by an energetic and effective prosecution of the war. The Congress, never meeting Congress. the heads of the departments face to face, and yet bound to provide for every executive need, was as wax in the hands of the Executive; it hardly carried weight enough to make an effectual resistance. At first some men of marked ability had entered it. But there seemed greater need for leaders in the field of battle than for leaders in counsel; the rewards of distinction were much greater at the front than in the debates at Richmond; and the Congress was left almost stripped of men of influence and initiative. Its weight in counsel was still further lessened by the somewhat fictitious character of its make-up. In both the first and second Congresses of the Confederacy members were present from Kentucky and Missouri. The people of certain portions of those States, in their passionate sympathy with the States which had seceded, had broken with their own state governments in revolutionary fashion, and had

sent representatives to the confederate House and Senate. And the confederate Congress had admitted them
to seats, upon the theory that they represented the real
popular authorities of their States.

From the first, when subjects of defence were under
consideration, the sessions of the Congress had been
Secret   secret; as the struggle advanced, this privacy
sessions.   of action was extended to a large number of
other subjects, and secrecy became more and more the
rule. This was due, no doubt, to a combination of influences. Military affairs engrossed most of the time and
attention of the body, and it was not prudent to discuss
military affairs in public. But, more than that, it became
increasingly difficult to command the approval of opinion out of doors for what was done by the government.
Whatever might have been the necessity for the executive domination which had been so absolutely established,
the people grew very restless under it. The writ of
habeas corpus had been early suspended in the South, as
in the North, and every one suspected of being out of
sympathy with the government was subject to arbitrary
arrest. A passport system, too, had been put in force
which placed exasperating restraints upon the free movement of individuals.

123. Opposition and Despair (1864).

It was not easy to bear, even for the purposes of the
war, so complete an absorption alike of all authority and
The minority.   of all the resources of the country into the
                 hands of the Executive as had taken place,
with the assistance of the Congress. Exhaustion and
despair began to supervene upon the terrible exertions
and sacrifices which the awful struggle had necessitated.
There was a certain, not inconsiderable, body of opinion
which from the first had not been convinced of the jus-

tice and wisdom of the war. It had yielded to the major
judgment under the exasperation of coercion by the
North and of federal emancipation of the slaves These
measures had set the faces of all alike as steel to endure
the contest. But conservative opinion had assented to
secession at the first only as a promised means of making new terms with the Union. After giving many
soundest proofs of its submission to the general will, it
at length grew impatient for peace.

As the war advanced beyond the disasters of 1863,
hope declined, and despair showed itself more openly.
Desperate
situation. The ports were closed, and the South was left
to eat its heart out with the desperate fighting.
There was no longer any shadow of hope of foreign recognition. For a time the English spinners had not felt
the pinch of cotton famine ; there was as much cotton in
Liverpool at the beginning of the year 1862 as there had
been at the beginning of 1861. And when the pinch did
come, the spinners declared themselves, nevertheless,
against slavery or the recognition of a slave government.
Except for the sake of the spinners, England had nothing
to gain by a recognition of the southern Confederacy.
The bulk of her trade was with the North, and the North
was powerful enough to resent interference. And so the
demand for peace at length grew clamorous even in the
South. Wholesale desertions from the confederate army
became common, the men preferring the duty of succor-
ing their starving families to the desperate chances of
further fighting.

And yet the end did not come until Sherman had made
his terrible march through Georgia and the Carolinas, —
Devastation. a march almost unprecedented in modern warfare for its pitiless and detailed rigor and thor-
oughness of destruction and devastation. It illustrated
the same deliberate and business-like purpose of destroy-

ing utterly the power of the South that had shown itself
in the refusal of the federal government to exchange prisoners with the Confederacy.   The southern prisons were
left full to overflowing with thousands upon thousands of
prisoners because the South was known to be using up
her population in the struggle, and it was not thought
best to send any fighting men back to her.   The southern troops were themselves enduring hunger for lack of
supplies ; and the prisoners too, of course, suffered severe
privations, aggravated by the necessity of placing large
numbers under the guard of small forces, by the difficulties of transportation, and by a demoralization in prison
administration inevitable under the circumstances.   It
was impossible that they should be well cared for in
such overwhelmingly burdensome numbers.   But General
Grant said that they were dying for the Union as much
where they were as if they died in the field.

And so the war ended, with the complete prostration
and exhaustion of the South.   The South had thrown
her life into the scales and lost it ; the North
had strained her great resources to the utmost; there had been extraordinary devotion and heroism
and mastery of will on both sides ; and the war was over
Nearly a million men had lost their lives; the federal
government had spent almost eight hundred millions of
revenue upon the war, and had accumulated, besides, a
debt of nearly three thousand million dollars.   Cities,
too, and States had poured out their revenues for the
purposes of the war   Untold amounts of property had
been destroyed.   But now it was over; the federal army
of over a million men was rapidly disbanded, being sent
home at the rate of three hundred thousand a month ;
and only fifty thousand men were retained as a standing
force   Now that the whirlwind had passed, there was
much to be reconstructed.

The end.

V.

REHABILITATION OF THE UNION

(1865–1889).

124. References.

Bibliographies. — Lalor's Cyclopædia (Johnston's articles on "Reconstruction," "Impeachments," "Crédit Mobilier," "Disputed Elections"); Foster's References to the History of Presidential Administrations, 49–58; Bowker's Reader's Guide, *passim;* John Fiske's Civil Government, 275, A. B. Hart's Federal Government, § 469.

Historical Maps. — No. 5, this volume (Epoch Maps, No. 14); MacCoun's Historical Geography of the United States, series "National Growth," 1853–1859, and series "Development of the Commonwealth," last two maps; Scribner's Statistical Atlas, plate 17; Johnston's School History of the United States, frontispiece.

General Accounts. — Johnston's American Politics, chaps. xxi.–xxvi., Patton's Concise History, pp. 963–990 (through Grant's administrations); Ridpath's History of the United States, chaps. lxvii.–lxx. (to 1881); Henry Wilson's Rise and Fall of the Slave Power in America, iii. 434–740 (1865–1869).

Special Histories. — Edward Stanwood's Presidential Elections, chaps. xxii.–end; Edward McPherson's History of Reconstruction; Walter Allen's Governor Chamberlain's Administration in South Carolina; R. H. Wilmer's Recent Past, from a Southern Standpoint; F. W. Seward's Seward at Washington, ii., xli.–lxxiii.; Taylor's Destruction and Reconstruction; E. B. Callender's Thaddeus Stevens; G. S. Merriam's Bowles, ii., Pleasant Stovall's Toombs, pp. 286–369; O. A. Brownson's American Republic (chaps. xiii.–xiv.); J. C. Hurd's Theory of Our National Existence; J. J. Knox's United States Notes, F. W. Taussig's Tariff History, pp. 171–256; Albert Bolles's Financial History, iii., book ii.; J. C. Schucker's Chase; D. B. Warden's Chase; Moorfield Story's Charles Sumner (in preparation), E. L. Pierce's Charles Sumner.

Contemporary Accounts. — Appleton's Annual Cyclopædia; Edward McPherson's History of Reconstruction, and Political Handbooks (biennial); Hugh McCulloch's Men and Measures of Half a Century (chaps. xxiii.–end), Autobiography of Thurlow Weed (chaps. lxvi.–lxviii.); S. S. Cox's Three Decades (chaps xvii.–xl.); J. G. Blaine's Twenty Years in Congress (1865–1885), Ben · Perley Poore's Perley's Reminiscences (chaps. xvii.–xlvii.); Alexander Johnston's Representative American Orations, in. (parts vii., viii.); G. W. Cable's Silent South, Negro Question ; Works of Charles Sumner, contemporary periodicals, especially Atlantic Monthly, Forum, North American Review, Nation, Political Science Quarterly.

CHAPTER XI.

RECONSTRUCTION (1865–1870).

125. The Problem of Reconstruction (1864–1865).

THE federal Constitution, no less than the confederate, had suffered severe strain under the weight of war. It had not been framed for times of civil strife. The President felt himself forced by circumstances to exercise an arbitrary power in many things. The Department of War became the real government of the country. Arbitrary arrests were made by the thousand, not only in the border States and where the federal armies were in occupancy, but also in the North. No one suspected of disaffection was safe. Judges were seized, mayors of cities, in Maryland members of the state legislature, and everywhere editors of newspapers and those who held " peace meetings," as well as those who were accused of being spies or deserters or of resisting the draft. The President suspended the writ of *habeas corpus* as he pleased, Congress following many months behind him in Acts validating what he

The Constitution and the war.

did. Men of all ranks and conditions lay imprisoned
without hope of trial. There was of course no purpose
of absolutism in all this. Mr. Lincoln did all things with
a wakeful conscience, and certainly without any love of
personal power for its own sake ; seeing substantial justice done, too, wherever he could. But the Constitution
was sadly strained, nevertheless.

The close of the war, while it removed the old stress,
put a new and even severer one upon the Constitution,
and Mr. Lincoln was no longer present to
exercise a restraining wisdom. Now that the
war was over, what was the status of the
States which had attempted secession? Were they still
members of the Union, and could their participation in
its affairs be resumed just where it had been left off?
Here was another situation for which the Constitution
had made no provision. If, as the Supreme Court subsequently held, in the leading case of *Texas* v. *White*, the
government from which they had sought to withdraw was
"an indestructible Union of indestructible States," they
had, in legal theory at any rate, succeeded neither in sever-
ing their connection with the federal government nor in
destroying their own existence as States. They were still
States, and States in the Union. But what sort of States,
and in what condition? In what relation did they now
stand to the government they had sought to destroy?
The President and Congress had not been in agreement
upon these questions. Congress had not even been careful to be consistent with itself in its actions concerning
them. It had recognized, as we have seen, the revolutionary government set up in the western counties of Virginia in 1861 as the regular government of the whole
State, and had acted upon its consent in erecting the
State of West Virginia. But when the officers of that
government afterwards removed to Alexandria and set up

Status of southern States.

its rule over such counties as were within the federal
lines, Congress began to withdraw its recognition. At
first it admitted both to the Senate and to the House persons sent to represent the "Virginia" of this government ; but after 1863 it declined any longer to receive its
representatives, although it meanwhile permitted one of
its senators to remain until his death, and the other
until the expiration of his term.

The President had held a very consistent theory, and
pursued a very consistent course, from the first. While
he conceived secession to have broken up the
governments of the States engaged against
the Union, he also deemed it his duty to re-
sume full civil relations with such portions of the South
as had been reduced to obedience, and to see that regular
and legitimate governments were constituted in them as
soon as possible. Acting under his constitutional power
to grant reprieves and pardons, as well as by authoriza-
tion of an Act of Congress of July of the previous year,
he had issued a proclamation of amnesty so early as December, 1863. Full forgetfulness and full restoration to
all property rights, except those in slaves, were offered to
all who would take oath faithfully to "support, protect,
and defend the Constitution of the United States, and
the union of the States thereunder," and "in like manner
abide by and faithfully support " all Acts of Congress or
proclamations of the President with reference to slaves,
"so long and so far as not repealed, modified, or held
void by Congress, or by decision of the Supreme Court."
Certain classes of persons who had taken a prominent
part in secession, or who had left the service of the
United States for the service of the southern Confederacy, were excepted from the amnesty ; but, for the rest, it
was declared that in any State which had attempted secession, so soon as one tenth of the voters of 1860 should

Lincoln's views and policy.

have qualified by taking the oath, and should have set up governments republican in form under the meaning of the Constitution, those governments would be recognized by the federal Executive, although Congress would have to determine for itself the question of admitting represen-
Preliminary reconstruc- tions. tatives elected under their authority to seats in the Houses. Arkansas had been reorgan- ized under the federal authority substantially after this fashion in 1863, before the proclamation; and before the presidential election of 1864 Mr. Lincoln had recognized new governments in Louisiana and Tennessee. But when electoral votes were sent in from Louisiana and Tennessee, the houses refused to receive them; and this notwithstanding the fact that representatives from Louisiana had been admitted to seats in the House dur- ing the last month of the preceding Congress.

126. Policy of Andrew Johnson (1865).

Mr. Lincoln's death made no break in the presidential theory with regard to the right constitutional method of
Johnson's character. reconstruction, for Mr. Johnson, the Vice- President, held views upon the subject prac- tically identical with those upon which Mr. Lincoln had acted. But the change of Presidents made all the dif-. ference possible in the manner and temper of executive action. Johnson had not a touch of Lincoln's genius for understanding and persuading men Of equally humble origin, he had risen, by virtue of a certain pugnacious force and initiative of character, to high posts of public trust; but his powers had never been schooled or refined as Lincoln's had been, — they always retained their na- tive roughness; he was rash, headstrong, aggressive to the last. The party which had elected him, too, was al ready inclined to suspect him. Although a Union man, he had been a Democrat. He had been Senator from

Tennessee when that State seceded, but had treated her act of secession with contempt, ignoring it, and remaining at his post in the Senate. He sympathized with southern men, however, in almost everything except their hostility to the Union; held strict views of state rights with an ardor and stubbornness characteristic of him; and was sure to yield nothing for the sake of accommodation. He could not be right without so exasperating his opponents by his manner of being right as to put himself practically in the wrong.

During the first eight months of his presidency there was no chance for Congress to interfere; until the houses should meet, Dec. 4, 1865, he could have his own way in dealing with the southern States. The governments of Arkansas, Louisiana, and Tennessee had already been reorganized by the voters who could take the oath of Mr. Lincoln's amnesty proclamation. In Virginia the "Alexandria government" had called together a convention, elected by the counties within the federal lines, in the spring of 1864; and that convention had adopted a constitution which embodied the ideas of Mr. Lincoln's proclamation, the abolition of slavery and the disfranchisement of those who had taken prominent parts under the Confederacy. In May, 1865, upon President Johnson's refusing to recognize the governor whom the Virginians had elected under the Confederacy, the Alexandria government became the regular government of the State. The constitution of 1864, with some modifications, but still retaining its prohibition of slavery, was adopted by the people.

The President pushed forward the processes of reconstruction in the other States. May 29, 1865, he put forth an amnesty proclamation, which was substantially the same as Mr. Lincoln's, although it considerably increased

Recognition of reconstructed States

the list of those who were to be excluded from its privileges.   By the middle of July he had appointed

Additional reconstruction.

provisional governors in all the States not yet reorganized.   The voters in those States who could qualify under the proclamation at once proceeded to hold constitutional conventions and erect governments under them, being assured of the President's recognition and support, should they agree to the abolition of slavery and establish governments which seemed to him republican in form within the meaning of the Constitution.   In every State, except Texas, these processes were complete by the autumn of 1865, and senators and representatives from the southern States were ready to apply for admission to their seats when Congress should convene

The new southern legislatures, moreover, had in the meanwhile ratified an amendment to the Constitution

Thirteenth Amendment.

which Congress had adopted the previous winter; and without their ratification this amendment would lack that assent of three-fourths of the States which the terms of the Constitution made indispensable to its validity.   Feb. 1, 1865, Congress had proposed to the States a Thirteenth Amendment to the Constitution, which should prohibit both slavery and involuntary servitude "within the United States or any place subject to their jurisdiction," except as a punishment for crime; thus recalling the terms of the Wilmot Proviso and of the celebrated Ordinance of 1787 for the government of the Northwest Territory.   West Virginia, Maryland, and Missouri, to whose territories Mr. Lincoln's emancipation proclamation had not applied, had by constitution or statute already begun a process of emancipation.   If the proclamation had legal validity, slavery existed only in Kentucky and Delaware.   Those two States refused to ratify the Amendment.   Texas, — which had not yet effected the organization of a new government, — and Mississippi and Florida did not act upon it at this time.   It was accepted by eleven of the former slaveholding States, however, together with sixteen free States; and on December 18 the Secretary of State, Mr. Seward, made official proclamation of its embodiment in the Constitution by the constitutional vote of twenty-seven of the thirty-six States   If the southern States did not have regular and legitimate governments, was this Amendment valid?

127. Acts of Southern Legislatures (1865–1866).

Congress had come together, however, on December 4, 1865, in no temper to look with favor upon the new governments of the southern States.   While the southern conventions, met for reconstruction, had adopted constitutions which abolished slavery, and the legislatures organized under those constitutions had adopted the
Status of   Thirteenth Amendment, and so apparently
the negro   given earnest of the acceptance by the South of the results of the war, those very legislatures had immediately proceeded to pass laws which seemed to embody a deliberate purpose to keep the negroes in "involuntary servitude," if not in virtual slavery.   In most respects the negroes were put at once upon a footing of equitable equality with the whites in all civil rights; but the southern legislatures could not but regard with profound apprehension the new, unaccustomed, unpractised, and yet wholly unrestrained liberty of so vast a "laboring, landless, homeless class."   In several of the States accordingly, — notably in Mississippi and
Labor   South Carolina, — statutes were passed with
system.   regard to employment, labor contracts, and vagrancy, which singled out the negroes for subjection to very stringent and exceptional restraints.   Those who

would not work at the current rates of wages were
to be considered vagrants, and subjected to unusual
penalties. A great number of the minor, but more an-
noying and demoralizing, offences likely to be committed
by the freedmen were made punishable by fine; and if
the fine could not be paid, the culprit was to be hired out
to work, by judicial process. An apprentice system was
in some instances adopted, by which all minor negroes
were made subject to be bound out to labor until they
should attain a certain age. Written contracts of labor,
or else licenses to perform job work, issued by the
mayors or police authorities of their places of residence,
were in a great many cases required, which the negroes
must show when challenged in that regard, to avoid
charge of vagrancy; and if proved vagrants, they could
be arrested, fined, and made to pay off the fine by compulsory labor.

128. The Temper of Congress (1865).

To the southern law-makers such restraint and compulsion seemed to be demanded by ordinary prudence
for the control and at least temporary discipline of a
race so recently slaves, and therefore so unfit to exercise their new liberty, even with advantage to themselves,
without some checks put upon them. But to Congress
they seemed plain and wilful violations of the freedom
of the negro, evidences of an open and flagrant recal-
citrancy against the results of the war. Opinions were
beginning to prevail among the members which looked
towards a radical policy of reconstruction which should
subject the southern States completely to the will of
Congress. The Constitution having, of course, failed
to provide for such a situation as that which now existed, many theories had been held with regard to the
status of the southern States after their defeat. Some

believed that, although the ordinances of secession had been legally null and void, the southern States had, by their resistance to the laws of the Union, di- vested themselves of statehood, and had, when defeated, become, not States again, but mere conquered possessions of the federal government. " A Territory by coming into the Union becomes a State, and a State by going out of the Union becomes a Territory." Others held, with Thaddeus Stevens of Pennsylvania, that the resistance of the South to the Constitution and laws of the Union had suspended all federal law so far as they were concerned; and that that law did not revive with regard to them until once more declared in force, because of fully renewed conditions of obedience, by the law-making and war-making power of the general government, — that is, by Congress. Congress, therefore, could reconstruct the southern States as it pleased, and revive the federal Constitution with regard to them only when it had finished.

Congressional reconstruction theories

This was the theory which Congress practically adopt- ed. It came together in December with a Republican majority obtained in 1864. A strong delegation of Re- publicans, chosen under military superintendence in the border States, raised that majority to more than two- thirds in both Houses, — a force strong enough, if united in opinion, to carry through any policy it chose, with the motto " Thorough." When organizing, the names of all of the States that had seceded were omitted in the roll-call ; and immediately upon effect- ing an organization, a concurrent resolution was passed by the two houses, appointing a joint committee, of nine representatives and six senators, to inquire into the con- dition of the seceding States, and to advise Congress upon the question of their being entitled to representa- tion under their existing organizations. By the opening

" Thorough."

of March, 1866, a joint resolution had passed, to the effect that neither senators nor representatives should be
received from the southern States until Congress should
declare them entitled to representation by full re-ad-
mission to the Union This was meant to checkmate
the presidential scheme of reorganization. The House
had already resolved that the troops should be kept at
their stations in the South until their recall should be
directed by Congressional action The temper of Congress had been raised to this pitch of authoritativeness by
the irritations to which it was subjected from two quarters. It was annoyed that the President should have
hastened to be beforehand with it in reorganizing and
practically reinstating the southern governments; and it
was exasperated by the laws which the southern legislatures had passed in despite of the freedom of the
blacks.

That legislation proved of comparatively little effect;
for the last Congress had, by an Act of March 3, 1865, es-
Freedmen's tablished in the War Department a " Bureau of
Bureau.　　Refugees, Freedmen, and Abandoned Lands,"
to which it had given very wide authority to assist the
somewhat bewildered and quite helpless hosts of liberated
slaves in finding means of subsistence and in establishing
their new privileges and immunities; and the officers of
this bureau had been even officiously active in securing
for the negroes the protection of federal authority against
all unfriendly discriminations of local law. But that the
southern legislation was of slight practical importance
did not render it the less offensive to the Republican majority in Congress.

129. The President vs. Congress (1866).

The law which established the " Freedmen's Bureau "
had limited its existence to one year. On February 6,

1866, therefore, another bill was passed, continuing it indefinitely. But, besides continuing it, the bill proposed Second Bureau Act. very greatly to increase its powers, and made any attempt to obstruct, interfere with, or abridge the civil rights and immunities of the freedmen a penal offence, to be adjudged and punished by federal military tribunals. The President vetoed the measure, alleging, among other reasons for his action, the fact that the bill had been passed by a Congress in which the southern States were not represented. An attempt to pass the measure over the President's veto failed of the necessary majorities; there were some members among the Republicans who were not yet prepared for an open breach with the Executive. But the President was rash and intemperate enough to force a consolidation of the majority against him. Having occasion to make a public speech on February 22, he spoke of Congress in the most bitter terms of contempt and condemnation, ascribing to its leaders disloyal and even criminal motives. In March Congress showed how it meant to respond by taking the government into its own hands and making law over his veto. It sent to the Civil Rights legislation. President a " Civil Rights " bill, declaring "all persons born in the United States, and not subject to any foreign power," citizens of the United States, denouncing penalties against all interferences with the civil rights of any class of citizens, and giving to officers of the United States the right to prosecute, and to the federal courts alone the right to try, all such offences. The President vetoed the bill as both unwise and in excess of the constitutional powers of Congress. It was promptly passed over his veto, and Congress moved on to complete its policy without his assistance.

130. The Congressional Programme (1866).

Not wholly undisturbed, it would seem, by the President's constitutional objections to the Civil Rights bill, Fourteenth Amendment Congress proposed to the States in June, 1866, the Fourteenth Amendment to the Constitution, to incorporate the principles of the bill in the fundamental law. It made "all persons born or naturalized in the United States, and subject to the jurisdiction thereof," citizens both of the United States and of the several States of their residence; provided for a reduction of the congressional representation of any State that should withhold the franchise from any male citizens of the voting age; excluded from federal office the most prominent servants of the Confederacy until Congress should pardon them; and invalidated all debts or obligations "incurred in aid of insurrection or rebellion against the United States." The acceptance of this Amendment by the southern States was to be regarded as a condition precedent to their recognition by Congress. In July a bill continuing the Freedmen's Bureau for two years, directing the sale of public lands to the negroes on easy terms, appropriating the property of the confederate government to their education, and providing military protection for their rights, was passed over the President's veto By an Act of July 24, 1866, Tennessee, which had already accepted the Fourteenth as well as the Thirteenth Amendment, was admitted to representation in Congress. Four days later Congress adjourned.

Before the adjournment the joint committee of fifteen which had charge of the Congressional policy of reconstruction presented a report, June 18, admirably adapted to serve as a manifesto and campaign document; for a new House of Representatives was to be elected before Congress should

convene again. It declared that the governments of the
States recently in secession were practically suspended,
by reason both of the irregular character of the new
governments which had been set up, and of the reluctant
acquiescence of the southern people in the results of the
war; and that it was essential to the preservation of the
Union that they should not be reinstated in their former
privileges by Congress until they should have given substantial pledges of loyalty and submission. The President's friends, on their part, both Republicans and
Democrats, got together in convention and
made a demonstration of adherence to the
President and his policy of reconstruction
which did not fail of producing a considerable impression.
But the President hastened to utter violent speeches,
which swelled the number of his radical opponents as
rapidly as the leaders of the Congressional majority could
have desired. On a midsummer trip to Chicago he
made coarse and intemperate attacks upon Congress at
almost every stopping-place. In October the southern
States began to reject, one after another, the Fourteenth
Amendment. In December Congress came together
triumphant and ready to push its triumph. The next
House had been elected, and was to contain as huge a
Republican majority as the present House. It now only
remained to formulate the means by which the southern
States were to be forced to accept the Amendment.

The President accepts the issue.

131. Reconstruction by Congress (1867–1870).

A caucus of Republican members framed a programme,
and Congress carried it out with a high hand over whatever vetoes Mr. Johnson ventured to interpose. It was provided that Congress should
convene on the 4th of March, instead of in December,
in order to deprive the President of the opportunity for

Acts to curb the President

the exercise of authority afforded by the long Congressional recess; the rules were strengthened which were to prevent southern members from getting their names upon the roll at the organization of the new Congress; an Act was passed, —known as the Tenure of Office Act, — making the President's power of removal from office, as well as his power of appointment, subject to the approval of the Senate; and a rider to the Appropriation Bill made General Grant, already in charge of the whole military force of the government, practically independent of the President in his command. Universal suffrage was established in the District of Columbia and in the Territories. Nebraska was admitted to the Union, March 1, 1867. Nevada had been added to the list of States, October 31, 1864. These measures were but to establish the authority and The Recon- prestige of the majority. They simply cleared struction Act the way for the great Reconstruction Act which became law March 2, 1867. On March 4 the new Congress convened: before the end of the month it had passed a supplementary Act which completed this extraordinary legislation; and the process of disciplinary and compulsory reconstruction went forward at once.

The southern States, with the exception of Tennessee, which had already been admitted to representation, were to be grouped in five military districts, which were to be The process. put under the command of generals of the army appointed by the President. These military commanders were themselves to conduct the process of reconstruction. They were to enroll in each State, upon oath, all the male citizens of one year's residence not disqualified to vote by reason of felony or excluded under the terms of the proposed Fourteenth Amendment; and they were then to hold an election in each State for delegates to a state convention, in which only registered voters should be permitted to vote or to stand as candi-

dates, the number of delegates to be chosen being apportioned according to the registered vote in each voting
district. These conventions were to be directed to frame
constitutions extending the franchise to all classes of citizens who had been permitted to vote for delegates; the
constitutions so framed were to be submitted to the same
body of voters for ratification, and, if adopted, were to be
sent to Congress, through the President, for its approval.
When its constitution should have been approved by
Congress, each of the reconstructed States was to be re-
admitted to representation so soon as its new legislature
had ratified the Fourteenth Amendment. Meanwhile its
government was to be deemed " provisional only, and in
all respects subject to the paramount authority of the
United States at any time to abolish, control, or supersede the same." Such was the policy of " Thorough "
to which Congress had made up its mind.

Its practical operation was of course revolutionary in
its effects upon the southern governments. The most
influential white men were excluded from voting for the
delegates who were to compose the constitutional conventions, while the negroes were all admitted to enrol-
ment. Unscrupulous adventurers appeared,
to act as the leaders of the inexperienced
blacks in taking possession, first of the conventions, and afterwards of the state governments; and
in the States where the negroes were most numerous, or
their leaders most shrewd and unprincipled, an extraordinary carnival of public crime set in under the forms
of law. Negro majorities gained complete control of
the state governments, or, rather, negroes constituted the
legislative majorities and submitted to the unrestrained
authority of small and masterful groups of white men
whom the instinct of plunder had drawn from the North.
Taxes were multiplied, whose proceeds went for the most

part into the pockets of these fellows and their confederates among the negroes. Enormous masses of debt were piled up, by processes both legal and fraudulent, and most of the money borrowed reached the same destination. In several of the States it is true that after the conventions had acted, the white vote was strong enough to control, when united; and in these reconstruction, when completed, reinstated the whites in power almost at once. But it was in these States in several cases that the process of reconstruction was longest delayed, just because the white voters could resist the more obnoxious measures of the conventions; and in the mean time there was military rule. By the end of June, 1868, provision had been made for the readmission of Arkansas, the two Carolinas, Florida, Georgia, Alabama, and Louisiana to representation in Congress Reconstruction was delayed in Virginia, Mississippi, and Texas because of the impossibility of securing popular majorities for the constitutions framed by the reconstructing conventions, and Georgia was again held off from representation for a time because her laws had declared negroes ineligible to hold office. It was not until January 30, 1871, therefore, that all of the States were once more represented in Congress

Meantime, however, a sufficient number of ratifications had been obtained for the Fourteenth Amendment; and on the 28th of July, 1868, it was finally proclaimed part of the fundamental law. A Fifteenth Amendment, moreover, had been added. February 26, 1869, Congress had proposed an amendment specifically forbidding either the United States or any State to deny or abridge the right of citizens of the United States to vote "on account of race, color, or previous condition of servitude;" and it was agreed to make it a further condition precedent to the admission of Virginia, Georgia, Mississippi, and Texas, belated in their reconstruction, that their legislatures should ratify this, as well as the Fourteenth Amendment. It was adopted by the necessary number of States, and finally declared in force March 30, 1870.

132. Impeachment of the President (1868).

The Congressional policy of "Thorough" had not been carried through without forcing to an issue of direct

Collision with the President. hostility the differences between Congress and President Johnson. The President's repeated vetoes of its most important measures, his open utterance of the most bitter contempt for it, his belligerent condemnation upon every ground of its policy of reconstruction, had rendered Congress as intemperate and aggressive as Mr. Johnson himself; and at last the unedifying contest was pushed to the utmost limit. The Tenure of Office Act of March, 1867, had sought to deprive the President of the power of removing even cabinet officers without the approval of the Senate. In August, during the Congressional recess, Mr. Johnson

Stanton episode. demanded the resignation of Edwin M. Stanton, the Secretary of War, whom he had retained in office along with the other members of Mr. Lincoln's cabinet. Mr. Stanton refused to resign, and the President suspended him from office, as the terms of the Act permitted him to do. But when Congress reassembled, the Senate refused to sanction the removal. Mr. Johnson thereupon resolved to ignore the Tenure of Office Act, which seemed to him a palpable invasion of his constitutional privileges, and force Congress to an issue. Again he removed Stanton; again Stanton refused to quit his office, appealing to the House for protection. On February 24, 1868, the House resolved to impeach the President for high crimes and misdemeanors. The trial was begun in the Senate on the 5th of March. A vote was reached on several of the articles of impeachment on May 16, and the vote stood, thirty-five for conviction, nineteen for acquittal. Five Republican senators had declined to vote with their party, and the two-thirds majority necessary for conviction could not be secured. A verdict of acquittal was entered. The Secretary of War resigned his office. The President had won the fight against the obnoxious Act. But he had hardly won it with dignity; for while the trial was actually in progress he had gone about the country, as before, pouring out passionate speeches against Congress.

Impeachment

133. Presidential Campaign of 1868.

Mr. Johnson was a Democrat, and the views which he had so passionately striven for in the matter of the reconstruction of the southern States were the views of the Democratic party. He had not won the confidence of the Democrats, however, by earning the hostility of the Republicans. So far as the presidency was concerned, he was, it turned out, as impossible a candidate for either party as Mr. Tyler had been. The Republican nominating convention, which met in Chicago on the 20th of May, 1868, just four days after the failure of the impeachment trial, unanimously and with genuine enthusiasm named General Grant for the presidency, trusting him as a faithful officer and no politician. The Democrats, who met in New York on the 4th of July, nominated Horatio Seymour of New York. Issue was squarely joined in the platforms upon the policy of reconstruction. But the result was not doubtful. Three of the southern States were shut out from taking part in the election because not yet reconstructed, and most of the rest were in possession of negro majorities; while most of the northern States were of a mind to support Congress in its policy of " Thorough "

Nominations.

The vote.

towards the South.   Two hundred and fourteen electoral
votes were cast for the Republican candidates, eighty for
the Democratic; though the aggregate popular majority
of the Republicans was but little more than three hundred thousand in a total vote of nearly six millions

The four months which remained to Mr. Johnson as
President passed quickly away, and on the 4th of March,
1869, General Grant assumed the responsibilities of successor to the stormy Tennesseean.   Mr. Johnson's four
years of office had certainly been among the most tem-
pestuous and extraordinary in the history of the country,
their legislative record crowded with perplexities for the
constitutional lawyer and the judicious historian alike.
One event of no little significance had marked the
foreign relations of the government.   In 1862 France
The French   had undertaken to interfere in the affairs of
in Mexico.   the distracted Mexican Republic by setting up
a throne there for the Archduke Maximilian of Austria,
—an amiable and enlightened prince who deserved a
function worthier of his powers.   French troops established and sought to maintain the monarchy in the interest of the clerical and landed classes of Mexico.   But
the United States viewed the movement with hostility from
the first; and so soon as the civil war was over, added
to protests a significant concentration of troops upon the
Mexican border.   The French thereupon withdrew.   But
Maximilian thought it his duty to remain, —only to fall
into the hands of ruthless opponents, and meet his death,
by condemnation of a military commission, June 19, 1867.
The Monroe doctrine had been successfully asserted, with
truly tragical consequences

The year 1867 saw a still further addition of territory to
Alaska   the United States by the purchase of Alaska
from the Russian government for a little more
than seven million dollars.

CHAPTER XII.

RETURN TO NORMAL CONDITIONS (1870-1876).

134. Restoration of Normal Conditions.

THE year 1876 marked not only a point of national sentiment, in the completion of one hundred years of in-dependence, but also a real turning-point in the history of the country. Normal conditions of government and of economic and intellectual life were at length restored. The period of reconstruction was past; Congress had ceased to exercise extra-constitutional powers ; natural legal conditions once more prevailed. Negro rule under unscrupulous adventurers had been finally put an end to in the South, and the natural, inevitable ascendency of the whites, the responsible class, established Something like the normal balance of national parties also had been restored; votes were beginning to lose their reminiscence of the war, and to become regardful first of all of questions of peace. Economic forces, too, recovering from the past, were gathering head for the future. The nation was made to realize this when it took stock of its resources at the great Centennial Exposition in Philadelphia. At last the country was homogeneous, and had subordinated every other sentiment to that of hope.

A new era

General Grant remained President for two terms, and the eight years of his incumbency were years at once of consummation and of recuperation, during which the Republican party completed its policy of reconstruction, and the country pulled itself together for the new and better career that was before it. Congress hastened, after the passage of the Fourteenth and Fifteenth Amendments, to support them by penal legislation. May 31, 1870, and April 20, 1871, laws were enacted, popularly known as the "Force Bills," which denounced fine and imprisonment against all hindrances or interferences, either attempted or accomplished, in restraint of the exercise of the franchise by the negroes, or the counting of the votes cast by them; and the courts of the United States were given exclusive cognizance of all offences under these Acts. There was unquestionably a deliberate Ku-Klux and more or less concerted effort made by the movement. whites of the South to shut the negro out by some means from an effectual use of his vote, and sometimes this effort took the most flagrant forms of violence. Presently, however, its more overt and violent features disappeared, and in the spring of 1872 Congress suffered some of the harsher portions of the force legislation of the previous year to lapse. May 22, 1872, it even passed a General Amnesty Act, which relieved of their Amnesty political disabilities most of those persons in Act the South who had been excluded from political privileges by previous legislation, excepting only those who had served the Confederacy after having been officers in the judicial, military, or naval service of the United States, or officials in the higher grades of administrative and political function.

The Supreme Court, moreover, began to throw its weight of authority decisively on the side of a conservative construction of the legal changes Influence of wrought by war, reconstruction, and constitu- the Supreme Court. tional amendment. While it sustained the political authority of Congress, in the matter even of its extreme policy of reconstruction, in *Texas* vs. *White*, holding that the law-making power could mend as it chose the broken relations of the southern States to the Union, it maintained, even in that case, that the States retained their statehood intact; and when it came, in the so-called " Slaughter-House Cases " (1873), to interpret the Fourteenth and Fifteenth Amendments to the Constitution, it pronounced the powers of the southern States unimpaired, declaring that their control over the privileges of their citizens was in no wise changed by the constitutional provisions which had placed the special privileges of citizens of the United States under the protection of the federal government. In subsequent cases it went even farther in recalling Congress to the field of the Constitution.

135. Election Troubles in the South (1872-1876).

Election troubles were of constant recurrence in those southern States in which the negroes were most numerous or most thoroughly organized under their Federal white leaders, and the federal government intervention. was repeatedly called upon to exercise the extraordinary powers which recent legislation had put into its hands. It would be very difficult to say with which party to these contests full legal right rested. On the one hand, the negro managers were in possession of the electoral machinery, were backed by the federal supervisors, marshals, and deputy-marshals whom Congress had authorized to superintend the voting, for the protection of the negroes, and were naturally bold to use such a situation for their own advantage. Their opponents, on the other hand, were able oftentimes, when they could not control the polls, to keep the negroes away from them by persuasion, reward, intimidation, or actual violence. In several of the States " Returning Boards " had been created by law to make final canvass

of the results of all state or federal elections, and even judicial determination of their validity. The control of
"Returning Boards." these boards became, of course, an advantage of the greatest strategic importance to the contending parties. In Louisiana, in the autumn of 1872, rival Returning Boards, both irregularly constituted, but both claiming full official authority, certified, the one a Democratic, the other a Republican, majority in the choice of presidential electors and state officers. Two rival governments were set up. Federal troops inter-
Intervention of federal troops vened in support of the Republican governor; and although a subsequent compromise, effected under Congressional direction, gave a majority of the House of Representatives of the state legislature to the Governor's opponents, he was himself left in office and authority. In 1874 and 1875 similar electoral difficulties led to calls for federal troops from Republican officials about to be ousted in Arkansas and Mississippi; but no troops were sent. The climax of the trouble was to come in connection with the presidential election of 1876.

General Grant was careful to justify his course in directing the interference of federal troops in the con-
The President's excuse. tested election troubles in Louisiana by an appeal to the "guarantee clause" of the Constitution, under which the United States guarantees to every State a republican form of government, and protection against domestic violence. But he declared that while he felt bound to intervene, he found it an "exceedingly unpalatable" duty; and when calls for troops came later from other States, he replied, with evident impatience, that the whole public was "tired out with these annual autumnal outbreaks in the South," and that the great majority were "ready now to condemn any interference on the part of the government." He had never shown

any vindictive feeling towards the South, and there can
be no doubt that in directing federal troops to interfere
to cut the puzzling knots of southern election snarls, he
acted with the same simple sense of duty towards the
laws that had characterized his soldier predecessors,
Jackson and Taylor.

136. Executive Demoralization (1869-1877).

During the first term of his presidency, this soldierly
simplicity and directness served the purposes of government sufficiently well, for the tasks of the moment were
not those of ordinary civil administration, in which he
had had no experience. The President, too, showed a
sincere desire to keep the public service pure and efficient. March 3, 1871, Congress, in tardy response to a
healthful movement of public opinion out of doors, passed
an Act which authorized the President to frame and ad-
minister through a commission such rules as he thought
The civil   best for the regulation of admissions to the
service   civil service; and the measure met with
General Grant's prompt and hearty approval. He appointed leading friends of the reform upon the commission, and for three years, after January 1, 1872, notwithstanding the opposition of the politicians, a system of
competitive examinations for appointments to office was
maintained by the President. In December, 1874, Congress refused any longer to vote money to sustain the
work of the commission.

Despite his honorable intentions, however, General
Grant did not prove fortunate in his selection of coun-
Official mal- sellors and subordinates. He found that
feasance.   choosing political advisers on the nomination
of politicians was quite different from promoting tested
officers in the army; and when his work was over, he
confessed, with characteristic simplicity and frankness,

that he had been deceived and had failed. In 1875 it was found that there was concerted action in the West between distillers and federal officials to defraud the government of large amounts in respect of the internal revenue tax on distilled spirits. The Secretary of War, W. W. Belknap, was impeached for accepting bribes in dispensing the patronage of his department, and resigned his office to escape condemnation. During the whole of General Grant's second term of office a profound demoralization pervaded the administration. Inefficiency and fraud were suspected even where they did not exist.

The soldier President showed no great wisdom, either, in such features of foreign policy as he sought to originate. San Domingo. It was his favorite idea that San Domingo (the "Africanized" republic of the Ostend Manifesto) ought to be annexed to the United States, because it might, in case of war, be used by a hostile power as a military rendevous at our very doors ; and he yielded very reluctantly, though gracefully enough, to the opposition which made the realization of the plan impossible Several serviceable treaties, however, marked the period of his incumbency. Of these the most worthy of Treaty of Washington. mention was the Treaty of Washington, concluded with Great Britain, May 8, 1871. This treaty provided for a clearer definition of the northwestern boundary, a portion of which had been too vaguely determined by the treaty of 1847; for the settlement of certain questions touching alleged interferences with American fishermen in Canadian waters; and for the arbitration of claims made by the United States against Great Britain on account of the fitting out in British ports of certain confederate vessels of war which had wrought havoc among the northern shipping. These last were called the "' Alabama' Claims," because they chiefly concerned the equipment in England of the confederate cruiser "Alabama." An amicable settlement of all the questions covered by the treaty was effected. In September, 1872, arbitrators appointed, under the terms of the treaty, by Brazil, Italy, Switzerland, Great Britain, and the United States, awarded to the United States fifteen million dollars in damages on account of the "'Alabama' Claims."

137. Legislative Scandals (1872-1873).

Congress, too, as well as the administration, had suffered a certain serious degree of demoralization, in consequence, no doubt, of the prolonged and unobstructed domination of a triumphant party majority. In 1869 both the Central Pacific and Union Pacific railways had been completed across the continent, by aid of enormous government grants. A corporation, known as "The Crédit Mobilier," chartered by the legislature of Pennsylvania, had taken charge of the construction of the Union Pacific and of its interests in the money market ; and in 1872 grave scandals began to come to light concerning its operations. It was publicly alleged that the Vice-President (Mr. Colfax), the Vice-President elect (Mr. Henry Wilson), the Secretary of the Treasury, the Speaker of the House of Representatives, and a number of senators and representatives had been bribed to further the interests of the company in Congress. Upon the convening of Congress in December, 1872, a committee of investigation was appointed in the House, upon the motion of the Speaker. Its report, made February 18, 1873, showed clear proof of guilt against two members of the House, exonerated others on the ground that they had had no knowledge of the illegitimate purposes of the operations in which they had confessedly taken part, and left resting upon a number of others a painful suspicion of disgraceful motives, even in the absence of conclusive proof of their guilt. The impression made upon the country was that a corrupt congressional " ring " had been partially unearthed. And this unfavorable impression concerning congressional motives was only heightened by an Act, passed the same session, which the public press very bluntly dubbed " the " Salary   salary grab." By this Act the compensation Grab "   of senators and representatives was increased, and the increase was made to apply retrospectively to the salaries of the members of the existing Congress. The next session saw this scandalous measure repealed.

138. Serviceable Legislation (1870-1875).

For the rest, Congress showed itself capable, during these eight years, of some very serviceable legislation, though it was not always steadfast in maintaining the good it did. It authorized a thorough reform of the civil service, as we have seen, in 1871, only to abandon it again for the spoils system in 1874. An Act of July Natural-   14, 1870, amended the naturalization laws ization.   It admitted to citizenship, besides " free white persons," "aliens of African nativity and persons of African descent." This was a completion of the policy of the Fourteenth Amendment to the Constitution. It also made stringent provision against the fraudulent naturalization and registration of aliens, appointing federal supervisors to enforce its regulations in that regard in cities of over twenty thousand inhabitants. January 14, 1875, an Act became law which provided for the resumption of specie payments by the government on the 1st Specie   of January, 1879. Congress had very narrowly payments.   escaped being deprived by the Supreme Court of the power of making its irredeemable paper issues legal tender for all debts, as it had done in 1862. A decision of that court, rendered in December, 1869, pro-

nounced such legislation unconstitutional. But the decision was agreed to by only a small majority of the justices;
Legal ten-　by the following spring the *personnel* of the
der cases.　court had been materially altered by the appointment of two new justices; and in March, 1870, the
court, thus re-organized, reversed the decision of December, and affirmed the constitutionality of the legislation
of 1862. The resumption of specie payments, however,
was none the less imperatively demanded by the business
sense of the country.

139. Reaction against the Republicans (1870–1876).

General Grant had been elected to his second term of
office in 1872 without formidable opposition. But there
Dissatisfied　had been signs even then of reaction against
Republicans　the Republican policy, and before the end of
his second term that reaction had gathered very formidable head indeed, having swept away the Republican
majority in the House of Representatives and brought
on a contested presidential election There had been an
influential element in the Republican party from the first
which, although it had supported the party cordially
for the sake of the Union, had given its support only
provisionally, with a potential, if not an actual, independence of judgment. There was another element, too, of
" War Democrats," whose allegiance was still looser, still
more openly conditional. These elements, as well as
a great many earnest, conservative men who accounted
themselves without qualification staunch Republicans,
were very soon seriously alienated from the party by its
extreme measures of coercion in the South in support
of the constitutional amendments, its constant military
interference there, in despite of the principle of local self-
government, the arrogant temper of mastery with which
it insisted upon its aggressive policy, and the apparent

indifference with which it viewed the administrative demoralization which so soon became manifest under General Grant.

So early as 1870 these forces of reaction had produced a " Liberal Republican " party in Missouri, which, by "Liberal Republicans" combining with the Democrats, presently gained complete control of the government of that State. By 1872 this "liberal republican " movement had greatly spread, assuming even national importance. In May, 1872, a general mass meeting of the adherents of the new party gathered in Cincinnati, and, after adopting a thoroughly Democratic platform, was led by a singular combination of influences to nominate for the presidency Mr. Horace Greeley, the able, erratic, stridently Republican editor of the New York "Tribune;" and for the vice-presidency Mr. B. Gratz Brown, the Liberal Republican leader of Missouri. The Democratic nominating convention accepted both the platform and the candidates of this meeting. But no Democrat could vote with real heartiness for the ticket. While the Republicans gained 600,000 votes over 1868, the Democratic vote increased only 130,000 ; and General Grant, who had been renominated by the unanimous choice of his party, was made President again. The most substantial result of the reaction was a perceptible increase in the opposition vote in Congress.

It was significant of the clearing away of the war influences that parties now began to form which manifested no great interest in reconstruction questions. 1872 saw conventions of a "Labor " party and of a " Prohibitionist " party, which framed platforms and nominated candidates for the presidency and the vice-presidency In 1873 and 1874 there emerged in the West an association of " Patrons of Husbandry," more generally known as " Grangers," which imperatively thrust forward the interests of the farmer in the politics of several of the western States, and induced there considerable legislative interference with railway transportation.

Although it miscarried in its attempts against the Republican strength in 1872, the opposition movement steadily gathered head. The corruption of the administration was brought more and more painfully to light; the financial distress of 1873 seemed to many who suffered from it to be connected in some way with the financial policy of the dominant party; influences large and Elections of small set against the Republicans; and in the 1874 and 1875 elections of 1874 and 1875 the Democrats, as it were suddenly and by surprise, carried their state tickets in many northern States, and even elected their candidate for governor in Massachusetts. In the Congressional elections, moreover, they were overwhelmingly successful, supplanting a Republican majority of almost one hundred in the House of Representatives by a Democratic majority almost as large. In the slowly changing Senate, however, the Democratic vote was still less than one-third. Before the presidential election of 1876 this "tidal wave" of success was running much less strongly, but it had by no means subsided.

140. Contested Election of 1876-1877.

The national Democratic convention of 1876 nominated for the presidency Samuel J. Tilden of New York, a man Popular who had proved both his ability and his integ-
election. rity in the highest administrative offices of his State. The Republican convention named Rutherford B. Hayes of Ohio. Once more Democratic majorities seemed to sweep the country, but the existence of three dual state governments in the South threw the whole result into grave doubt, and produced one of the most extraordi-

nary situations in the history of the country. In Louisiana the official Returning Board, through whose hands

Louisiana. the votes of every voting precinct in the State must pass, was under the absolute control of W. P. Kellogg, the Republican governor who had been recognized by the federal government and supported by federal troops in 1874. This board, after refusing to comply with the law in several respects, declared the Republican presidential electors chosen, and the governor signed their certificates. Mr. McEnery, however, of the opposite party, claimed to have been elected governor, and gave certificates to the Democratic electors. Two sets of votes, therefore, were sent to Congress from Louisiana. There had been similar double returns from Louisiana in 1872, and the houses had then

Florida refused to count the electoral vote of that state at all. In Florida the Returning Board contained but one Democrat, the Attorney-General, and its majority, exercising judicial prerogatives in counting the votes which the supreme court of the State had forbidden the board to assume, declared the Republican electors chosen. The Attorney-General, the Democratic member of the board, gave certificates to the Democratic electors. As in Louisiana, so here, the governor of the State was a Republican, and signed the certificates of the

South Carolina. Republican electors. In South Carolina, too, as in Louisiana, there were two governors and two legislatures, each claiming to have been elected and to constitute the only legitimate government of the State. The Republican government was protected and supported in effecting its organization by federal troops, who had also in many places guarded the polls at the elections, where, the Democrats claimed, they had made a free election impossible. Just as in Louisiana, therefore, each set of electors received their certificates of elec-

tion, the one from the Republican governor, in possession of office, the other from the Democratic governor, de-
Oregon.
manding possession of office. There was a complication, besides, in Oregon. There the Republican electors had secured a majority; but one of them was thought to be disqualified under the law from serving in the capacity of presidential elector, and the governor gave a certificate to the Democratic elector who had received the highest number of votes. The Secretary of State, however, the official canvassing officer of the State, gave certificates to all three of the Republican electors. If these disputed votes should all be given to the Republican electors, the Republican candidates for the presidency and vice-presidency would be chosen by an electoral majority of one; but if any one of them should be lost to the Republicans, they would lose the election also.

The House of Representatives was Democratic, the Senate Republican; and it was impossible that the two Houses should agree with reference to the nice questions which would arise in counting the votes from the States from which there were known to be double returns. In
Electoral
January, 1877, therefore, an Electoral Com-
Commission
mission was created by Congress, to consist of five members chosen by the Senate, five members chosen by the House of Representatives, and five Justices of the Supreme Court, in the hope that the puzzling and intricate questions involved might be decided with judicial impartiality. Unhappily, however, every vote of the Commission was a vote upon partisan lines. It contained eight Republican and seven Democratic members, and in each case all disputed questions were decided in favor of the Republicans by a vote of eight to seven The process of decision was very slow, and, of course, generated the most profound excitement. Not

until the second day of March, — two days before the date set by the Constitution for the inauguration of the new President, — was the counting finished, and the result officially determined in the joint session of the houses. The feeling was universal that, leaving aside all questions of fraud in the elections, — which affected both parties almost equally, — the whole affair threw profound discredit upon those concerned. A perilous conflict had no doubt been avoided; but it had proved impossible to get a commission from Senate, House, and Judiciary in which either the majority or the minority would vote upon the legal merits of the cases presented   Even members of the Supreme Court had voted as partisans.

141. The Centennial Year.

Soon after his inauguration, President Hayes very wisely ordered the withdrawal of the federal troops from the South; and the Republican governments of South Carolina and Louisiana, — upon whose *de facto* authority his election had turned, — were quietly superseded by the Democratic governments which had all along claimed the right to occupy their places. In Florida, too, decisions of the courts effected the same result. The supremacy of the white people was henceforth assured in the administration of the southern States.

Troops withdrawn.

May 10, 1876, had witnessed the opening of an International Industrial Exhibition at Philadelphia, which had been arranged in celebration of the centennial anniversary of the adoption of the Declaration of Independence. It was a fit symbol and assurance of the settled peace and prosperity which were in store for the country in the future. All the great commercial and industrial nations were represented in its exhibits, among the rest, of course, England, whose defeat the Exhibition

Centennial Exhibition.

was planned to celebrate. Her presence made it also a festival of reconciliation. It spoke of peace and good-will with all the world. It surely is not fanciful to regard it, besides, as a type and figure of the reconstruction and regeneration of the nation. The Union was now restored, not only to strength, but also to normal conditions of government. National parties once more showed a salutary balance of forces which promised to make sober debate the arbiter of future policies. It showed the economic resources of the South freed, like those of the North, for a rapid and unembarrassed development. The national spirit was aroused, and conscious now at last of its strength. The stage was cleared for the creation of a new nation.

CHAPTER XIII.

THE NEW UNION (1876-1889).

142. Unstable Equilibrium of Parties (1876-1889).

THE first Congress of Mr. Hayes's administration was made up of a Democratic House and a Republican Sen-
Democratic   ate; the second Congress of his term was
Congress.   Democratic in both branches. But the Demo-
crats gained no permanent advantage by their control of legislation. They were not yet a compact or homo-geneous party. They were, on the contrary, a party made up of various elements, some of which were noto-riously inclined to financial and other experiments in legislation with which conservative opinion could have no sympathy. They sought, too, to force some of their political measures upon the President by attaching them as riders to the appropriation bills; and the President's steady resistance to these irregular means of mastery served to consolidate the Republicans and put them upon their mettle. The Democratic majorities in the House were no longer large; they had steadily grown smaller from election to election, since the great "tidal wave" of 1874. The Republicans won the presidential election
Election   of 1880 by a majority of fifty-nine in the elec-
of 1880.   toral vote, overcame the Democratic majority in the House of Representatives, and brought parties to a tie in the Senate.

Then once more, by the operation of causes hardly to be discerned with certainty in the absence of direct is-sues of policy between the parties, another wave of Dem-

ocratic success swept over the country in 1882, creating
a Democratic majority of more than eighty in the House
Republican   of Representatives, though the Senate passed
losses.   under the control of the Republicans   There
had been ignoble dissension among the Republicans
over the distribution of offices by Mr. Garfield, the
new President ; Mr. Garfield had been assassinated by a
disappointed and desperate office-seeker; and Mr. Arthur,— who had been made Vice-President to please that
branch of his party which was least in the confidence of
the country, — had succeeded to the office of President.
Election   Once again, however, in the elections of 1884,
of 1884   when another President was to be chosen, the
Democratic majority in the House fell off. But such
advantage as the Democrats had lost, the Republicans
enabled them to regain by nominating for the presidency
and vice-presidency candidates who represented seriously
discredited elements within the party; and the Democrats,
for the first time since Buchanan, elected their candidates,
— Grover Cleveland of New York, and Thomas A Hen-
dricks of Indiana. Until Mr Cleveland's term of office
closed, with the first century of the Constitution, they
maintained their supremacy in the House, although they
failed to increase their strength materially in the
Senate.

The presidential elections of 1876, 1880, and 1884 had
shown a singularly nice balance between the two na-
Popular vote.   tional parties in the aggregate popular vote.
Popular vote.   That vote, which was about eight million three
hundred thousand in 1876, had swelled to nine million
two hundred thousand in 1880, and to more than ten
millions in 1884; but the relative strength of parties had
changed scarcely at all while it grew. In 1876 the
Democrats had had a majority of a little more than two
hundred and fifty thousand in the aggregate vote; in 1880

the Republicans had a plurality of nine hundred and fifteen, more than three hundred thousand votes having gone to the " Greenback " party ; and in 1884 the Democrats had a plurality of less than sixty-three thousand, some three hundred thousand votes having again been diverted to other parties.

143. New Economic Questions (1880–1889).

While parties were thus held in equilibrium, most of the men who had guided the legislation of the war and

Economic questions of reconstruction passed out of politics, and their places were taken by new men. Old questions, now practically settled, fell into the background; new questions, bred of the new times, thrust themselves imperatively forward. By an Act passed in 1880 the use of federal troops at the polls had been forbidden ; and with the abandonment of federal interference with elections, the " southern question " fortunately lost its prominence in party programmes. Financial, economic, and administrative interests produced the problems of the day. The most prominent of these questions were the coinage of silver, the reform of the civil service, the reduction of tariff duties, the control of corporations, particularly the great interstate railways, and the purification of the ballot. Divisions of opinion concerning these matters by no means coincided with party lines. The platforms of the two parties became singularly alike, and upon many points alike ambiguous. Neither party could feel sure beforehand of its vote upon particular questions.

Upon the most familiar of the subjects of debate, the tariff, there existed, of course, traditional views. The Democratic party had always in the past been a low-tariff party, its utterances upon this head had been more consistent, and more unbroken in their consistency, than its deliverances upon any other point of policy. The Republicans, on their part, had not only inherited the doctrines of the Whigs, but had also put them into practice to an extent hitherto unprecedented, in the financial legislation of the war times. But nothing had shown more extraordinary growth since the war than manufacturing industry, and there was now an influential section of the Democrats also, led by Mr. Samuel J. Randall, of the great mining and manufacturing State of Pennsylvania, which was opposed to a reduction of the tariff duties. While repeated efforts were made, therefore, by the advocates of tariff reform to secure legislation upon this subject during the period we have now under consideration, nothing of any consequence was accomplished. In 1882 a Tariff Commission, constituted by Act of Congress, travelled through the country, taking testimony as to the state of industry and the effect upon it of the existing tariff laws; and in the session of 1882–1883, acting upon the report of this Commission, Congress provided for a slight reduction of duties. But beyond this nothing was done. The tariff question can hardly be said to have become definitively a party question until Mr. Randall's death broke the influence of the protectionist minority among the Democrats, and President Cleveland's message of December, 1887, finally committed his party to the old doctrines by its explicit and outspoken advocacy of tariff reform.

The tariff.

The question of silver coinage confused party lines more than any other. By an Act of July 14, 1870, it had been provided that the bonds of the United States should be paid "in coin;" and an Act of February 12, 1873, had suspended the coinage of silver, except for subsidiary coins; the value of silver, therefore, as compared with gold, had very greatly depreciated, — to the detriment, of course, of the silver mining inter-

Silver coinage.

ests of the West. Gold was regarded, therefore, by that large class of persons who cannot comprehend monetary questions as "dear" money, and the coinage of silver was demanded, in order that the country might have an abundant supply of "cheap" money. This demand came, not from the commercial portions of the country, of course, where money was understood, but from the agricultural and mining regions of the South and West. The earnest opposition of the "moneyed interest" of the East to the legislation proposed, only confirmed its advocates in their conviction that it was necessary for their protection against financial tyranny, — against a government of the country from Wall Street. In February, 1878, a Republican Senate and a Democratic House united in passing the "Bland-Allison Silver Bill" by heavy majorities over the President's veto. As originally proposed in the house, by Mr. Bland of Missouri, the Bill provided for the unlimited coinage of silver at the old ratio of 16 to 1. In the Senate, upon the motion of Mr. Allison of Iowa, the provision for unlimited coinage was stricken out, and a clause was substituted which required the purchase of a large amount of silver bullion every month by the Treasury, and its steady coinage into money. Thus amended, the Bill became law. It obliged the Secretary of the Treasury to purchase at least two million dollars' worth of silver bullion every month, and authorized him to expend, if he should see fit, as much as four millions monthly for that purpose. The bullion bought was to be coined into dollars, each of which should contain 412½ grains of standard silver; and these dollars were made legal tender, without restriction of amount, in payment of all debts.

Bland-Allison Bill.

144. The Civil Service and the Ballot (1880-1889).

In the matter of the reform of the civil service there had been equally confusing party divisions, but more satisfactory progress in legislation. Congress had with-
Civil service drawn its support from the reform, as we have
reform. seen, in 1874 (§ 136), and the members of both houses had too keen a relish for their part in dispensing the patronage of the government to wish to see legislation upon the subject revived. But after the scandalous and tragical events of the spring and summer of 1881 it was impossible to resist any longer the pressure of opinion. Almost immediately after Mr. Garfield became President, in March, 1881, both of the Senators from New York resigned their seats in the Senate because he would not allow them to dictate his choice of a collector for the port of New York. The country had dramatic evidence of the extent to which Congressional control of appoint-ments had been carried. On the second of July of the same year Mr. Garfield was shot by a man who had failed to obtain an appointment, receiving wounds of which he died in September The country had tragical proof of what clamor for office meant. On January 9,
The "Pen- 1883, therefore, the "Pendleton Civil Service
dleton Act." Act" passed Congress, with the support of both parties. It was proposed by a Democratic Senator, Mr. Pendleton of Ohio, in a Republican Senate; passed the Senate and the Democratic House by good majorities; and was promptly signed by the Republican President, who had previously declared his willingness to put such an Act into execution. It authorized the President to order appointments to the civil service to be made by competitive examination, and to constitute a Civil Service Commission for the management and development of the system. President Arthur put it immediately into force.

and under his Democratic successor, Mr. Cleveland, its administration was extended and perfected. The system did not gain full acceptance or support at once, of course, from either party, neither was it made to include all grades and branches of the service; but steps were taken towards the completion of the reform which could not be retraced. They were taken also with courage and in good faith.

The purification and protection of the ballot lay with the States, not with Congress; and the period is made noteworthy by reason of the adoption by State after State of the "Australian" system of voting. An impetus was given and an example set in this reform which assured its final universal adoption throughout the Union. The main features of the reform were, the facilitation of independent nominations for office, the official printing of the ballots to be used, their distribution to the voters by sworn officers of election, and the isolation of the voter while preparing his ballot.

Ballot reform

145. Interstate Commerce Act (1887).

That Congress should occupy itself with economic questions was made imperatively necessary, not only by the extraordinary growth of economic interests, but also by the portentous concentration of capital in the hands of corporations and of small groups of capitalists. Both capital and labor were effecting their own organization independently and upon the grand scale. It was necessary to see to it in the interest of society that they should not be too far beforehand with the law. Some means of controlling them in the common interest it became imperative to devise. On the one hand, not only trades unions, but also vast federations of unions, national associations of the trades, were forming; and, on the other hand, great combinations of capi-

Economic changes.

talists, not only into corporations, which the law already undertook to control, but also into " trusts " and " combines," for which the law had as yet devised no machinery of control. The invention of elaborate and costly machinery for all branches of manufacture was steadily increasing the amount of capital necessary for even the initial steps in establishing industries of all sorts, great and small; and for the maintenance of the greater sort associations of individuals were giving place to associations of companies. It was against these great combinations of capital that the laborers were themselves combining, to resist the attempts then already a-making, and sure to be made upon an even greater scale thereafter, to control rates of wages against the influence of competition for labor.

For Congress the whole question was typified by the concentration under the management of a few companies The great of the great railway systems of the country. railways. As the enormous growth of railways continued, and link after link was completed in the great systems of road which were binding the country together in all its parts, the old order of separate lines of railway, under the management of separate companies, was rapidly giving place to joint management under monster corporations. The trade of the country was largely in their hands. They could discriminate as they pleased in both their passenger and their freight rates between individuals, and even between regions. They could make or ruin particular regions or persons or companies as their interest suggested. Congress had constitutional power to legislate concerning post roads and interstate commerce. Interstate The States had many of them sought to regulate the railways already ; and in 1887 Congress passed an Interstate Commerce Act which forbade discrimination in rates, the " pooling " of rates

by competing lines of railway, or the division among
them of earnings. A semi-judicial tribunal was constituted to enforce the provisions of the Act. This Interstate Commerce Commission speedily became one of the
most important tribunals of the country, administering
the provisions of the law with both firmness and discretion, to the fortunate correction of many abuses.

146. Administrative Questions (1886, 1887).

The disputed presidential election of 1876 had rendered painfully evident to the whole country the necessity for more satisfactory provisions with regard to count-
Electoral   ing the electoral votes which had long been
count.   evident to thoughtful public men; and Congress presently undertook to legislate upon the subject, —
not promptly, as might have been expected after the hazards of the Electoral Commission, because it was difficult
to agree upon details, but with a satisfactory discernment
of the proper remedy. By an Act approved Feb 3, 1887,
it was provided that each State might determine under
its own laws the manner in which definitive judicial decision of every contest arising out of a presidential election
should be made, and that the houses could not reverse a
decision which had been reached in accordance with such
state laws, except in cases where there was a conflict of
tribunals within a State and the houses could not agree in
deciding the question which of those tribunals was the
lawful tribunal under the laws of the State concerned.
By a concurrent vote of the two houses, however, electoral votes not protected by state judicial determination
of their validity might be rejected.

An earlier law, approved Jan. 18, 1886, had made sensible provision for the official succession to the presidential office in case of the death or disability of both the

President and the Vice-President. The Secretary of State was put first in order of succession, and after him the Secretary of the Treasury, the Secretary of War, the Presidential Attorney General, the Postmaster General, the succession Secretary of the Navy, and the Secretary of the Interior, in the order named, provided, in each case, of course, that the officer upon whom the succession devolved were otherwise eligible for the office of President under the terms of the Constitution. Upon such administrative measures the two parties did not find it difficult Tenure to agree. They agreed also, during the clos- of office ing days of the session of 1887, to a repeal of the Tenure of Office Act by which Congress had sought to control President Johnson's dismissals from office in 1867.

147. Pensions, Immigration, Polygamy.

The other leading questions of these years were the granting of pensions and the regulation of immigration. Pensions. Congress had hastened from one lavish vote to another in providing pensions for the soldiers who had fought in the civil war, until at length generosity had passed into folly. President Cleveland for the time put a stop to the reckless process by a vigorous use of his veto power. Immigration had long Immigration. since become a threat instead of a source of increased wealth and material strength, bringing, as it did, the pauperized and the discontented and disheartened of all lands, instead of the hopeful and sturdy classes of former days; and public opinion was becoming very restless about it. But Congress did little except act very harshly towards the immigrants from a single nation. By an Act of 1888 the entrance of Chinese into the country was absolutely cut off.

Congress undertook, too, under the leadership of Sen-

ator Edmunds of Vermont, to deal in summary fashion
with polygamy among the Mormons of Utah.   The charter of the Mormon church was declared forfeit, polygamy
Polygamy.   was made criminal, and all persons were
              excluded from the elective franchise in the
Territory who would not take oath to obey the stringent
provisions of the federal statutes (of 1882 and 1887) aimed
at the principal domestic institution of the Mormon sect.

In November, 1889, four new States entered the Union,
— North and South Dakota, Montana and Washington.
The tale of States had now reached forty-two.

148. End of the First Century of the Constitution (1889)

The end of the first century of the Constitution had
come.   It was but twenty-four years since the close of
Transforma-   the war between the States ; but these twenty-
tion of the   four years of steam and electricity had done
South.   more than any previous century could have
done to transform the nation into a new Union   The
South had been changed, as if by a marvel, into likeness
to the rest of the country.   Freed from the incubus of
slavery, she had sprung into a new life; already she
promised to become one of the chief industrial regions of
the Union.   She had discovered resources of coal and
iron beneath her rich soil of which she had never dreamed
before.   Manufactures sprang up on every hand.   She
lost her old leisure and her old-time culture, but began
very fast to build the material foundations for a new leisure and a new intellectual life.   In the presence of such
changes the old alienation of feeling between the sections
could not survive.   Northern capital poured into the
South; northern interests became identified with southern interests, and the days of inevitable strife and permanent difference came to seem strangely remote.

The growth of wealth throughout the country was unprecedented, marvellous. Individual fortunes came al-

Conclusion. most suddenly into existence such as the country had not dreamed to see in former times, such as the world had seldom seen since the ancient days of Eastern luxury or Roman plunder. Self-indulgence and fashion displayed and disported themselves as never before in the sober republic; and the nation felt itself big and healthy enough to tolerate even folly for the sake of freedom. New troubles came, hot conflicts between capital and labor; but the new troubles bred new thinkers, and the intellectual life of the nation was but the more deeply stirred. As the equilibrium of parties tempered political action, so the presence of new problems quickened sober thought, disposed the nation to careful debate of its future. The century closed with a sense of preparation, a new seriousness, and a new hope.

INDEX.

———◆———